6588   692   £29.99   Jan 15.

BIM DESIGN

Library of Congress Cataloging-in-Publication Data

Garber, Richard, 1971–
    BIM design : realising the creative potential of building information modelling / Richard Garber.
        pages cm
    Summary: "This book emphasises the potential of BIM for architects as designers"-- Provided by
        publisher.
    Includes bibliographical references and index.
    ISBN 978-1-118-71980-0 (hardback) -- ISBN 978-1-118-71976-3 (ebk)
    1. Building information modeling. 2. Building--Superintendence--Data processing. 3. Architects
    and builders. 4. Buildings--Computer-aided design. 5. Building information modeling--Case
    studies. I. Title.
    TH438.13.G37 2014
    720.285--dc23
                                                                                          2014012683

Executive Commissioning Editor: Helen Castle
Project Editor: Miriam Murphy
Production Editor: Andrew Hallam
Assistant Editor: Calver Lezama

Page design by Emily Chicken
Cover design and layouts by Artmedia, London
Printed in Italy by Printer Trento Srl

Front cover image © Henry Grosman, BanG studio

SMART02

BIM DESIGN

Realising the Creative Potential of Building Information Modelling

WILEY

Richard Garber

Acknowledgements

Books, like buildings, need to be actualised through material processes, and the creative procedure of writing, editing, formatting and ultimately printing, undertaken by many, shares similarities with the processes of building actualisation described herein.

I would like to express my gratitude to the many people who have lent their thoughts, comments, time and inspiration to the actualisation of this book:

Helen Castle has been a wonderful and thoughtful editor, and she and her staff at Wiley have twice now made this process fun and enjoyable. Mario Carpo has always been willing to review and comment on my work, and has written a generous introduction. Urs Gauchat has offered his comments on early drafts, and has been a great supporter and advisor for many years. Karen Franck has been a fantastic colleague, who has offered much advice on this and other projects. My staff at GRO Architects past and present, especially Scott Corey, for their dedication to our work and for the generation of the many images and illustrations made especially for this book. The faculty, students and staff at the New Jersey Institute of Technology have created an incredibly stimulating home for me there, and have provoked many of the thoughts articulated here. And of course, Nicole Robertson, who won't let me fall down.

Dedication

For the people of the world who are suspicious of the digital …

CONTENTS

FOREWORD

MARIO CARPO

When I started my architectural studies in Italy, in the late 1970s, one of the first assignments I was given was to make a model of a circus tent. The mimeographed instructions specified that the model had to include poles, either vertical or slanted, suspended ropes or wires with load-bearing functions, and a canopy; the scale of the model and the choice of materials were up to the students. I vividly remember being perplexed from the start; my frustration then grew along with my evident inability to make that bizarre contrivance stand up – in any configuration. I did not know how to saw wood, cut canvas or tie ropes. I had no experience as a *bricoleur*, no skill as a handyman, nor any desire to become one; and I stood up and said exactly that the second or third time the class met. The professor, a stern melancholy man of solid Tuscan stock, severely reprimanded me, accusing me of being an elitist, an urban intellectual, or worse. By contrast, he praised his own rural upbringing in a family of farmers and woodworkers, hence his spiritual understanding of the nature of the materials of which architecture is made and their inner workings – or something like that. I was not persuaded and, back home, I fine-tuned my arguments in preparation for another round. I do not remember what those arguments were, as no further debate ensued.

The week after that memorable confrontation, the Department of Architecture, together with most of the university, was occupied by Communist guerrillas. When the same professor tried to go to his office, the Proletarian Avant-Garde of the Irascible Non-Tenured Lecturers (an approximate translation from the original Italian) smashed him over the head with a heavy wooden chair. His ancestral familiarity with timber, however, did not save his skull; he was taken to hospital and kept there for almost as long as the school's occupation. When courses restarted, months later, all assignments were due the same week. I teamed up with other students, better *bricoleurs* than me, the model was produced collectively and my task in the group was to write the presentation text.

For the remainder of my studies in architecture I was never asked to produce another physical object – other than drawings, of course – and so never had the opportunity to revisit and further investigate the causes of that altercation and the nature of my objections. Had I been more perspicacious, or more conversant with the history of architecture – which I wasn't at the age of 18 and after barely a month of classes – my retort to that blundering craftsman-turned-architectural-educator should have been: architecture as an art of design was invented by Leon Battista Alberti, and a few others, during the Renaissance. Alberti and his humanist friends thought that architects should not make physical buildings, but concentrate only on drawing them. For the humanists, the complete separation between designers and makers, both ideological and practical, allowed no exceptions: designers should do the drawings and send them to the builders for execution; designers should not make objects and makers should not design them. Thus, architects are not craftsmen but thinkers, which is why, unlike plumbers or bakers, they prepare for their profession by studying at university, instead of training in a shop or on site.

This 'Albertian paradigm' is the foundation of modern architecture as an art of design, and when the humanists invented it, it was a revolution against the medieval and traditional way of building as a mechanical craft. When I enrolled in the Department of Architecture of an Italian university to become an architect, I was the product of five centuries of Albertian humanism in the arts of design: I wanted to become a maker of notations, expressed through words, numbers and drawings. I had no interest whatsoever in making buildings with my own hands, and I was even less interested in learning from, or even simply dealing with, the scores of builders and makers and craftsmen and contractors that at some point would, somehow, translate my drawings into physical objects. Alberti would have said that if I had felt so inclined, I should have gone back to live in the Middle Ages (not the exact words he used) to train as an apprentice in the guild of the stonecutters. There I would have found dust and dirt, blood, sweat and tears and much gnashing of teeth. Instead, in the modern, Albertian way, the tools of my trade had to be strictly limited to sound ideas and clear lines ('*fidum consilium*' and '*castigataque lineamenta*').

Approximately two decades after the rise of computer-based design, we now fully appreciate that digital design and fabrication do not work that way. The technical logic of digital tools runs counter to, and indeed negates, the Albertian principle of separation between design and making. Computers can notate any three-dimensional physical object using as many X-Y-Z coordinates as necessary (or using mathematical functions to generate them). These digital notations, when sent to a computer screen, create 2-D images, and when sent to a 3-D printer, create 3-D objects. When the architectural avant-garde of the early and mid 1990s began to use digital design and fabrication tools, this process was called 'file-to-factory', implying that the fabrication of the real object, in real size, is just one of the many instantiations of the same digital file, and can be managed by the same person. This person used to be called a designer, but in this seamless digital process the designer is also the maker, and this digital designer-and-maker is de facto a digitally empowered craftsman, who using the same digital tools can design and make at the same time.

Today, a 3-D printer can fabricate almost any one-piece object that a computer screen can represent with images. Designers can then manipulate the physical object and send the changes back to the digital file, if necessary, by scanning it in 3-D, and so on

PROCESS

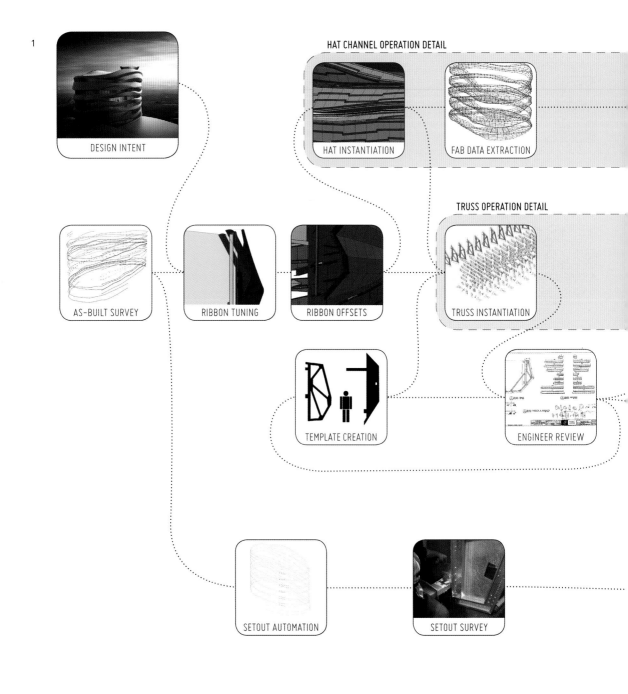

1

DESIGN INTENT

HAT CHANNEL OPERATION DETAIL

HAT INSTANTIATION

FAB DATA EXTRACTION

TRUSS OPERATION DETAIL

AS-BUILT SURVEY

RIBBON TUNING

RIBBON OFFSETS

TRUSS INSTANTIATION

TEMPLATE CREATION

ENGINEER REVIEW

SETOUT AUTOMATION

SETOUT SURVEY

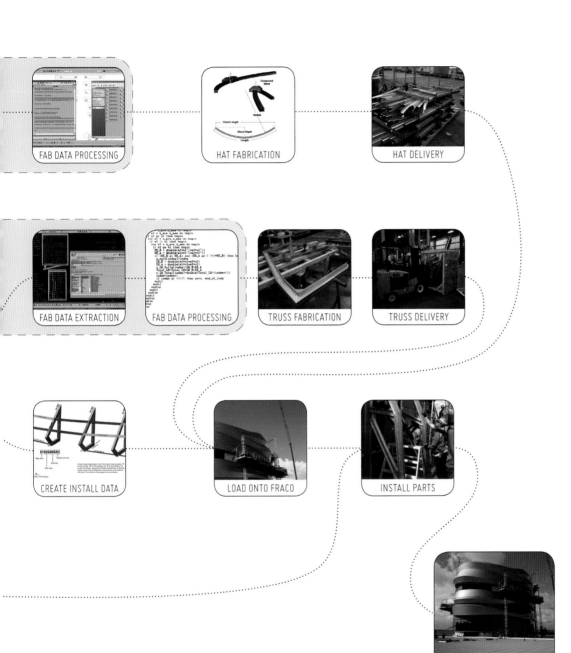

FAB DATA PROCESSING

HAT FABRICATION

HAT DELIVERY

FAB DATA EXTRACTION

FAB DATA PROCESSING

TRUSS FABRICATION

TRUSS DELIVERY

CREATE INSTALL DATA

LOAD ONTO FRACO

INSTALL PARTS

COMPLETION

1 Gehry Technologies, Edmonton
International Airport, Edmonton, Alberta 2013
An important role of so-called BIM consultants
is to conceptualise the whole process of
information flow across an entire project.

ad libitum. The digital avant-garde was quick to grasp the creative potential of the 'file-to-factory' model, and a comprehensive new theory of digital design and making, or digital craftsmanship, was formulated in the course of the 1990s, despite the limited technical possibilities that 3-D printers of the time (mostly CNC milling machines) could offer. Experimental product design also blossomed at the time, mostly in small sizes, small batches and at the small scale of prototyping, which early digital fabrication technologies could more easily support. A bigger scale and bigger objects, it was then thought, would come in time, with bigger and more powerful machines.

This did not happen. Using any cheap 3-D printer today, anyone could – if so inclined – design and print a teapot, for example, on his or her desk. But no machine can 3-D print a real building in one big piece (even though, using a technology called 'contour crafting', some are still trying). In the summer of 2012 a group of 13 Yale students used state-of-the-art digital technologies to design and build an elegant pavilion made of laser-cut metal parts, which they assembled with their own hands on the New Haven Green, Connecticut. But the success of this experiment does not mean that a hundred students could conceive and make a housing project, nor that a thousand students could conceive and make a skyscraper. Today's building and construction industry does not yet work that way, and chances are it never will, as buildings are not big teapots, nor the assembly of many smaller ones – no matter how customisable. A building is in most cases made from many very different parts, which in turn are made of different materials, provided by different industries or crafted by different contractors, following the rules of different trades, and frequently redesigned and fine-tuned all along this process in ways that may in the end match, somehow, the intentions of the original designer – but often don't.

This is one reason why, to 'close the gap' between design intentions and project delivery, the building and construction industry has looked for other ways to reunite design and making, based not on single-actor, or single-piece, fabrication, but on a different strategy of information sharing. This followed from the assumption that the many and diverse actors participating in a complex design process would remain separate but use the same digital models from the start, and that these models should make all technical and financial information accessible to all at all times. In more recent times, this managerial approach has merged with the avant-garde experiments of a new generation of digitally intelligent designers under the generic name of Building Information Modelling (BIM). The spirit of BIM posits that designers, builders and theoretically other agents as well, such as customers or clients or users, should participate in the collaborative making of the digital model of a future building, and that contractors in particular – thanks to this new, interactive digital platform – may enter the design process from the very start. Given the unprecedented power of digital simulations, one may surmise that at some point virtual models may become perfect duplicates of, and substitutes for, the buildings they represent – embodying and enacting all and every aspect of them. Designers could then 'make' a digital model just as builders would once have made an actual building, and the final translation from model to building would entail no intellectual (or informational) added value whatsoever.

As in Jorge Luis Borges's famous paradox of the map that becomes identical to the territory it portrays, this final culmination of the Albertian notational paradigm appears ontologically problematic. Phillip Bernstein of Autodesk has also recently suggested that this new participatory way of building invites a new business model as well as a new legal framework for project delivery, where authorship may no longer be the privilege and monopoly of traditional designers, and more participants may in turn lead the design and construction process – thus phasing out the traditional, humanistic and modern modes of 'design by notation' on which the architectural profession has been predicated, since its early modern, Albertian beginnings. In such instances, BIM could be seen as, potentially, one of the strongest manifestations of the collaborative spirit that has pervaded digital culture and technology (and upended whole swaths of the global economy) in the early years of the new millennium.

The idea of reuniting design and making on a collaborative building site (albeit today a digitally simulated one) may revive the utopian dream of communal creation which made medieval arts and crafts so appealing to Victorian Romantics such as John Ruskin; but today's design professions should also note that designers did not exist before the Renaissance, and if we revert to a digitally re-enacted, pre-Albertian mode of 'design by making', we usher in the obsolescence and disappearance of design itself – or at least of design in the humanist and modern sense of the term. Without any idealistic ambition, this is what the corporate drive of the building and construction industry is already doing, for better or worse, in many parts of the world where the humanist tradition, and the humanist authorial premises of the architectural profession, are less rooted and less influential than in the West.

This book by Richard Garber – which follows a seminal issue of AD, pertinently titled 'Closing the Gap', which he guest-edited a few years ago – is a passionate and persuasive plea not to go that way. As Garber argues, and the examples he shows suggest, it is possible to use BIM technologies to the full, with all the advantages they entail, and still remain faithful to our traditional notion of design – in Alberti's words, 'conceived in one mind, then expressed through drawings and models'. Today's new models are digital, and they offer unprecedented venues for interactive simulation, optimisation and collaboration. Garber suggests that today's digital tools expand, rather than constrain, the authorial ambit of architectural design. Architects will have to learn all the rules of the new game to prove him right.

Image: pp 10–11 © Gehry Technologies

1 | INFORMATION MODELLING TODAY

We are in the midst of a virtual re-contextualization or re-embedding that, although it is in no way a return to the premodern contextualization or interlinking of science, religion, art, etc. is nevertheless a stepping beyond the specific autonomies of modernity. As one aspect of this phenomenon one can note that modern technology no longer exists as such – or at least is more and more ceasing to exist. Technology proper has been or is in the process of being supplanted by a post-technology, a hyper-technology, or what I prefer to call a meta-technology. Under such historical conditions the philosophy of technology can be seen as an epoch-specific event that is coming to an end, that is petering out in a kind of exhaustion or displacement. If this is true, then the philosophy of technology may well be in the process of being replaced – not with a philosophy of meta-technology but by philosophy in a general sense that re-incorporates into itself reflection on the meta-technical condition of the postmodern techno-lifeworld.[1]

Carl Mitcham, 1995

Building information modelling (BIM) provides the entire design and construction team with the ability to digitally coordinate the often complex process of building prior to actual construction. As a new design methodology rooted in the technological advances afforded to design practice in the 1980s and 1990s, BIM allows the designer to examine 'many more facets of the project, at the initial sizing stage, using sophisticated computer graphics tools'.[2] This method of construction delivery has become known as *integrated project delivery*, or IPD. Unlike computer-aided drafting, which simply allowed documentation to be *drawn* in the computer, BIM links three-dimensional geometry with real-time databases. Through this single, shared *information model*, the design team can iterate, simulate and test all aspects of construction prior to their operation on the project site. If inaccuracies can be corrected *virtually* prior to construction, material and time savings can be passed on to the architect, general contractor and owner – the three parties typically involved in a construction project. BIM is a technology that not only affects how we construct buildings (the efficiencies and operations), but how we design them as well. For Mario Carpo, 'digitally designed architecture is even more prone to participatory modes of agency, as from its very beginning the theory of digital design has posited a distinction in principle between the design of some general features of an object and the design of some of its

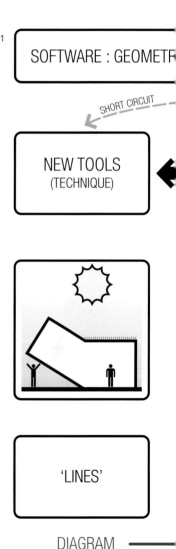

1

SOFTWARE : GEOMETR

SHORT CIRCUIT

NEW TOOLS
(TECHNIQUE)

'LINES'

DIAGRAM

VIRTUAL

1 GRO Architects, book organisation, 2012
The development of a building information model from design to construction, will be characterised as virtual geometry, the *line*, which begins to accept additional data, or *constraints*, as it is refined from sketch form to building proposal. Two-dimensional drawing production can be accommodated, via the *profile*, or sectioning of virtual geometry, and leads to the generation of the *toolpath* for computer numerically controlled actualisation or analogue construction.

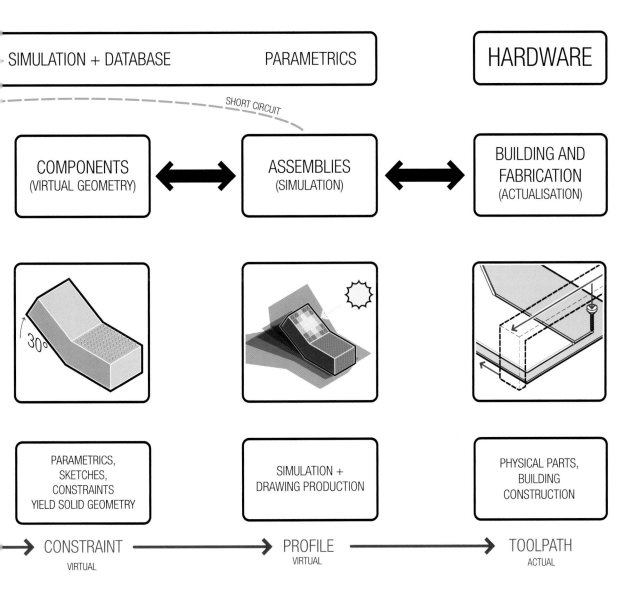

SIMULATION + DATABASE   PARAMETRICS

HARDWARE

SHORT CIRCUIT

COMPONENTS
(VIRTUAL GEOMETRY)

ASSEMBLIES
(SIMULATION)

BUILDING AND
FABRICATION
(ACTUALISATION)

30°

PARAMETRICS,
SKETCHES,
CONSTRAINTS
YIELD SOLID GEOMETRY

SIMULATION +
DRAWING PRODUCTION

PHYSICAL PARTS,
BUILDING
CONSTRUCTION

CONSTRAINT
VIRTUAL

PROFILE
VIRTUAL

TOOLPATH
ACTUAL

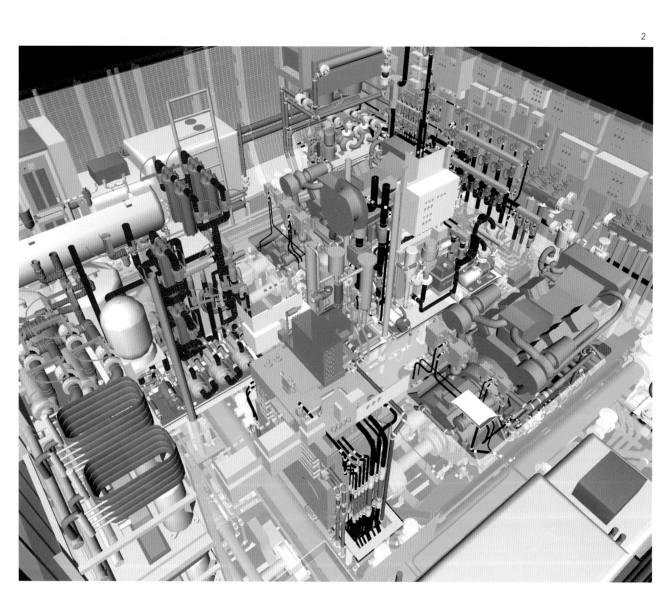

ancillary, variable aspects'.[3] The duality inherent in BIM brings construction and design together under the rubric of a shared information model, while still promoting the architect as a creative director of sorts – who authors design intent, or a project's general features, and then supervises a collaborative team of experts who each input data, or variable aspects, into the model.

WHAT CAN THE DESIGNER EXPECT?

Building information modelling promises that a single, intelligent model can contain and coordinate the following information:
- Construction documentation
- Visualisation (design and construction)
- Material and equipment quantities
- Cost estimates
- 4-D construction sequencing and reporting
- Scheduling
- Fabrication data and toolpaths.

By adopting an information-modelling platform, architects and designers can:
- Visualise multiple design organisations
- Simulate alternatives
- Identify clashes between building equipment
- Communicate design intent three-dimensionally
- Improve productivity.

For David J Andrews, Professor of Engineering Design at the University College of London, 'The general standardizing of software practice, operating systems, data exchange formats and general purpose CAD systems is so pervasive that the practice of design is effectively dominated by its capabilities, which the computer revolution now provides.'[4] Information modelling tools ultimately replace the CAD tools adopted towards the end of the 20th century with an integrated, parametric database that is shared and refined during the design process, taking advantage of the enhanced graphic, memory and storage capacities of desk- and laptop computers. This database – or *information model* – contains specific three-dimensional geometric information such as sizes, areas and volumes as well as: cost data, material and component quantities, zoning analysis, environmental performance and instructions for fabrication and construction. While such a model may 'look like' the three-dimensional visualisations possible in CAD packages, information models contain an inherent design intelligence that fosters collaboration between those on the design team and those who build the design itself. In addition to a three-dimensional modelling environment, information modelling packages include workspaces for sketch design, simulation for sustainability or construction purposes, two-dimensional drawing output and numeric export to spreadsheets or other hardware for scheduling or digital fabrication. Each of these aspects of designing within the building information modelling environment will be explained.

2 Vripack, system piping production information, Sneek, the Netherlands, 2013
The shipbuilding and aerospace industries have relied heavily on two aspects of BIM that are only now having an impact on architectural design and the construction industry. First, ship designers have created integrated virtual models that take into account routing of all systems within a boat hull and allow for checks against collisions. Such models allow for the production of shop drawings used by the fabrication team that include individual part information and bills of quantities. Second, these models allow for both automated and manual prefabrication of these ship systems.

3 Studio Daniel Libeskind with architect-of-record Davis Partnership Architects, extension to the Denver Art Museum, Frederic C Hamilton Building, Denver, Colorado, 2006
By understanding the museum as a virtual three-dimensional construction prior to building, Studio Daniel Libeskind was able to translate the sweeping forms of the building's exterior to interior spaces, such as this contemporary art gallery.

3

A commonly referred-to example of this process is the Denver Art Museum by Daniel Libeskind and a large US general contractor, Mortenson Construction. Though Libeskind developed a preliminary digital model, the contractor invested the time and effort to develop a complete virtual model that contained not only geometric information – like Libeskind's – but also complete '4-D' (time-based) clash reporting and construction sequencing so that the entire building process could be studied virtually before construction began. The investment paid off; the Denver Art Museum was completed in 2006, three months ahead of schedule and with no cost overruns despite the building's daring geometric form. The conceptual ambitions of the designer-author who uses BIM tools still cannot be replaced.

Still, this early success story only begins to describe the potentials of the building information modelling paradigm we have entered. While there have already been several books taking a case-study approach to how BIM promises amplified efficiencies to architects, contractors and owners from a cost-saving point of view, very little has been written about how these tools allow for rationalisation and optimisation of design intentions for architects at far earlier points in the project development process. How the architect as *author* can take advantage of these tools to amplify qualitative intentions that are not necessarily quantifiable in terms of cost savings or more pragmatic efficiencies is an area of BIM that is underexplored. The aim of this book is to further expose pragmatic efficiencies while expanding the notion that BIM allows for an entirely new type of design process using an augmented suite of tools that engage issues of contemporary design.

For Kenneth Frampton, speaking at Yale University in 2010:

> *Architecture by definition aspires to a state of cultural synthesis and so cannot be made totally consistent in terms of criteria whose sole aim is to optimize production as an end in itself, since at its best, building culture incorporates values that transcend our current proclivity for maximizing the production/ consumption cycle in every facet of life. At the same time, the material and operative transformations taking place in the building industry cannot be ignored by the profession, if for no other reason than that many of these innovations are coming from the profession itself.*[5]

Through cohesive integration, BIM has the ability to resolve traditionally oppositional aspects of architecture such as theory/ practice, academy/profession and design/construction. This resolution may yield a redefinition of what we think buildings should *look like* and how they should *perform*. As such, this book is organised to accommodate those already adept at using three-dimensional tools, and those just beginning the transition to information modelling. Information modelling and operations are broken down in the following way:

4 Studio Daniel Libeskind with architect-of-record Davis Partnership Architects, extension to the Denver Art Museum, Frederic C Hamilton Building. Denver, Colorado, 2006
For the construction of the 13,500-square-metre (146,000 ft²) project, the general contractor, Mortenson Construction, adopted BIM technologies and developed the three-dimensional model supplied by Libeskind to support the building's construction. Mortenson's team created building information models of the concrete and steel structure for quantification, formwork design, shop drawings and coordination. The building, and ultimately its design and construction process, received recognition from the American Institute of Architects' fifth annual Technology in Architectural Practice (TAP) Building Information Model (BIM) Awards in 2009.

5

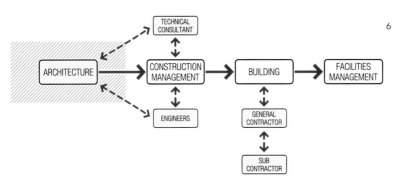

6

TECHNICAL CONSULTANT

ARCHITECTURE → CONSTRUCTION MANAGEMENT → BUILDING → FACILITIES MANAGEMENT

ENGINEERS

GENERAL CONTRACTOR

SUB CONTRACTOR

TRADITIONAL DESIGN PROCESS ◄►◄ TRADITIONAL SITE ACTIVITIES AND POTENTIAL FIELD ERRORS ►

7

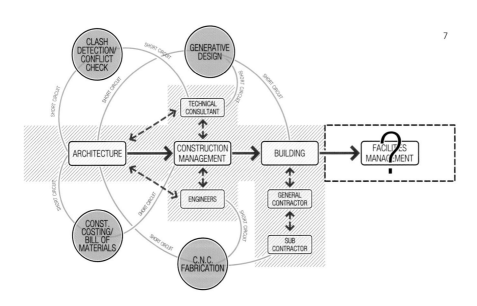

CLASH DETECTION/ CONFLICT CHECK

GENERATIVE DESIGN

SHORT CIRCUIT

TECHNICAL CONSULTANT

ARCHITECTURE → CONSTRUCTION MANAGEMENT → BUILDING → FACILITIES MANAGEMENT?

ENGINEERS

GENERAL CONTRACTOR

SUB CONTRACTOR

CONST. COSTING/ BILL OF MATERIALS

C.N.C. FABRICATION

OPPORTUNITY FOR EXPANSIVE DESIGN PROCESS AND FURTHER ITERATION ◄►◄ TRADITIONAL SITE ACTIVITIES AND POTENTIAL FIELD ERRORS ►

1 The introduction of new tools and (virtual) techniques;
2 The use of parametrics and constraints to produce (virtual) building components;
3 The aggregation of these components into building assemblies that can be simulated;
4 The translation of virtual components and assemblies to actual buildings, increasingly with prefabrication occurring off-site;
5 The real-time management and simulation of the building construction process and life-cycle management of the building.

The purpose of this organisation is to find consistency with the way different BIM software functions. Specifically, four protocols that compress the gap between design and construction will be explored. These are: generative design; construction costing and bills of quantities; model simulation including clash detection and environmental analysis and computer numerically controlled (CNC) fabrication. By introducing these operations through both historic context and contemporary application, it is anticipated that the reader will not adopt information modelling simply as a way to execute conventional design processes *in a more efficient way*, but consider instead how information modelling technologies allow the architect to operate in truly novel ways to achieve new building efficiencies and organisations. The consequences of how we consider problems of design with these tools will have an impact on what buildings look like and how they perform, thereby charting a new course for contemporary architectural practice.

THE DIGITAL DESIGN ENVIRONMENT

As the construction industry has traditionally been slow to adapt to change, advances in digital design and delivery, and the changes they have allowed in building construction, are still novel. As such it is helpful to study how the digital environment has brought about process change in other design-intensive industries. David J Andrews has written extensively on the shift in the shipbuilding industry that digital design tools have enabled. His work will serve as a sounding board for some of the operations introduced here. On a grand scale, he signals that digital technologies have enabled ship designers to move away from engineering design processes and embrace those found in architectural design.[6] In his book *Design in Architecture: Architecture and the Human Sciences*, Geoffrey Broadbent refers to architectural design as 'complex design with human habitat/environment' that is bespoke with a complex procurement process.[7] This classification becomes interesting when it is contrasted with concepts of engineering design as articulated by Vladimir Hubka. Engineering design is 'mechanistic', with machine products and mass-produced components having a 'clear economic basis'.[8]

What becomes clear about the comparison between these two design processes is the multi-faceted, and perhaps open-ended, development of the architectural project. This is not to say that optimisations do not occur within the architectural design process – they do and can at earlier points in the process with information

5 Future Home Technology, prefabricated wall production, Port Jervis, New York, 2013
Increasingly, buildings are being constructed in factories using strict digital controls, much like the shipbuilding and aerospace industries. Future Home Technology, one of several prefabricated building manufacturers that have emerged in the greater New York City metropolitan region, promises customised design and engineering in its 9,300-square-metre (100,000 ft²) 'state of the art' construction facility. The company, as well as others like it, has adopted BIM technologies to communicate better with architects and streamline the design and production process. Here a series of pre-framed walls are being prepared and will be attached to pre-framed floors.

6 GRO Architects, traditional architectural design, 2012
The traditional architectural design and delivery process tended to minimise time for design operations and to marginalise the impact of the architect on a building project.

7 GRO Architects, design iteration with BIM, 2012
The architectural design and delivery process utilising information modelling and shared responsibilities. In this paradigm, design operations are iterative and expansive, and data is shared and used in downstream simulation and fabrication operations.

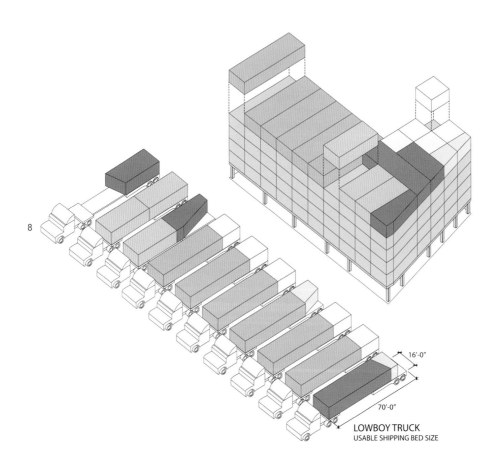

8

16'-0"

70'-0"

LOWBOY TRUCK
USABLE SHIPPING BED SIZE

16 x 54
MOD

16 x 54
MOD MOD

16 x 35
MOD

16 x 35
MOD MOD

16 x 16
MOD

16 x 16
MOD MOD

modelling technologies – but that optimisation itself is far more complex because of the multiple effects that architectural design must produce. Information modelling operations, in this sense, must then allow the designer to customise the manner in which she/he works with tools – in effect to reinforce the notion of the architect as an *author*. It is the more broad design operations enabled by information modelling, as opposed to its latent management capabilities, that offer the most opportunity to the architect and that will therefore be focused on. Another clear distinction made by Andrews is the bespoke, or mass customisable, aspect of architectural design as compared with engineering design. The reader will find opportunities for mass customisation to be abundant in the design processes described.

BIM: A BLIND EMBRACE OF NEW TECHNOLOGIES?

In addition to the examples and modelling operations discussed, this book is grounded by a conceptual explanation of the paradigm shift to information modelling. The *virtual* building information model is, within computer software, a fully formed thing that needs only to be *actualised*, or made physical. Such modelling operations no longer fall into the trope of representation we are familiar with – that a building is made via the interpretation of the architect's drawings by others. This point will be elaborated in great detail throughout the book.

One of the promises of information modelling software is that architects can better simulate their intentions virtually and exert a far greater degree of control over the translation and actualisation of their work. This notion of control should not be understood as a futile attempt by architects to take responsibility away from others involved in the construction process, but serve to inform and coordinate more completely those allied in the process itself. As a consequence, new digital protocols and techniques to interface with those of the construction industry have emerged, giving us the opportunity to move away from, or integrate variably with, traditional methods of building.

If BIM is indeed a paradigm shift for the profession of architecture and the allied engineering and construction industries, then the information contained herein will be timely and of interest to architects who are transforming their practices from traditional computer-aided design (CAD) tools to more integrated BIM technologies, specifically with an interest in novel and contemporary design techniques that have been made possible through these technologies – particularly addressing the notion of 'authorless results' as Frampton cautions, through the blind embrace of these new technologies.[9] Building, though often the goal of an architectural endeavour, should not be the only reason for information modelling to be broadly adopted. Other aspects of information modelling, such as parametric capacities to constrain or relate geometry or other organisational elements, will prove useful and strategic to designers at project stages well before the selection of a general contractor – a *builder* – is required.

8 GRO Architects, multi-family housing project, Jersey City, New Jersey, 2013
Diagram showing variation of prefabricated construction modules in a multi-family housing project. In contrast to 20th-century production ideals, BIM allows for mass customisation of building components that can be developed and rationalised virtually, and then transmitted digitally as a set of instructions for actual building. Increasingly, this has required the designer to take into account building logistics, such as the transport of prefabricated building components to a project site.

The builder stands to benefit equally from the virtues of information modelling. While new contractual organisations between architects, builders and owners are beyond the scope of this section, it is important to note that during the development of the information model – which is accessible to all parties involved in a building project – attributes such as cost data and construction sequences can be input. These aspects of building, which generally have been undertaken by general contractors or their consultants (cost estimators, subcontractors) will prove in several of the case studies shown in this book to alter the conventional development of a design project.

MOVING FORWARD

This book takes a different track from others in that it does not presuppose that everything the designer needs exists within a library stored within BIM software. Instead, it discusses how geometry is built to take on specific attributes, thereby advocating the creation of custom libraries when called for. The Carl Mitcham quote that opens the chapter is timely for several reasons. First, it was written in 1995, the year I graduated from undergraduate school and it is quite incredible to understand how the practice of architecture has changed since then, specifically through information modelling technologies and the impact they have had on the design process. Next, it makes distinctive the difference between the current landscape of technology and the one that existed during the rise of humanism in the early Renaissance – a time that many look to specifically when linking information modelling concepts to the activities of the master builder. The possibility to put forth more comprehensive and integrated designs for buildings, through software, does have similarities with the work done by the master builder – usually an artisan trained in the guilds who spent much of his entire career on the site of a single construction project. Finally, it suggests that a post-technological milieu 'reincorporates into itself reflection', or perhaps intuition, that can reposition the use of technology to the hands of the designer-author as opposed to the technical consultant or draftsperson. That technology, specifically technologies used to support architectural design, has developed to a point where it is flexible enough to be engaged within intuitive design strategies that foster novelty.

In his 2012 book *Future Perfect: The Case for Progress in a Networked Age*, Steven Johnson suggests a phenomenon he calls 'peer progressivism' in which problems are solved incrementally by many, in a decentralised way not unlike web networks.[10] This is a useful way to think about a design and construction team developing BIM, where specialists can add to the model within their scope and expertise. This has interesting implications for authorship, but instead of BIM simply giving way to 'design by many' scenarios, it seems the architect or designer, by imparting design intent, can guide the development of a building information model while still relinquishing a certain amount of the control traditionally associated with the development of a building design.

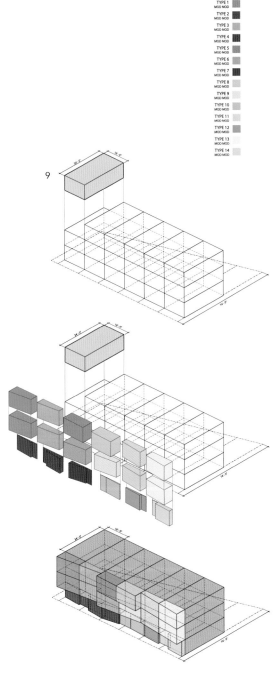

9

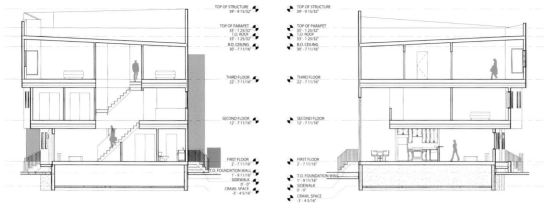

UNIT 4 - LONGITUDINAL SECTION

UNIT 3 - LONGITUDINAL SECTION

9 GRO Architects, modular housing project, Jersey City, New Jersey, 2013

BIM makes mass customisation of building projects possible in a variety of ways. In a separate housing scheme, GRO Architects uses a standard 4.9 x 10.4-metre (16'–0" x 34'–0") unit module, optimised for shipping, and then attaches a series of differentiated 'clips' to provide interior distinction between units and bring variation to the building facade.

10 GRO Architects, modular housing project, Jersey City, New Jersey, 2013

Unit sections, cut from the building information model, show differentiated living spaces and variation along the building facade. Ultimately, two-dimensional drawings such as these are still required in most jurisdictions in the United States and Europe, but are less critical to the construction process, especially when buildings are prefabricated, or manufactured off-site.

NOTES

1 Carl Mitcham, 'Notes Toward a Philosophy of Meta-Technology', *Society for Philosophy and Technology*, D Baird (ed), Nos 1–2, Fall 1995.

2 DJ Andrews, 'A Comprehensive Methodology for the Design of Ships (and Other Complex Systems)', *Proceedings of the Royal Society: Mathematical, Physical and Engineering Sciences*, Vol 454, No 1968 (8 January 1998), p 194.

3 Mario Carpo, 'Digital Style', *Log* 23, Fall 2011, p 47.

4 DJ Andrews, 'Simulation and the Design Building Block Approach in the Design of Ships (and Other Complex Systems)', *Proceedings of the Royal Society: Mathematical, Physical and Engineering Sciences*, Vol 462, No 2075 (November 2006), p 3416.

5 Kenneth Frampton, 'Intention, Craft, and Rationality', *Building (in) the Future: Recasting Labor in Architecture*, P Deamer and P Bernstein (eds), Princeton Architectural Press (New Haven), 2010, p 31.

6 Andrews, 'A Comprehensive Methodology for the Design of Ships', p 188.

7 Geoffrey Broadbent, *Design in Architecture: Architecture and the Human Sciences*, John Wiley & Sons (Chichester), 1973.

8 Vladimir Hubka, *Principles of Engineering Design*, Butterworth-Heinemann (London), 1982.

9 Frampton, 'Intention, Craft, and Rationality', p 30.

10 Steven Johnson, *Future Perfect: The Case For Progress In A Networked Age*, Penguin Group (New York), 2012, p 48.

IMAGES

2 | THE MASTER BUILDER AND INFORMATION MODELLING

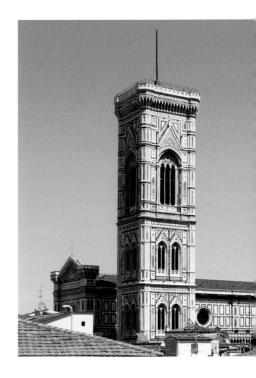

So we talk, because the experience of American beauty is inextricable from its optimal social consequence: our membership in a happy coalition of citizens who agree on what is beautiful, valuable, and just. In this we are the direct descendants of those Renaissance artists, mercantile princes, and connoisseur churchmen who spoke of beauty the way we do.
Dave Hickey, 'American Beauty'[1]

The emerging discussion of information modelling has rekindled an interest in the pre-Renaissance idea of the architect as the master builder – one who was intimately involved in the holistic process of creating a building, beginning with design and continuing through construction. This suggests, as others have implied, that the more hands-on approach of the master builder is likened to the designer using information modelling technologies. What is more interesting is that both our pre-Renaissance counterparts and designers today needed an extended field of knowledge to execute complex building projects – further suggesting a break with the architect's representational activities of the 20th century. The introduction of perspectival drawing and the printing press in the 15th century drastically changed the *design-to-construction* process and the roles and relationships of the people who undertook that work. This recent and 21st-century return to a three-dimensional and model-based – albeit digital – method of designing and virtually constructing buildings is perhaps even more significant in the way it will affect the practice of architecture and the construction industry.

The continuum in the late Middle Ages was largely dictated by powerful guilds that, especially in northern Italy where the Renaissance was born, prepared young men for work in the trades without differentiating between technological and artistic tropes. It has already been documented that there was not a guild or path of training for those who wanted to build buildings, and most *architects* of the time were trained in allied arts such as sculpture or goldsmithing. In his influential volume *The Architecture of the Renaissance*, Leonardo Benevolo reminds us that craftsmen were generally given membership in certain guilds based on the materials they were trained to work with. Those who worked in wood and stone belonged to the guild of masons and carpenters; while goldsmiths – those who worked with metals – were members of the Arte della Seta, the guild associated with the production of various luxury items.[2]

Further, 'the technical activities known, after the fifteenth century, as the "fine arts" were not seen, in the late Middle Ages, as a single group, but appeared as scattered throughout the broader grouping of the "mechanical arts". The Florentine guild organization distinguished the Arti in relation to their economic importance, and did not originally recognize an independent position for either painters or sculptors, while it did distinguish the architect from workers of the building guilds, subdivided in their turn into several groups.'[3] At the time, it has been suggested, most architects were probably given the title *magister*, signalling that they were master guildsmen who were in appropriate employ of the task at hand. The term *architector* was used in Tuscany in the early 14th century prior to its broad adoption in the Renaissance brought about by Alberti and others.[4]

Perhaps the most notable master builder from the period immediately prior to the Renaissance was Filippo Brunelleschi. While Brunelleschi is most noted for his work vaulting the massive dome over Santa Maria del Fiore in Florence between 1419 and 1436, he also worked on many other projects of varying scales and media and is the first person in history to obtain a patent. Like many master builders of the time, Brunelleschi was originally trained as a goldsmith and by way of projects, for which he was employed as a sculptor, began working on architectural commissions by the time he was about 42 years old. He was hired in 1419 to design and build the Ospedale degli Innocenti (the Foundling Hospital) and the Basilica of San Lorenzo, both in Florence. It was also in 1419 that Brunelleschi submitted designs to a competition organised by the wool merchant's guild, the Arte della Lana, to erect a dome over Santa Maria del Fiore, the Florence Cathedral. This project would not only occupy most of the rest of his life, it would gain him fame and fortune in Tuscany and beyond for his ingenious solution.

In an early essay on the practice of architecture in the pre-Renaissance, 'Gothic Architecture by Remote Control', Franklin Toker tracks the development of the term 'architect'. As related to the master-builder practices of the pre-Renaissance, the term *magister* often referred to the individual who was responsible for the design and construction of a building. The example used within this context is Filippo Brunelleschi in his work between 1419 and 1436 on the design and the technical execution of the massive dome at Santa Maria del Fiore. Though not directly making reference to this project, Toker demonstrates the relationship between the word *magister* (master, manager) and the term *architector*. It was at this time that the architect increasingly became known as the individual who could create and organise a building as well as execute it.[5]

1

1 Filippo Brunelleschi, Santa Maria del Fiore, Florence, Italy, 1419–36
The dome of Santa Maria del Fiore, as it stands today, was perhaps the greatest single building achievement of the Renaissance. Though the cathedral had been under construction for some time prior to Filippo Brunelleschi's appointment in 1419, it was the master builder's work through 1436 that revolutionised construction technologies of the day and elevated the position of the architect in society.

For the competition entry and subsequent work on the vaulting of the dome of Santa Maria del Fiore, Filippo Brunelleschi used at least one large *information* model, a 'big model in brick and stone, apparently with wood framing, and begun on September 1, 1418'.[6] In the case of Brunelleschi's first documented model of the dome of Santa Maria del Fiore, the master was lent four bricklayers by the Florentine Building Commission.[7] This model was some 18 metres (60'–0") in length and approximately 3.5 metres (11'–6") in diameter and sought to ease the concern of Brunelleschi's patrons – the Opera del Duomo – that the use of wooden, and possibly stone, tension chains within the cavity of the dome itself would be sufficient to support the structure without the use of internal vaulting or external Gothic buttresses. The model ensured an architectural precision about the whole volume of the proposed dome, as well as its sequence of construction without vaulting, and information about its construction details. The model also contained intricate patterns of brickwork believed to help arrest the massive outward stresses of the structure. As such, the model presented the designer's intentions for the overall geometry of the dome while giving a sense of the construction details that would be used in its construction.

The working methods and processes of Brunelleschi have been exhaustively speculated on in many texts, but it is important to remember that even in the early Renaissance, building was a 'collaborative undertaking: patron, architect, contractor and workmen share in the collective task of raising new shelter'.[8] The master builder, slowly through his authority and knowledge, emerged from the relative autonomy of the guilds to adopt the title of Architect to signal that *he* is *author* of the building. Brunelleschi seemed to know the importance of surrounding himself with competent workmen – the masons and carpenters who would help him to realise the vaulting of the dome at Santa Maria del Fiore also assisted in the construction of his model. Further, evidence suggests that *abaci*, or mathematicians, were also present at certain building sites.[9] The *abaco* is thought to have assisted in the estimation of material quantities or costs of these materials; however, as the architect became a distinguished figure in the age of humanism, one must consider that Alberti and others were developing a coherent theory of beauty and ornament in architecture that was based on the *mathematical system of proportion*, as its scope was codified from secretive practices held by guilds to the profession it has become today. Indeed contemporary information modelling's impact on new design processes stems in part from the computer's ability to manage geometry in ways that would be difficult to achieve otherwise.

Frank D Prager writes that while building the dome, Brunelleschi 'supervised the work done by carpenters, stone masons, and bricklayers, sent messengers to stone quarries, contracted both personally and through others for the supply of materials, and built a powerful hoisting machine'[10] – his oxen hoist.

2

The historian James S Ackerman suggests that within the relatively short expanse of time between Brunelleschi's work and that of the 'High' Renaissance in the late 16th century, there are actually three periods through which the profession of architecture developed.[11] The first period, of which Brunelleschi and Lorenzo Ghiberti were products, involved the transformation of the apprenticed guildsman to building expert. This individual – the master builder – primarily worked on the building site and instructed others while managing all aspects of construction. Brunelleschi's work on the dome, his ingenious creation of new construction techniques, and his inventions to move materials hundreds of feet in the air to the masons above, certainly falls in this category.

Next is the period following Alberti's 1452 treatise *De re aedificatoria* (English: *On the Art of Building in Ten Books*) in which the practice of architecture is codified. Architects 'like poets and men of letters, were now moving outside the professional classifications of the Middle Ages, and had already entered the sphere of humanistic culture, which set individual talent against all collective traditions'.[12] The printing press had arrived in Italy around this time and allowed for the broad dissemination of information relating to the working methods of architects and contemporary methods of construction. Brunelleschi's earlier work was paramount in fostering this period, as was the development of new technologies such as the printing press. We will see that this period in a way underpinned the work of the architect that continued through the 20th century. It is interesting to note that Ackerman suggests Antonio Sangallo, who would figure prominently in the development of St Peter's Basilica in Rome, is most significant in this period because 'he deserves distinction for being one of the few architects of his time who never wanted to be anything else'.[13] This indicates a growing separation from the guilds that allowed architecture to emerge as its own independent profession.

Finally, in the later 16th century the codification by Alberti and others would come full circle with the establishment of academies that would train architects and further codify theories about building and form. Thus, the education of the architect had moved from the secretive basis of the guilds to something like the accredited programmes of architecture we see today.

But what was practice like for the master builder or nascent architect? There are varying accounts from the historical records of how architects worked, but it seems there was a general move away from the building site and the managing of multiple projects remotely that corresponds somewhat to Alberti's *Ten Books*. The duties of an architect were devoted mainly to design and supervision, as other duties on the building site – especially a significant building site like Santa Maria del Fiore – were carried out by people in the employ of the benefactor. Supervision included looking after the responsibilities of these people, who included a co-architect, foremen, specialists such as carpenters, stone carvers and bricklayers, record keepers and treasurers.[14] The architect would also be responsible for cost estimation, keeping

2 Filippo Brunelleschi, Santa Maria del Fiore, Florence, Italy, 1419–36

Wooden model of the lantern of Santa Maria del Fiore by Filippo Brunelleschi. The lantern was the last portion of the massive dome to be completed. Brunelleschi won this commission via competition, remaining the project's master builder until its completion in 1436.

track of materials and supplies, and the staking of the building plan at full scale on the site. In this sense, he resembled an estimator, contractor or surveyor we might work with today. A section of a text attributed to Brunelleschi and his friend, the marine engineer Mariano Taccola, entitled *Problems of Inventors and Builders* gives some additional information about collaboration and construction technology at the time. First, they write of the importance of *not* sharing inventions with many – a clear example that the guild tradition of secrecy still flourished around the time of construction of the dome; and they also speak about the importance of strategic site procurement and proper cost estimation.[15] Brunelleschi indicates that a proper shed should first be erected to protect tools and provide a place where the masters can work. He goes on to suggest that proximity to forests for timber, and gravel or sand for masonry is important. Finally, he states that the architect must consider many things when considering the cost of a project, including materials, pack-hauling, transportation, habitation and sustenance. Curiously absent is discussion on drawings – though drawings remain from the second and third periods as suggested by Ackerman above, it seems from the pre-Renaissance through to the 16th century, architects relied primarily on scaled models to convey their intentions to both patrons and their building team.

BROAD USE OF (PHYSICAL) MODELS

As the rise of the contemporary architect-designer separated that individual from the building site, models would have ensured a three-dimensional understanding of the scope of the work at a time when drawings did not figure prominently in the planning of buildings. The historian Martin S Briggs suggests that writers on architectural production have concerned themselves with the 'decorative effect' of this work; however, the late medieval architect used models to explain both the architectural geometry and materials to clients or patrons and, more importantly, to work procedurally through the problems and sequences of construction. For Briggs, a 'model made afterwards is a mere mechanical reproduction of the original building on a smaller scale, and has no interest as an evidence of the process of design'.[16] Models used in the 14th and 15th centuries were built by designers and small groups of craftsmen, masons or woodworkers, from the various guilds who would often carry out the actual construction work sequenced within the model. Briggs, speaking specifically about Brunelleschi's model of the dome, proposes a 'model gives to a layman the clearest notion of a building in three dimensions, and though we know that Brunelleschi was regarded as an expert in perspective, on this occasion he is evidently relying on a model and a utilitarian plan rather than on a skillful perspective drawing'.[17]

While this large-scale model of the construction procedures and materials of the dome no longer exists – Briggs suggests it was removed when the building sufficiently resembled the model – a second model of the dome's lantern, also made as a competition entry, remains on display at the Museo dell'Opera del Duomo

3 Kevin Kuziola and Eugene Dassing, three-dimensional printed model of Santa Maria del Fiore, College of Architecture and Design, New Jersey Institute of Technology (NJIT), Newark, New Jersey, 2013
Students from the NJIT's College of Architecture and Design worked from the historical archive to produce a digital model of Brunelleschi's dome at Santa Maria del Fiore, and imagined how the inner and outer shells were tied together with a system of wooden and possibly stone tension rings. The digital model was ultimately actualised via a three-dimensional printer as a scaled physical model. Digital fabrication – the ability to produce physical parts or models via additive or subtractive material processes – is an important way architects and designers are leveraging BIM today.

4 Kevin Kuziola and Eugene Dassing, three-dimensional printed model of Santa Maria del Fiore, College of Architecture and Design, New Jersey Institute of Technology (NJIT), Newark, New Jersey, 2013
Detail of the NJIT 3-D printed Santa Maria del Fiore model showing interior and exterior ribs as well as the series of wood tension chain rings.

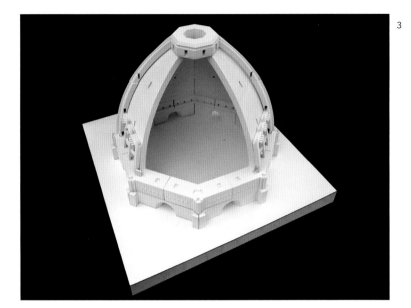

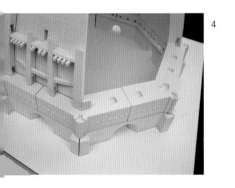

in Florence. According to Leader Scott, Brunelleschi's winning design for the lantern was made by a skilled woodworker named Antonio Manetti, who had himself competed unsuccessfully in the competition. The model is important as Brunelleschi would not live to see the actual lantern completed, but according to his biographer Giorgio Vasari, 'he left directions in his will that it should be built as the model showed, and as he had directed in writing'.[18]

Vasari's quote brings us to another point – that late-medieval models were sometimes accompanied by the designer's *written intentions*, forming the basis of a specification. Brunelleschi's 1419 model for the dome included with it a written description of the masonry model that was also tendered to the Opera del Duomo. According to Frank D Prager, the 'document exists in the form of a notarial record preserved by the Woolen Guild, which generally states'[19] what was shown in the masonry model. This document, reprinted in Prager's *Brunelleschi: Studies of his Technology and Inventions*, in clear and concise detail states what should be done in actual construction. On drainage at the cupola Brunelleschi writes, 'The water falling on the Cupola collects in a marble gutter two thirds of a foot [200 millimetres] wide, which discharges the water by suitable drain-spouts of tan sandstone below the gutter.'[20] Of the construction sequence of the cupola he writes, 'The Cupola shall be built in the aforesaid manner, without any armature, but at least up to a height of 58 feet [17.5 metres], but with platforms in such manner as will be counseled and deliberated by the masters who will have to construct it, and from 58 feet upwards, as will then be counseled, because in masonry work practice will teach how to carry it out.'[21]

Several things stand out in this text. First, in many instances the platforms and equipment used in construction were designed, through models, for the specific task at hand. Next, and equally interesting, is that certain aspects of the text are written in explicit detail: 'two thirds of a foot wide', while others such as, 'platforms … as will be counseled', suggest that precision in certain aspects of the design and construction is less critical. This is consistent with the new design pedagogy laid out by Manuel DeLanda in his 'Philosophies of Design' text, that with new technologies the designer becomes a manager or guide of data, so that an overall strategy of formal-material becoming is articulated; however, the actual development of that form can take on its own local logics within the designer's guided framework.[22] Finally, certain aspects of the text are left completely ambiguous, 'masonry work practice will teach how to carry it out'. This phrase could also be consistent with the then-still-prevalent practice of secrecy, or trade knowledge carried out by master builders. Construction knowledge prior to the Renaissance, and the printing press, was largely disseminated verbally by masters to those being trained in the guilds, and kept secret from those outside that particular establishment. This esoteric custody of knowledge is also consistent with some master builders carving their models out of wax so they could be melted down once their content was learned by the tradesmen, and only the tradesmen, who carried out the particular construction problem.

ALBERTI AND *DE RE AEDIFICATORIA*

About six years after Brunelleschi's death in 1446, Leon Battista Alberti published *De re aedificatoria*. These *Ten Books* were the first major theoretical works on the art and science of building since Vitruvius's treatise, of approximately the same name, from antiquity. In the text Alberti codified the still young practice of architecture. Interestingly, it is in his earlier publication from 1435,[24] *Della Pittura* (English: *On Painting*), that he includes the following compliment to Brunelleschi:

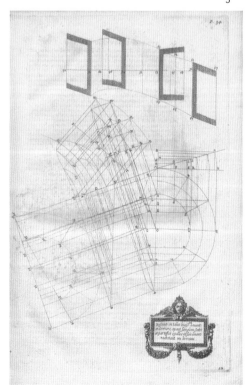

> *Who is so dull or jealous that he would not admire
> Filippo the architect, in the face of this gigantic structure,
> rising above the vaults of heaven, wide enough to
> receive in its shade all of the people of Tuscany; built
> without the aid of any truss work or mass of timber – an
> achievement that certainly seemed impossible?*[25]

It is curious to note that he spoke so highly of his colleague Brunelleschi – whose achievement could be seen by anyone in and around Florence – and the vaulting of the dome as a technical achievement, while also referring to him as an *architect*. In the 17 short years between 1435 and 1452, Alberti's own ideas about architecture culminated in the *Ten Books* which argued for the clear distinction of architect from the building trades, a split still seen in contemporary practice today. Alberti is equally adamant, however, about the architect's required knowledge in both design and construction, thus he defines architecture as a humanistic profession that merges art and science.

Diagram labels:

RHINO | 3D STUDIO **VISUALIZATION**

INNOVAYA | AFFINITY **QUALIFICATION**

EXODUS | RADIANCE | ECOTECT | FLUENT | THERM **BUILDING PERFORMANCE SIMULATION & ANALYSIS**

PROJECT WEBSITE BUZZSAW/CONSTRUCTWARE

MODEL CHECK NAVISWORKS/SOLIBRI

TRANSITION LAYER

SKETCH INFORMATION MODEL — DIGITAL PROJECT / RHINO / SKETCHUP

BUILDING DEVELOPMENT INFORMATION MODEL — ARCHITECTURAL / DIGITAL PROJECT / REVIT / STRUCTURAL / MEP

REVIT AutoCAD — TRADITIONAL DELIVERABLES

E-SPECS

THINK3 | IMAGINE &SHAPE | STUDIO TOOLS **INDUSTRIAL DESIGN**

TEKLA STEEL | INVENTOR | RHINO | SOLIDWORKS | TEKLA CONCRETE **FABRICATION INFORMATION MODEL**

INTERNET COMPONENT SEARCH TECTONIC NETWORK

INTERNET COMPONENT PROCUREMENT GOOGLE

WORKING TODAY

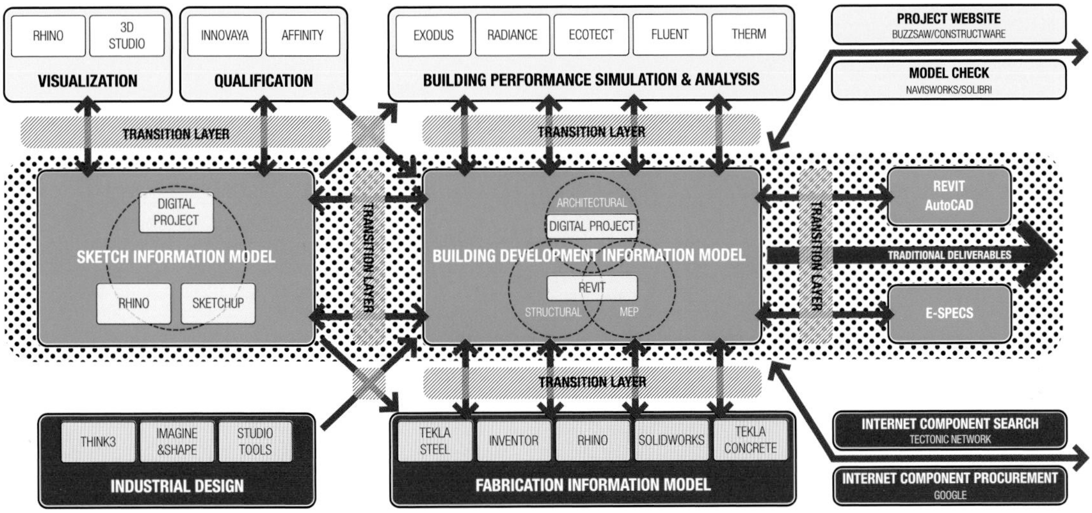

5 The noted architectural historian Robin Evans reveals an operative history of the profile as the 'template' or 'trait' used by master stonemasons. 'Traits were layout drawings used to enable the precise cutting of component masonry blocks for complex architectural forms, especially vaults. Thereby accurate fabrication of parts could be achieved prior to construction. Traits are not illustrations and yield little to the casual observer. They are orthographic projections, but they are not like other architectural drawings.'[23]

6 Paul Seletsky, BIM operations used by SOM, 2007
Two-dimensional drafting practices have clearly been replaced by three-dimensional modelling and simulation activities.

… in free matter, energy and information become perfectly coextensive fluxes, the translation of one into the other is simultaneous, and events are 'computed' instantly. Speed and space were the new materials of which the future would be made.
Sanford Kwinter, 'Flying the Bullet'[26]

In the 1990s, computer technologies equipped designers with a new series of design and construction techniques that were esoteric to many – just like the secret construction techniques and procedures of the guilds used by the master builders before them. What followed the guilds were a rapid democratisation of construction and a codification of the practice of architecture via thinkers like Alberti. What follows the digitalisation in the '90s is a user-friendly and easy relationship to software; one that allows for a closer understanding of materials, their constraints and assembly potentials.

Perhaps the most interesting similarity between the master builder and the architect using information modelling technologies today is the *expanded field* of knowledge required when the responsibilities of building fall on the designer. While these discussions will ultimately arrive at the question of risk taken by those on the design team, it is useful to suspend this aspect of the technology and focus on how it integrates with building knowledge.

THE MASTER BUILDER AND INFORMATION MODELLING 34–35

7 Jonathan Van Ostenbridge and Thomas Yeh, digitally fabricated marble panel, College of Architecture and Design, New Jersey Institute of Technology (NJIT), Newark, NJ, 2013
Students from the New Jersey Institute of Technology with Richard Garber and Yale University with Mark Foster Gage attended a workshop in digital stone manufacturing coordinated by the US-based Digital Stone Project in June 2013. Students were tutored by a group of stonemasons – who work exclusively with computer numerically controlled (CNC) milling equipment at the Garfagnana Innovazione in the Tuscany region of Italy – to produce a series of marble sculptures directly from digital three-dimensional model data. Here a five-axis robot arm removes stone in a process called '3D roughing' while a stream of water removes heat from the cutting tool. Project by Yeh and Van Ostenbridge.

An irony that seems destined for this discussion is that master builders applied years of experience and esoteric technical training in the guilds to the construction problems of the time. Today it is generally the younger and less experienced designer-builders who have the most experience with software. Some contemporary firms have addressed this issue through the creation of a new role and new job title, namely 'building information model manager'. Such a person would be responsible for the integration of digital content from all design and technical consultants – BIM software packages such as Autodesk® Revit® have distinct environments for architectural, structural, and mechanical, electrical and plumbing (MEP) objects that can all be referenced into a single file. The efficiency of this arrangement, however, especially on larger projects, approaches the representational trope that BIM promises to move our profession away from. While affording the designer the ability to make informed decisions during design development by allowing them to engage larger amounts of information, the BIM manager doesn't necessarily need to understand how to *build*. This has implications on what exactly we teach students of architecture, and the kinds of experience that will be valuable in the future. Recall the scene in the 1999 film, *The Matrix*, when Trinity has downloaded her instructions to pilot a helicopter. While it might not be a direct replacement for actual experience, information modelling points to a new combination of experience, so-called *pre-modern* intuition, and data in the development of a design scheme. It might be that younger practitioners gain the necessary experience mature architects have acquired in a very different *virtual* manner. Therefore, the manner in which we work today becomes differentiated from that of the master builder, but more strikingly from the way we practised in the 20th century.

Perhaps it is useful here to re-establish what exactly is meant by *design*. On a recent trip to the New Jersey Institute of Technology, Robert Aish, Director of Software Development at Autodesk, posited that design can be defined via three constraints applicable to any designed system:

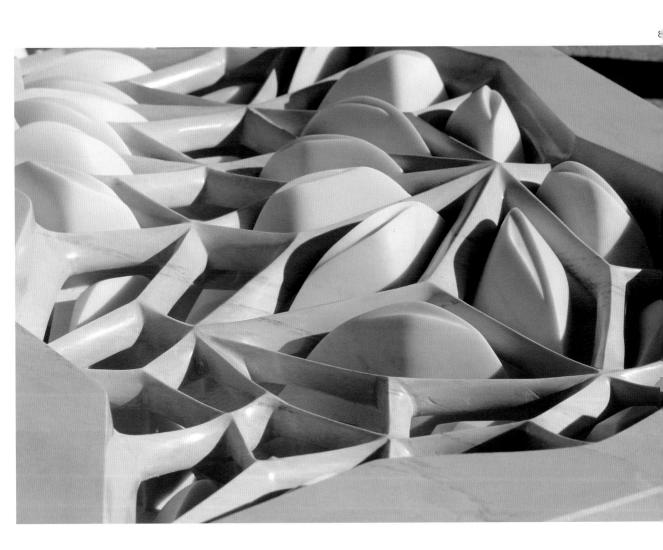

8 RJ Tripodi and Nicholas Kehagias, digitally
fabricated marble panel, Yale School of Architecture,
Yale University, New Haven, Connecticut, 2013
Digitally fabricated marble panel by Yale University
students produced at the Digital Stone Project stone-
milling workshop held at the Garfagnana Innovazione in
Italy, June 2013. The project was originally executed as
part of the 'Disheveled Geometries' seminar at the Yale
School of Architecture, taught by Mark Foster Gage.
Project by RJ Tripodi and Nicholas Kehagias.

1 How well does the system satisfy internal criteria of the designer?
2 Is the system an exemplar internally of itself as a strategy given development criteria?
3 Does the system display *protean* characteristics?

To make some sense of this, one must assume that through internal criteria, Aish is referring to the ideas or desires of the designer her/himself, establishing intuition as important in early design stages. As an exemplar of itself, the system might be considered a prototype for a design solution that meets development criteria established outside the designer's desire. Finally, by suggesting the design needs to be *protean*, Aish suggests that there should be some variability embedded in the logic of the system itself so as to respond to development criteria as the design develops. By example, this can be formally variable, such as a housing prototype for different sites, or systemically variable as in the design's ability to make use of different subsystems, such as building systems. Interestingly, this notion of design occurs outside a more technical definition and, as we will see, can be broadly applied to designed objects and not limited to works of architecture.

MASTER BUILDER > MASTER MODEL

Recall that the first CAD packages were a sort of analogue for what designers traditionally did manually, meaning that they provided a virtual working environment; however, they did very little to challenge the design process itself. When applied to design computation and rule-based architecture, information modelling allows designers to write algorithms to generate buildings. By creating a rule-based environment, designs can be virtually developed based on specific criteria such as environmental orientation or site complexity. An advantage is that design computation is inherently parametric – changes can be applied to the system automatically, so designers no longer have to manually update aspects of the design. For instance, by numerically changing the size of a window type, a parametric model will update every instance of that window that exists within the model. By changing the design rules, aspects of a design can be automatically changed.

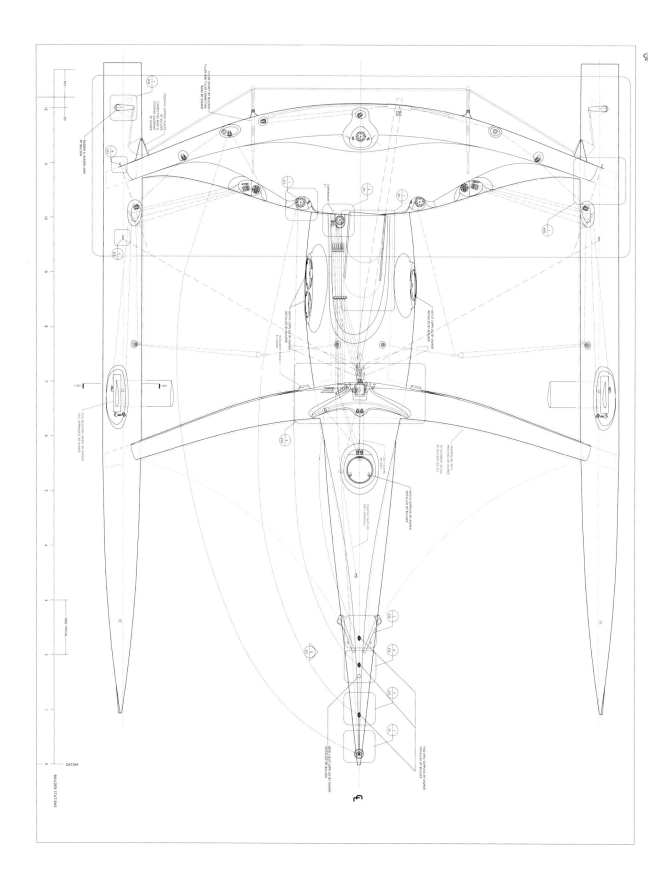

As a way of exploring the potentials of new information modelling technologies, and re-evaluating traditional design development, it is helpful to look at how information modelling has transformed other industries that are more inclined to change with technology, most notably the shipbuilding industry. In the design of yachts, spaces are limited and need to be optimised for both performance and efficiency. Some designers, such as Greg Lynn, have explored these topics in their own work and in design studios recently, and have suggested that new technologies have augmented the traditional role of the designer. It is interesting, however, that optimisations for performance in, for instance, how a boat hull cuts through water are first intuitively modelled by designers and then optimised through simulation software.

David Andrews, in his musings on shipbuilding, advocates the use of a virtual three-dimensional modelling environment – a *master model* – to achieve what he refers to as *architectural synthesis*, including material production and assembly, suggesting 'computer-aided design and production (CADAP) systems foster a better approach to definition, both for manufacturing and ensuring that the whole design is thoroughly and effectively integrated'.[27] By *integration*, Andrews refers to multiple aspects of design that are directly applicable to architecture. First, an iterative dialogue can be achieved with the building owner, or architect's client, so that suggestions and changes can easily be integrated into the virtual design. Next, the integration of the model with various databases allows for real-time costing and material lead-time estimations. Finally, the possibility of simulating the virtual design downstream in the design process allows for the understanding of manufacturing and other support processes.

CONCLUSION: TOWARDS A MORE HOLISTIC AND CREATIVE WAY OF DESIGNING

In the design of any large and organisationally complex system, such as a building or large ship, refinement of the system, both formally and numerically, has largely occurred *downstream*, that is at a later point in the design process when a multitude of consultants are involved with a system's optimisation. How could the design process change if during the earliest concept stages aspects such as environmental performance, formal organisation and human interface and interaction are studied virtually? It seems logical that the earliest stages of design development – preliminary or schematic design – are critical in determining large-scale aspects of a system, such as its organisation, so as to make more efficient the later design phases where the majority of consultants have traditionally worked. By using simulation techniques graphically within the computer, and engaging consultants at earlier stages of the design process, a shift in optimisation and efficiency should then occur. The next chapters will identify specific places in a conventional design process where information modelling can radically change the way the designer works, and suggest methods for the generation and simulation of information models.

9 Greg Lynn yacht, GF 42 Trimaran, 2013
In a very literal crossover, the architect Greg Lynn has formed a yacht design company with several key marine partners including Westerly Marine, located in Santa Ana, California and Kreysler & Associates, located in American Canyon, California. The latter uses Lynn's building information model to perform CNC tooling of the hulls and arms.

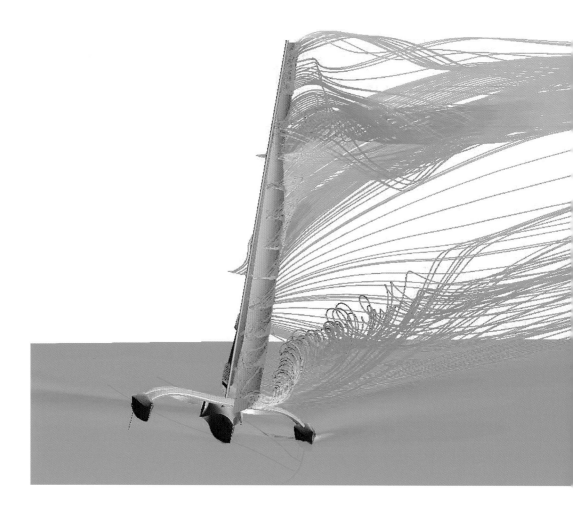

NOTES

1 Dave Hickey, 'American Beauty', *The Invisible Dragon: Essays on Beauty*, University of Chicago Press (Chicago), 2012, p 70.

2 Leonardo Benevolo, *The Architecture of the Renaissance*, Routledge (London), 2002, p 20.

3 Ibid, p 19.

4 This is suggested by Franklin Toker in 'Gothic Architecture by Remote Control: An Illustrated Building Contract of 1340', *The Art Bulletin*, Vol 67, No 1 (March 1985), pp 67–95.

5 Toker, 'Gothic Architecture by Remote Control', pp 67–95.

6 Martin S Briggs, 'Architectural Models – I', *The Burlington Magazine for Connoisseurs*, Vol 54, No 313 (April 1929), p 174.

7 See Frank D Prager, 'Brunelleschi's Inventions and the "Renewal of Roman Masonry Work"', *Osiris*, Vol 9, March 1950, pp 457–554.

10 Greg Lynn yacht, GF 42 Trimaran, 2013
As the geometry of boat hulls and sails must be precisely understood to gauge performance, Lynn's team simulated how the vessel would perform. Simulations included a computational fluid dynamics (CFD) model to assess how the boat will sail through the water. The boat's hull, deck and internal structure are vacuum consolidated E-glass/epoxy/PVC carbon/foam sandwich construction from computer numerically controlled (CNC) tooling.

8 Nicholas Adams, 'The Life and Times of Pietro dell'Abaco, a Renaissance Estimator from Siena', *Zeitschrift für Kunstgeschichte*, Vol 48, No 3 (1985), p 384.
9 Ibid, p 386.
10 Frank D Prager and Gustina Scaglia, *Brunelleschi Studies of his Technology and Inventions*, Dover Books on Architecture (New York), 1970, p 42.
11 James S Ackerman, 'Architectural Practice in the Italian Renaissance', *Journal of the Society of Architectural Historians*, Vol 13, No 3 (October 1954), p 3.
12 Benevolo, *The Architecture of the Renaissance*, p 20.
13 Ibid.
14 Ibid, p 5.
15 Frank D Prager, 'A Manuscript of Taccola, Quoting Brunelleschi, on Problems of Inventors and Builders', *Proceedings of the American Philosophical Society*, Vol 112, No 3 (21 June 1968), pp 131–49.
16 Briggs, 'Architectural Models – I', p 174.
17 Ibid, p 180.
18 Giorgio Vasari, *Lives of the Painters, Sculptors, and Architects*, quotations taken from Briggs, 'Architectural Models – I'.
19 Frank D Prager and Gustina Scaglia, *Brunelleschi: Studies of his Technology and Inventions*, p 31.
20 Ibid, p 39.
21 Ibid, p 41.
22 Manuel DeLanda, 'Philosophies of Design: The Case of Modeling Software', Alejandro Zaera-Polo and Jorge Wagensberg (eds), *Verb: Architecture Boogazine*, Actar (Barcelona), 2002, p 141.
23 Robin Evans, 'Drawn Stone', *The Projective Cast: Architecture and its Three Geometries*, MIT Press (Cambridge, MA and London), 1995, p 179.
24 Fillipo Brunelleschi lived until 15 April 1436.
25 Leon Battista Alberti, *On Painting*, revised edition, Yale University Press (New Haven, CT), 1966, p 40.
26 Sanford Kwinter, 'Flying the Bullet, or When Did the Future Begin?', in Rem Koolhaas and Sanford Kwinter (ed), *Rem Koolhaas: Conversations with Students (Architecture at Rice 30)*, Princeton Architectural Press (New York), 1996, pp 68–94.
27 DJ Andrews, 'A Comprehensive Methodology for the Design of Ships (and Other Complex Systems)', *Proceedings of the Royal Society: Mathematical, Physical and Engineering Sciences*, Vol 454, No 1968 (8 January 1998), p 205.

IMAGES
pp 28–29 © Thomas Yeh; p 30 © Scala, Florence 2013; p 33 (t& b) © GRO Architects, PLLC; p 34 Courtesy of ETH Zurich; p 35 © Scott Corey for Paul Seletsky; p 36 © Jonathan Van Ostenbridge; p 38 © RJ Tripodi and Nicholas Kehagias; p 40 © 2012 Greg Lynn YACHT & Courouble Design: Yacht & Aerospace; pp 42–43 © 2012 of GF42 Trimaran designed by Greg Lynn YACHT & Courouble Design: Yacht & Aerospace.

10

ARCHITECTS,
CONTROL AND
CONSTRUCTION

THE BARCLAYS CENTER

1

1 SHoP Architects, Barclays Center,
Brooklyn, New York, 2012
SHoP Architects completed the Barclays
Center in Brooklyn in September 2012.
SHoP Construction Services worked
closely with structural engineers Thornton
Tomasetti and used highly controlled
digital direct-to-manufacture processes
to deliver a high degree of design-build
project integration.

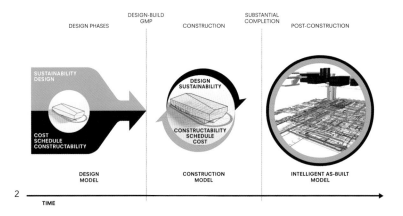

About 12 years ago, SHoP Architects became interested in development work such as the Porter House and 290 Mulberry Street, and consequently became an equity partner in those projects. As such, the practice had a responsibility to take on the typical risks associated with construction projects, seeing them as an opportunity to leverage a robust set of digital tools effectively to facilitate the delivery of these projects on cost and budget. There is very early integration in the SHoP design process of material specifications, costs and fabrication; this process has been explored in various subcontractor relationships, where the practice will engage these fabricators and use their expertise, software and hardware in the design process. This allows for the rationalisation and integration of a variety of building components and systems sometimes as early as the design development stage of a project. SHoP's hands-on approach to building construction differs greatly from the way architects have operated in the last 500 years, in which a set of two-dimensional documents is created to be interpreted by others, which is many times 'value-engineered' after construction documentation is complete. The practice began regularly to produce shop-drawing or fabrication quality documentation early in the design process to bring cost certainty to their work and to deliver a level of comfort to their development partners while producing novel designs.

SHoP's interest in these activities in some ways predates building information modelling (BIM) as a software phenomenon; while the practice always leveraged digital tools in their work, their novel approach came at a time when digital fabrication technologies were only beginning to be widely used by architects. BIM followed a few years later and allows the practice to take this interest further with the ability to coordinate and integrate full building systems virtually. It is important to note that it was an interest in digital fabrication that set the practice on the path it has followed. In fact, most of the practices profiled here have adopted a design-centric approach to using BIM through an interest in digital fabrication

2 SHoP Architects, New York, 2010
The SHoP Architects/SHoP Construction Services relationship allows the firm to use digital technology tools to engage in sustainable design activities while virtually controlling construction costs in project design phases. During construction, the virtual model is used to check design assumptions and construct the building virtually, allowing the firm to control construction methods, cost and schedule. Post-construction, the model can be used to record as-built changes and manage the facility.

3 SHoP Architects, A-Labs at the Fashion Institute of Technology, New York, 2008
SHoP Architects was an early adopter of virtual construction and greater coordination between the design and construction phases of a building project. SHoP Construction Services created a virtual model to track construction progress at SHoP's A-Labs project, a renovation of lab and studio spaces at the Fashion Institute of Technology, which was completed in 2011.

technologies. Interestingly, this approach has not only allowed these practices to exert more control over the construction process as architects, it has also allowed them to work in a more sustainable way through the simulation tools BIM systems afford.

SHoP also served as a construction manager for its early development projects. Traditionally, construction managers worked manually with printed two-dimensional drawing sets for measuring bills of quantities. This role, and the use of digital tools to perform management responsibilities coupled with the digital fabrication explorations in this early work, naturally led the practice to BIM systems and to the creation of SHoP Construction Services (SC) in 2007. The practice had gained experience in construction management, but came about it via digital modelling tools and if they were using software to rationalise the geometry of a specific part of a building, such as a panelised metal facade, it made sense to expand the use of such tools to understand the whole building as a series of integrated yet discrete systems. Digital tools allowed the practice to take more responsibility in the actualisation of their projects and therefore exert more control in the project development than had typically been seen in 20th-century practice models in which architects generally attempted to reduce their risk and exposure in the construction aspects of a building project.

3

BIM AS A DRIVER FOR VIRTUAL CONSTRUCTION

Jonathan Mallie, Principal of SHoP and Managing Director of SHoP Construction, used experience he gained as a project designer on these early projects to conceptualise an augmented role for the architect. Mallie suggests that the preparation and training architects obtain is well suited to project management roles and has found in SHoP and SC creative solutions to design and deliver novel building solutions at a large scale.[1] This approach to authorship should be underscored; by actively participating in the design and construction phases of a building project the two companies ensure that design intent is novel, but also efficient and cost-effective. This partnership goes beyond having highly technical expertise on the design team, because SC necessarily takes on risk on the construction side of a building project as a contractor or manager, it is required to take on additional scope in a project's resolution. This has expanded their digital palette to include 4- and 5-D construction scheduling, and very precise cost estimation that is driven by data included in the information models the practice produces on the design side. It has also required the practice to set high standards in the quality of its design documentation as this will be the foundation of information modelling activities on the construction side. The opportunity to have a separate entity such as SC allows for an almost internal budgeting process for projects, enabling the practice to be contracted by others on the construction team, such as a subcontractor or a construction manager, ensuring the practice can achieve its design goals.

Early on it became important for SHoP to convince their clients that this model and working relationship was cost-effective, especially on projects that were increasing in size and complexity. While this model begins to look like a traditional architect-led design-build scenario, it is the use of digital tools that makes it different. In the Barclays Center in Brooklyn, completed in 2012, SA initially brought in SC to protect their design intent and convince the project owner, Forest City Ratner, that the practice could manage all quantities and materials included in the architect's scope of work, which was the wrapping of the area's exterior and the development of a series of interior spaces within the sports arena. The building information model created by SC needed to take into account all costs associated with the project at a schematic level of design. Once the practice was able to show proof of this concept, the level of trust that was built between architect and owner became significant.

SC is different from other contractors or construction management entities in that the digital technologies used to actualise a building have been digested into SHoP's design process. Still today, many similar companies will use BIM tools in their work, but at an additional short-term cost to the owner offset by long-term savings in the building through cost and time efficiencies. New technologies, when properly implemented in a design-build process, will generally yield efficiencies and cost savings that could

4

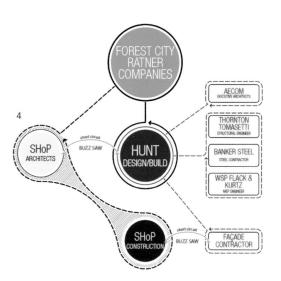

not be realised in an analogue method of working. This attests to the SHoP/SC working process being still novel in many ways, and, counterintuitively, there remaining a belief that the use of digital tools brings an added cost to the overall hard and soft costs of a building project. BIM is not an additional line item in a construction budget, instead it is something far more transformative in that the design and construction team can at any time during project development query attributes in real-time and make better informed decisions about the actualisation of a project. It drives virtual construction prior to fieldwork. This ability can lead to a reduction of change orders and requests for information during the construction process, thereby decreasing the amount of time allotted for construction itself.

Mallie feels that BIM has a role in all design and construction, not solely novel or 'high' design projects. Increasingly, the coordination that these tools afford is being used to prefabricate more and more parts and assemblies in factories where higher tolerances can be maintained and costs are generally lower. (See GRO Architects' work on modular construction.) While an architect's BIM may contain data for bills of materials, SC is linking this data to procurement strategies for suppliers as a way of generating very precise cost analyses of their projects. Mallie sees this as moving the construction industry further in the direction of off-site manufacturing – so the construction industry may indeed become more like the shipbuilding industry, it may become primarily a manufacturing industry.

THE BARCLAYS CENTER, DESIGN AND BIM EFFICIENCIES

The design of the Barclays Center achieves a balance between the building's iconic facade and flying canopy with the engagement of a busy urban intersection. It is legible at multiple scales while maintaining an identity that delights visitors, neighbours, fans and spectators. Integrated into one of the busiest urban intersections in the New York metro area, the Center will sustain a healthy, interactive dialogue with the surrounding streets and neighbourhood.

When SHoP Architects was awarded the contract to complete the design of the Barclays Center, the practice quickly realised that SC would be a critical element to the project's success. Given the scheduling pressures the practice inherited when it became involved, it naturally turned to BIM strategies to manage the construction process virtually. At that point, the structural steel for the building had already been ordered and previous architects had planned much of the project. The project's structural engineer, Thornton Tomasetti in New York, had created a structural steel model using Tekla® Structures, which was shared with the design team at SHoP so the practice could assess the design while planning the exterior wrapper of the building. Mallie feels the most fluid and integrated work on the project occurred between SC, which was contracted by the facade contractor, and Thornton Tomasetti, the structural engineers on the design team. Once

4 SHoP Architects, Barclays Center, Brooklyn, New York, 2010
Contractual relationships between SHoP Architects, design team, construction team and SC (SHoP Construction) allowed for a seamless transfer of information between all entities engaged in the design and fabrication of the pre-weathered steel panels, even though SC worked only and directly for the facade contractor.

5

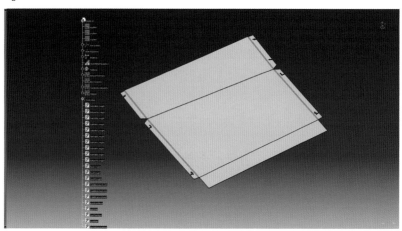

6

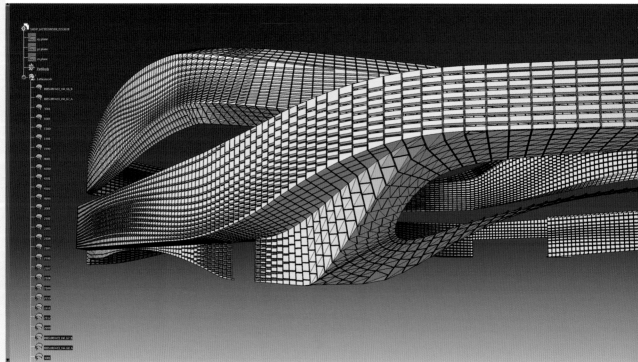

SHoP Architects began working on the project, SC worked on the facade integration with the design team to support the development of the design. This work was ultimately added to a guaranteed maximum price (GMP) estimate that had been previously undertaken, so a new, revised cost estimate took into account the SHoP design proposal. The facade contractor worked with Hunt Construction Group to complete the facade construction and SC ultimately performed consulting work for them. This scope of work included the secondary steel system required to support the pre-weathered steel facade panels – work that had to be coordinated with the Thornton Tomasetti Tekla® model. The facade contractor used a facade-engineering firm, Curtainwall Design Consulting (CDC) as engineer of record.

The design of the Barclays Arena is a new collaborative model enabled by digital tools. SC's scope was ultimately defined by the facade contractor and initially pertained to the geometric definition of the curving pre-weathered steel facade panels. In defining the panel shapes for CNC-cutting, SC developed the complex geometry with Dassault Systèmes CATIA® and used SigmaNEST® AutoNEST® to nest the facade panel shapes efficiently on sheets for water-jet cutting. In doing so, they demonstrated the power of the technology used to the facade contractor, who originally intended to order a 1.524-metre (5'–0") wide coil width of A588 pre-weathered sheet steel, at a 4.77-millimetre (³/₁₆") thickness, to address both a 1.524-metre (5'–0") panel-spanning requirement and blast mitigation requirements. Using the nesting software, SC demonstrated that all panels could be efficiently nested in a 1.505-metre (4'–11") coil width, the 44.45-millimetre (1¾") decrease in width saving the facade contractor approximately $250,000 USD in material costs on the facade panels. This three-day exercise in efficiency and cost-savings led the facade contractor to rely heavily on SC's expertise for the remainder of the design and build project phases, and demonstrated for the construction team that standardisation was no longer a requirement of the facade panels: with the digital control exerted by the SHoP Construction team, panels could be mass-customised – made unique – while still ensuring an efficient material yield. In some ways SC provided an avenue for the design intent to exceed the intentions of SHoP Architects as it was initially thought that SC would help rationalise or optimise panel yield through standardisation. Instead, they found efficiencies through nesting software that allowed for uniqueness of the pre-weathered steel panel shapes, and then the attachment of these panels to a unitised curtain wall and the secondary steel – which was all under the scope of the facade contractor. This process didn't merely protect the design intent – it advanced it.

The facade contractor took design intent from SHoP Architects, and knew that they wanted to unitise the curtain wall, which was something that they had experience with on other projects. The attachment of the secondary steel to the primary steel and coordinating the unitised curtain wall between them fell under SHoP Construction's coordination scope.

5 SHoP Construction Services, Barclays Center, Brooklyn, New York, 2010
The surface panels were given a 4.77-millimetre (³/₁₆") thickness by offsetting the original surface. At this point in geometric development it was important that the team take into account bend radii that would occur in panel actualisation. Each panel was unfolded in CATIA® so that it was flat and could be nested onto a virtual material sheet. These files were then used for water-jet cutting of each panel.

6 SHoP Architects, Barclays Center, Brooklyn, New York, 2010
The SC team moved from the Rhinoceros® surface model to CATIA® for specific weathered-steel panel development, by extracting surface edge curves and importing them. A script was developed to instantiate the panels on the global surfaces developed from the Rhinoceros® edge curves; this script also ensured that the edge curves would remain parametric. The facade pattern development was part of the Knowledgeware platform in CATIA®. Once the panels were deployed on the CATIA® surfaces, each panel needed to be developed in terms of its fold geometry and tabs for mounting, and given thickness – turned from a surface model into a solid model. A prototypical panel was first developed to understand the amount of geometric bending necessary for each panel. The SC team then deployed the panels over the surface geometry in CATIA® that was translated from Rhinoceros® edge curves.

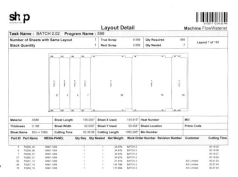

7

8

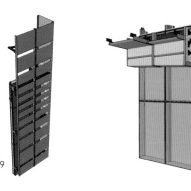

9

7 SHoP Construction Services, Barclays
Center, Brooklyn, New York, 2010
A digital fabrication ticket, or 'FAB Ticket',
shows nested panels on sheets of raw material
for water-jet cutting. The facade contractor
used this data for panel production.

8 SHoP Construction Services, Barclays
Center, Brooklyn, New York, 2011
The formed facade panels of A588 steel
were pre-weathered using a wet-dry cycle
process. The facade contractor used 12 to 16
wet/dry cycles per day for each panel for a
period of three months. This occurred for four
batches of approximately 3,000 panels each.
Pre-weathered steel was selected due to the
contextual character of historic downtown
Brooklyn and the industrial waterfront of the
Brooklyn Navy Yard. SC developed an iPhone
application for tracking the forming and
weathering processes – each panel could be
tracked on a smartphone to understand where
the fabricator was in the process of fabricating
and pre-weathering each panel.

9 SHoP Construction Services, Barclays
Center, Brooklyn, New York, 2012
The facade contractor pushed a prefabrication
agenda in delivering facade panels. These
assemblies, which the team referred to as
'mega-panels', were assembled off-site,
shipped and craned into place on site. The
method of attachment for each of these panels
needed to be considered with an already
unitised curtain-wall assembly process, making
a modular solution ideal.

10 SHoP Construction Services, Barclays
Center, Brooklyn, New York, 2011
Each vertical mullion was spaced on an
approximately 1.524-metre (5'–0") grid that
was maintained along the exterior of the
building. This served as a way of attaching
the non-regular pre-weathered steel panels
back to a uniform grid for the unitised curtain
wall. The panels were shipped in widths of
3.05-metres (10'–0") or two-panel assemblies.

10

As SC became more engaged with the general contractor and
subcontractors, it became clear that the complex panelisation on
the building's facade would not only be controlled but would
exceed design intent. The level of confidence this instilled in the
building owner and contractors led SC to begin interfacing with
additional scope in the project's design and construction. The
interior design would ultimately need to respond to the exterior
building shell and technology enabled SHoP/SC to design and
develop more complex interior systems, such as the system of light
rails on the concourses and the arena concession modelling
program, for which SC did a high-level coordination of all food
services spaces with the building's mechanical, electrical and
plumbing (MEP) equipment. On this coordination effort, the
building's general contractor remarked that Barclays was the most
efficient concession installation they have done in over 30
concession installations. Using Autodesk® Revit® software, SC
additionally provided digital as-built models to the facility managers
that were linked to project data such as submittals and cut-sheets.

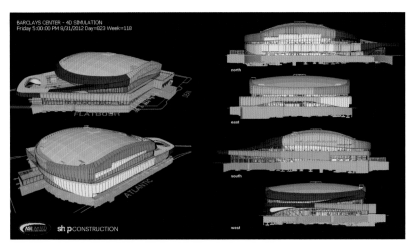

11 SHoP Construction Services, Barclays
Center, Brooklyn, New York, 2011
SC created a 4-D construction-sequencing
model, which included primary structural
steel, secondary steel, unitised curtain wall
and the pre-weathered steel skin. The model
enabled the construction team to make
informed decisions on a daily basis. All parties
involved in the construction process embraced
responsibility in order to mitigate the risk of
such an innovative process.

12 SHoP Architects, Barclays Center,
Brooklyn, New York, 2012
Light rails on the main concourse illuminate
the space and were also designed to light the
facade itself.

13 SHoP Architects, Barclays Center,
Brooklyn, New York, 2012
Coordination between the secondary structural
steel, the pre-weathered steel panels and the
shape of the oculus itself was required and it
was also one of the last aspects of the arena
to be constructed. Here the secondary steel
is installed and gives form to the canopy in
March 2012.

SPECIFIC BIM PROCESS

SC developed a Revit® model that took key criteria from the exterior facade design and integrated it with the base building model. For this model, SC imported facade data from their CATIA® V5 model that delineated different scopes within the contract for construction including a 'face of curtain wall' model, a 'line of secondary steel model' and a 'line of pre-weathered steel panel' model. This was combined with the model used to coordinate SHoP's interior design and construction scope. The interface between each of these components ensured a designed relationship between interior and exterior components. The pre-weathered steel facade was originally developed in Rhinoceros® and then moved into CATIA® V5 and coordinated with Thornton Tomasetti's Tekla® structural model.

The Barclays Center was opened in September 2012 and has successfully hosted professional sporting events as well as concerts.

NOTE

1 Discussion with Jonathan Mallie in New York, 4 June 2013.

IMAGES

pp 44–45 © SHoP Architects, photos Bruce Damonte; pp 46, 47, 50, 53, 54 © SHoP Construction; p 48 © GRO Architects, PLLC; pp 54–55 © SHoP Architects, photo Julie Jira; pp 55, 56–57 © SHoP Architects, photos Bruce Damonte.

12

13

14

14 SHoP Architects, Barclays Center, Brooklyn, New York, 2012
The canopy soars 9.144 metres (30'–0") high and contains the oculus that frames the view of the arena. This public entry plaza links Atlantic and Flatbush Avenues while creating a grand civic space. The canopy is used for image projection and infographics, as seen here during a Brooklyn Nets game.

3 | THE C(REATIVE)ONSTRUCTION PROCESS, THEN AND NOW

THE CURIOUS CASE OF CONSTRUCTION DOCUMENTS IN 20TH-CENTURY PRACTICE

As the profession of architecture matured in the late 19th and 20th centuries, so did the architectural office and its concomitant contractual responsibilities. As analogue production tools and methods developed, so did the deliverables generally required of architects by their clients and those who constructed their designs. The notion of phasing in architectural design became codified, in which architects generally completed contract deliverables in three specific design phases that followed initial project development. These three phases: schematic design (SD), design development (DD) and construction documentation (CD), often took place discretely, with the inclusion of engineering consultants in design development, or more often, during construction documentation. This mode of working also maintained separation from a liability standpoint, the architect from the general contractor, who would receive at the end of these phases a set of two-dimensional drawings to, in theory, fully cost and deliver the building.

Schematic design is concerned generally with the determination of large-scale design organisation and the development of architectural plans, while design development takes this work further with the production of exterior and interior elevations, determination of large-scale building systems and preliminary coordination with consultants such as structural and mechanical engineers. Material selections and a preliminary cost estimate can also be accomplished during design development. During construction documentation, two-dimensional drawings that depict, dimension and notate all significant aspects of the building so that precise costing of the project can be accomplished are fully developed. The work of other technical consultants, such as facade/curtain wall consultants and acoustic consultants is fully integrated in this phase, as is the final development of building systems chosen in the previous phase.

1

1 Budd Company, drafting room, Philadelphia, Pennsylvania, 1916
The early 20th-century drafting room further codified the work of the architect as distinct from the work of the builder. The majority of draftsmen worked away from project sites largely on the representation of a building project. This practice allowed for interpretation by those who built the work and could not ensure the architect's intentions were being followed. Pictured is the drafting room of the Budd Company's Hunting Park plant in Philadelphia, PA in 1916. Nowadays the company is called ThyssenKrupp Budd and is a prominent manufacturer of building elevator systems.

2 McKim, Mead & White, drafting
room, New York, 1891
The drafting room in the offices of
McKim, Mead & White at 1 West 20th
Street in Manhattan, 1891. At the time
the firm was the largest architectural
practice in New York. It was not
uncommon then for drafting rooms in
such large firms to encompass whole
floors of a building.[6]

2

According to the American Institute of Architects, which has been developing contract and construction document standards for over 120 years:

> More than 100 forms and contracts comprise AIA Contract Documents. These forms and contracts define the relationships and terms involved in design and construction projects. Contract Documents provide assistance to users who otherwise could not obtain knowledgeable legal counsel in a timely or economical fashion by (a) providing standard documents as an alternative to expensive, custom-drafted documents, and (b) promoting flexible use through the publication of supplemental guides demonstrating, with model language and instructions, the adaptability of the standard documents to particular circumstances.[1]

The notion of the drafting room evolved in the early 20th century much like the assembly line, where a team of men layered cloth and Mylar® and documented with pencils the *majority*[2] of the graphic and written information necessary to build a building. Structural grids were drawn and dimensioned, and two-dimensionally coordinated with information and features of the architectural plan. Building sections displayed the two-dimensional elevational relationship between the architectural ceiling, building infrastructure such as lighting, the sprinkler system, and mechanical ducting to the structure of the floor above. Reflected ceiling plans sought to two-dimensionally organise equipment and features in the architectural ceiling like fire and smoke alarms, lighting fixtures, vents and registers, and sprinkler system heads, with the complex arrangement of ducts, piping and structure above.

During this time, drafting rooms varied in size based on a firm's project load, and as larger firms increasingly augmented their own body of work, they referred to that body of work in the production of new projects. Writing about Raymond Hood's office in 1929, when he and several associated architects were designing Rockefeller Center, Daniel Okrent notes, 'On the twenty-fifth floor, one enormous drafting room contained forty-two identical drawing boards, each the size of a six-seat dining room table; another room harbored twelve more, and an additional fourteen stood just outside the principal's offices or at the top of the principal's offices.'[3] In the mid-1890s, McKim, Mead & White was the largest architectural firm in New York with a staff of over 100, the majority being draftsmen.[4] In reflecting on the work and the drafting room of McKim, Mead & White during the 1880s, Mosette Broderick writes, '… McKim, Mead & White became image people, bringing European splendor to the New World. Their drafting room moved from creativity to conformity, with each detail being verified to ensure it had appeared in the office library of Renaissance architecture books.'[5] In some ways, this profession in transition began to move backward as it increasingly relied on *images of buildings* and became further removed from their construction.

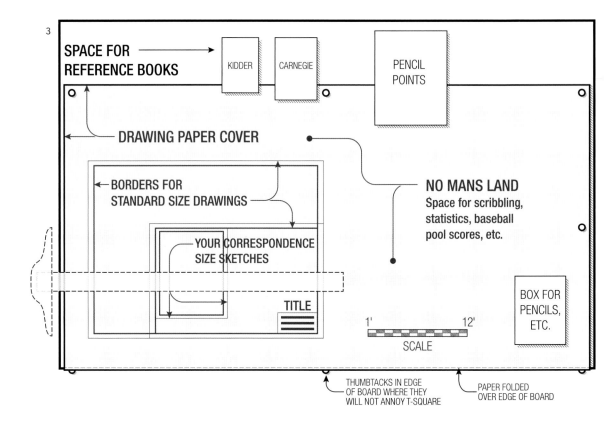

3

SPACE FOR REFERENCE BOOKS

KIDDER

CARNEGIE

PENCIL POINTS

DRAWING PAPER COVER

BORDERS FOR STANDARD SIZE DRAWINGS

YOUR CORRESPONDENCE SIZE SKETCHES

TITLE

NO MANS LAND
Space for scribbling, statistics, baseball pool scores, etc.

BOX FOR PENCILS, ETC.

1'   12'

SCALE

THUMBTACKS IN EDGE OF BOARD WHERE THEY WILL NOT ANNOY T-SQUARE

PAPER FOLDED OVER EDGE OF BOARD

To further complicate this situation of distance, it seems some in the early 20th century sought to make distinctions between the architect and the draftsman – elaborating the differences between the 'incommensurable process of artistic creation and the quantifiable technical production in the drafting room'.[7] This distinction, one of professional training in the academy versus vocational training, perhaps at night school, helped to portray the architect as a model of 'historic resistance',[8] whose authority as author was made manifest through the tools of the era, mainly the pencils and film on the drafting board, which were used by others – the draftsmen – to create a possibility of the architect's vision. Inherently, these layered sheets of drafting film composed the possible and intended organisation of a building and its components. Construction documents at best represented design intentions in a comprehensive way. These instruments of the architectural contract were more often than not then transmitted.

physically, to clients or others ultimately for the construction of a building. These layers of professional organisation served to enforce the notion of the time that architecture was an epistemological practice, as opposed to a *material* one.

It has been necessary for contract documents to adapt to the requisites of more complex building programmes and requirements, and the emergence of new 20th-century building types – the airport, the factory, the car wash – and the increasing demands of the market. Specialists that handled specific aspects of building design, technical consultants such as structural and mechanical engineers, planners, interior designers – all inadvertently contributed to the increasingly difficult task of coordinating the construction document set. Not only did a two-dimensional representation of a building require many translucent drawing sheets, but they were also often produced remotely from one another.

INSTRUCTIONS FOR BUILDING?

Typically, once the construction documents were tendered in a building project, architects had little to do with the day-to-day progress of building construction. Contracts at times stipulated for site visits and other involvement, such as shop drawing review and procurement of funds for the contractor for work completed; however, the representational nature of these documents more often than not led to interpretation on the project site by those charged with building the designs. Building construction is usually divided into various trades, and often two trades cannot work on a building at the same time simply due to the fact that they work within the same space. For instance, a sprinkler systems subcontractor and a mechanical subcontractor work within the cavity of the architectural ceiling and the floor above; the former needs a certain amount of work by the plumbing subcontractor to be complete prior to commencing their work. The complexity of these situations has led to field errors that have proved costly in time and expenditure to the owner, general contractor and even the architect. This is not to champion the work of the architect over others in the messy process of building, but more importantly to reiterate the gap that has historically existed between design production and building construction.

Perhaps the most remarkable aspect of contract documents in the 20th century is that they really had little to do with the responsibility of building. According to the authors of *The Architect's Handbook of Professional Practice*, James B Atkins, FAIA, and Grant A Simpson, FAIA:

> *The documents are not issued for construction per se, but instead, they are issued to facilitate construction by expressing the design concept. The documents do not contain sufficient information to construct the project, and much more information is required before the work can be done …*[9]

3 GRO Architects, plan of a drafting board, New York, 2013
This 'roof plan' of a drafting board was recreated from a sketch depicted in *Pencil Points*, the journal for the architectural draftsman in 1929. In some ways, the drafting board is analogous to the desktop or home screen of an architect's computer today, the software of which – the digital tools of the 21st-century architect – has replaced the T-square, drawing sheets and box of pencils shown on the draftsman's desktop. The original sketch included in its captioning advice for replacing drawing paper covers and advocated the use of a rational proportion system for tracings, based on standard sizes used by the architectural firm.

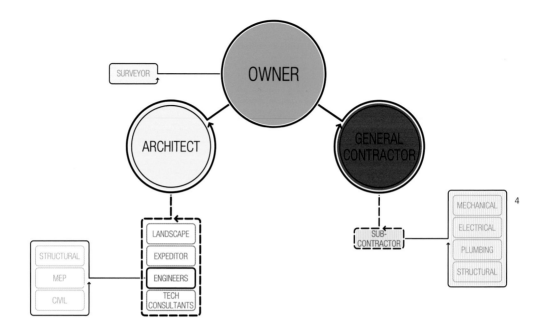

4

5

Further, the same book elaborates, 'It is important that all parties understand that construction documents are not intended to be a complete set of instructions on how to construct a building. Construction means, methods, techniques, sequences, procedures, and site safety precautions are customarily assigned as responsibilities of the contractor to give the contractor full latitude in preparing bids and carrying out the construction phase.'[10] Both of these quotes enforce the notion that construction documents demonstrate a possible design and construction solution, but more importantly form a basis, along with the written contract(s), of a binding and legal agreement between an owner and general contractor, with the architect representing the owner's interest in the building project. Design intent has to do with desired outcome, not the means by which it is achieved, however, as any designer knows, the design process can heavily influence that outcome. It is not a coincidence given this agreement that in the case of arbitration or a construction error or omission, that the written word, either in contracts, notes or architectural specifications, prevails over the abstract graphical notion of the construction documents.

CONVENTIONAL ARCHITECT – OWNER – CONTRACTOR RELATIONSHIPS

As interpretations readily emerged and conflicts in large building projects became more prevalent, additional specialists were added to the architect-owner-contractor relationship. Through the emergence of the construction manager, who represents the general contractor and serves as a liaison between contractor and owner or architect; and the owner's representative, who is installed largely to work with, or against, the construction manager, the layers of individuals or teams responsible for constructing a building began to thicken. Beginning in the 1960s, the conflux of the high cost of cash in the credit markets, an increase in the construction of large and complex projects, and a rise in litigation over construction projects (often directed at general contractors), the concept of the professional construction manager was born. This individual, incentivised by time and cost controls, would act as intermediary between the project owner and general contractor, serving as a manager of construction procurement and the construction process.[11] The addition of construction management services became a serious consideration for large projects following the construction of the Atlanta and Fulton County Stadium in Georgia, which was 'designed in secret and built within one year as part of the Braves baseball team's move from Milwaukee to Atlanta' in 1965.[12] This large sports complex was constructed in only 51 weeks.

The addition of these specialists – often trained as architects or professional engineers themselves – was meant to streamline the building process by making others accountable for aspects of construction, changing costs of materials, managing lead times for materials or equipment and making substitutions, or even challenging design decisions made in the construction documents, but it did little to increase trust between owner, architect and contractor – in fact often it made the building process more contentious.

4 GRO Architects, typical owner-architect-general contractor relationship, 2013
In a typical owner-architect-general contractor (GC) relationship, the owner legally acts as liaison, or perhaps more appropriately barrier, between the architect and general contractor. This distance regularly results in interpretations of the architect's intentions by others and can lead to costly (in time and expenditure) errors on project sites.

5 Heery International, Inc, Atlanta and Fulton County Stadium, Atlanta, Georgia, 1965
The Atlanta and Fulton County Stadium, seen under construction looking north, was constructed in just under a year to attract Major League Baseball's Braves from Milwaukee and is an early example of how construction management services enabled greater efficiency in the delivery of 20th-century construction projects. Heery, at the time teamed with Finch, Alexander, Barnes, Rothschild and Paschal, and known as Heery-Fabrap, performed architectural, engineering and construction management services. The stadium held both baseball and American football games until 1996 and was demolished in 1997.

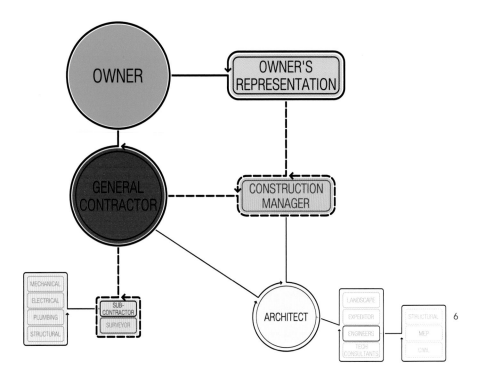

6

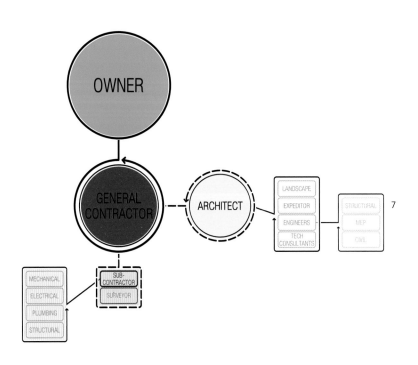

7

6 GRO Architects, conventional owner-architect-general contractor relationship with construction manager, 2013
As traditional building contracts failed to provide equal incentives to the three main parties – owner, architect and general contractor – and documentation technologies could not fully encapsulate all conditions and methods on the project site, others in the employ of owners or general contractors such as owner's representatives and construction managers *thickened* the construction process. The use of such overseers for a specific party both complicated the building process and further diminished the importance of the architect on the 20th-century building site.

7 GRO Architects, conventional design-build relationship, 2013
In a typical design-bid-build owner-architect-general contractor relationship, the architect's contractual relationship is with the general contractor, as opposed to the owner. Project consultants remain in the employ of the architect. This organisation sought to streamline construction communication between the general contractor and architect but falls short of the shared responsibility contracts that can be utilised through building information modelling.

CONCLUSION: NEW TOOLS, NEW RELATIONSHIPS AND NOVEL FORMS

The first wave of three-dimensional modelling tools largely sought to mediate this construction landscape; interestingly, however, many architects did not implement them for this explicit purpose. The adoption of modelling software in the 1990s by many schools of architecture, as well as notable firms large and small, allowed for the quick visualisation of intended buildings, while also creating the opportunity for new and novel forms that were difficult to describe two dimensionally. The idea of adopting three-dimensional modelling tools to better manage a project digitally has merit: designers could find problems in their virtual models and correct them prior to building; however, what is overlooked is precisely what empowered Brunelleschi in the 15th century – at the time when the profession was being codified. Recall again that, as a master builder, Brunelleschi was entrusted with the conceptualisation of the dome at Santa Maria del Fiore (building *ART*) and the direction of its means of actualisation (building *SCIENCE*).

Large general contracting companies are increasingly imposing BIM, and the particular form it takes, on architects. In this sense it is the contracting company that drives the virtual development of the project, at least from a construction standpoint. Ultimately, this could open up a sharing of responsibilities between project development entities, with the virtual model being circulated for information purposes to entities responsible for a specific scope. It also has the potential to create hybrid entities, such as architect-developer as seen in the successful design and delivery of the Porter House by SHoP Architects in 2003.

No discussion of BIM should be complete without a reconceptualisation of how new digital tools augment, challenge and change the authorial process of design. In charting the development of more progressive design practices over the last 10 years, it is apparent that such firms are not adopting BIM simply to be more efficient – they understand that BIM tools have the capacity to change radically the way designers conceive of, develop, iterate and share design solutions. Intrinsic to this point is a new process of *verification*: as the design methodology using new tools is codified, projects can be managed during preconstruction stages so as to ensure their viability in terms of cost and schedule, thereby assuring owners that architects are identifying and engaging in risks. Examples of new relationships between architect, owner and contractor that these technologies have brought about should be considered.

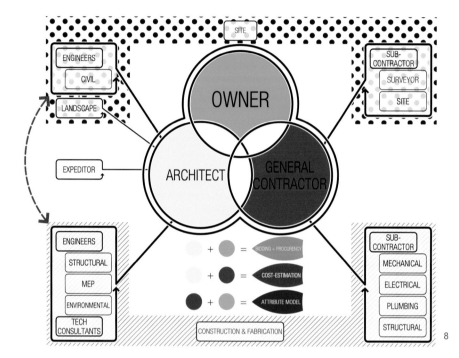

Diagram labels:

SITE

ENGINEERS
CIVIL
LANDSCAPE

OWNER

SUB-CONTRACTOR
SURVEYOR
SITE

EXPEDITOR

ARCHITECT

GENERAL CONTRACTOR

ENGINEERS
STRUCTURAL
MEP
ENVIRONMENTAL
TECH CONSULTANTS

○ + ○ = BIDDING + PROCUREMENT
○ + ● = COST-ESTIMATION
● + ○ = ATTRIBUTE MODEL

SUB-CONTRACTOR
MECHANICAL
ELECTRICAL
PLUMBING
STRUCTURAL

CONSTRUCTION & FABRICATION

8

8 GRO Architects, incentivised design-bid-build, 2013

In a revised design-bid-build scenario, the architect, owner and general contractor share a series of risks in the delivery of a construction project. Firms, such as SHoP Architects in New York, are exploring such relationships as a way of giving parties on the design and construction team an incentive to find ways to operate more efficiently in terms of project costs and schedule.

9 SHoP Architects, Porter House, New York, 2003

The Porter House, a residential project by SHoP Architects, is an example of a hybrid development model where the architect and developer worked closely together and shared risks and responsibilities to design and deliver the project. The architects, with the development team of Jeffrey M Brown Associates, were active in the day-to-day management of site construction. The team also used three-dimensional tools to design and deliver the building, and more specifically, its varied zinc facade, in 2003, at a time prior to more common usage of BIM platforms. The project, shown under construction, led the firm to launch SHoP Construction Services LLC four years later.

NOTES

1 http://www.aia.org/contractdocs/AIAS076682

2 I suggest 'majority' here as it is impossible in an abstract documentation medium to 'draw' a fully complete and realisable building.

3 Daniel Okrent, *Great Fortune: The Epic of Rockefeller Center*, Viking Penguin (New York), 2003, p 147.

4 Gail Fenske, 'The Beaux-Arts Architect and the Skyscraper: Cass Gilbert, the Professional Engineer, and the Rationalization of Construction in Chicago and New York', in Roberta Moudry (ed), *The American Skyscraper: Cultural Histories*, Cambridge University Press (New York), 2005, p 25.

5 Mosette Broderick, *Triumvirate: McKim, Mead & White: Art, Architecture, Scandal, and Class in America's Gilded Age*, Alfred A Knopf, a division of Random House, Inc (New York), 2010, pp 241–2.

6 Ralph W Liebing, *The Other Architecture: Tasks of Practice Beyond Design*, Springer (Vienna, New York), 2011, p 83.

7 George B Johnston, 'Dialectics of the Architect and the Draftsman in *Pencil Points*, 1920–1932', *Drafting Culture: A Social History of Architectural Graphic Standards*, MIT Press (Cambridge, MA), 2008, p 59.

8 Ibid, p 2.

9 http://info.aia.org/aiarchitect/thisweek05/tw0902/tw0902bp_riskmgmt.cfm

10 American Institute of Architects, *The Architect's Handbook of Professional Practice*, 13th edition, John Wiley & Sons, Inc (Hoboken, NJ), 2001, p 532.

11 George T Heery, 'A History of Construction Management, Program Management and Development Management', 2011, p 2. Accessed via http://www.brookwoodgroup.com/index.php?sec=2&sub=7#histCMPM

12 Ibid, p 3.

IMAGES

pp 58–59 © Hagley Museum and Library; pp 60–61 McKim, Mead & White / Museum of the City of New York; p 62, p 64 (t), 64, 68 © GRO Architects, PLLC, image by Scott Corey; p 64 (b) © Kenan Research Center at the Atlanta History Center; p 69 © SHoP Architects PC, photo Jeremy Bitterman.

9

PEROT MUSEUM OF
NATURE AND SCIENCE

Morphosis is a highly regarded interdisciplinary practice that has been actively producing celebrated works of architecture for over 30 years. The practice, originally based in Santa Monica but now in Culver City, also maintains a New York office, to handle the firm's ever-growing body of international work. Morphosis, which was an early adopter of digital technology, characterises these tools as being both project and goal specific. Their work remains largely driven by the design agenda of founder and Design Director Thom Mayne. This is a very important distinction because the practice does not use digital tools to dictate design, nor do the geometries and aesthetics come about because of their use. Under Mayne's direction, the *design intent* – formal geometries and spatial characteristics of a building – comes first, and then digital tools become the means by which the firm brings resolution to that design intent.

Typically, a project is set up with Mayne and a senior designer defining intent, and a small team of junior designers working closely with them. As the firm has come to rely heavily on parametric design, digital fabrication and building information modelling, it has recently assigned Cory Brugger as Director of Technology at Morphosis. Brugger works with the individual project teams to deploy and create the basic organisation of the design and building information models, setting out strategies for design development, which could be specific levels of automation, or generative or parametric design.

Each project the practice undertakes brings a different way of defining digital development logics, but all projects to some degree are executed as building information models because of the emphasis on three-dimensional design methodologies. There is not a heavy agenda of scripting or automation in the office, and parametric modelling does not necessarily drive the development of every project, but it may drive certain areas of a project, such as a geometrically complex facade.

1

1 Morphosis, Perot Museum of Nature
and Science, Dallas, Texas, 2012
Morphosis relied heavily on digital
tools and worked closely with a precast-
concrete manufacturer to achieve the
undulating precast-concrete exterior of the
16,700-square-metre (180,000 ft²) museum.

2 Morphosis, Perot Museum of Nature and Science, Dallas, Texas, 2010
Morphosis still creates two-dimensional geometric drawings as part of their design scope, charting dimensions in X, Y, Z coordinate systems for geometry set out, or for organisational relationships of the key formal design surfaces of the building. This series of patterning diagrams for the museum's foundation conveyed very specific dimensional criteria for a family of precast components.

C4.1 POSITIVE PROTRUSION ADD SECTION

E4 POSITIVE PROTRUSION GEOMETRY FAMILY - ADD

C4 POSITIVE PROTRUSION FAMILY - ADD

C3.1 NEGATIVE RECESS MIRRORED SECTION

E3 NEGATIVE RECESS GEOMETRY FAMILY - MIRRORED

C3 NEGATIVE RECESS GEOMETRY FAMILY - MIRRORED

C2.1 NEGATIVE RECESS SECTION

E2 NEGATIVE RECESS GEOMETRY FAMILY

C2 NEGATIVE RECESS GEOMETRY FAMILY

C1.1 POSITIVE PROTRUSION SECTION

E1 POSITIVE PROTRUSION GEOMETRY FAMILY

C1 POSITIVE PROTRUSION GEOMETRY FAMILY

STRUCTURE OF DESIGN SERVICES AND RISK MITIGATION

The majority of the practice's projects are still typically organised in a design-bid-build process for contracts, meaning the deliverables are still two-dimensional documents derived from three-dimensional models that are tendered to the client and the contractor and subcontractors. The practice continues to rely heavily on two-dimensional drawings to ensure that they cover the required scope of work; they use the 2-D drawing set as a way of mitigating their own risk.

As part of these services, Morphosis provides a three-dimensional model for information purposes, resulting from an early tendency of the practice to produce digital structural steel models in-house. As consulting engineers have more fully adopted BIM platforms, the practice now provides the technical consultants with a digital model as a basis for their scope of work. For facade development, the design team will provide the facade consultant with the parametric three-dimensional model for the design surface and the facade patterning scheme to be used as a reference for starting their own model. The Morphosis model is not used for fabrication, rather this is a way for the practice to separate liabilities among the design team as all consultants are required to build their own model. This is an important distinction for different scopes of work as a design building information model would not necessarily be built to the required tolerances or accuracy of one used for fabrication. Each consultant models their BIM differently based on their own scope of work, however, model sharing ensures that a consultant does not have to start a new model from a two-dimensional set of drawings.

A BRIEF HISTORY OF INFORMATION MODELLING AT MORPHOSIS

In the mid-1990s the practice's original Director of Technology, Marty Doscher, was already pushing the office in a digital direction. On projects such as Caltrans District 7 Headquarters in Los Angeles, the practice had embarked on three-dimensional development processes. For that project a 3-D model was used for the coordination of many trades; specifically by overlaying digital CAD drawings on the structural steel model and looking for any discrepancies, the design team was bypassing the traditional shop drawing review process. Caltrans was being developed in 1997, and construction was ultimately completed in 2004. The building is important because it is a good example of Morphosis's desire to use digital tools to protect its design intent – in many of their projects the structural steel is exposed in what Brugger described as the 'backend tectonic side of the building'.[1] Ensuring a level of control to achieve that level of architectural intent ensures the building aesthetics and ultimately the quality of the architecture.

The model, and its development to a high level of detail, provides knowledge across the design team of all relationships within each project component and assembly. Morphosis partnered early on with Bentley Systems, using its architectural solution

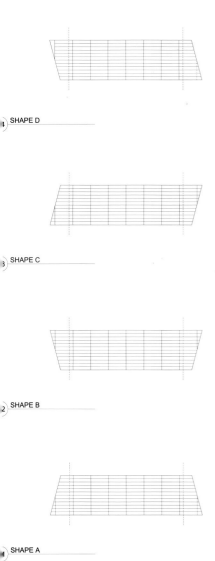

SHAPE D

SHAPE C

SHAPE B

SHAPE A

3

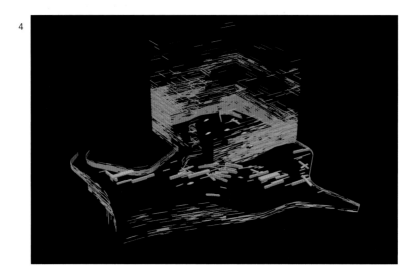

	ATRIUM
	CORE
	CUBE
	STRUCTURE
	PLINTH

4

3 Morphosis, New York, 2010
Morphosis's Master Model serves distinct but interrelated roles during different project phases. During design phases, the design team uses the model to focus on design iteration, geometric rationalisation, analysis, coordination, clash detection, cost estimation, two-dimensional documentation and prototyping. During construction phases, the construction team uses various models for data extraction, detailed review and coordination, mock-ups, constructability and field (as-built) verification.

4 Morphosis, Perot Museum of Nature and Science, Dallas, Texas, 2010
Morphosis's building information model for the museum with the 'cube' or precast-concrete facade geometry isolated. BIM was primarily used for steel coordination and the fabrication of precast panelling, which was developed fully during the construction documentation phase of the project. The building's primary structure is both steel and cast-in-situ concrete, while the geometrically complex atrium is steel framing with precast panelling.

5 Morphosis, Perot Museum of Nature and Science, Dallas, Texas, 2010
The design of the museum included five key building components. The building's atrium, core, exterior 'cube', steel structure and plinth were all geometrically coordinated within a building information model through both design and construction.

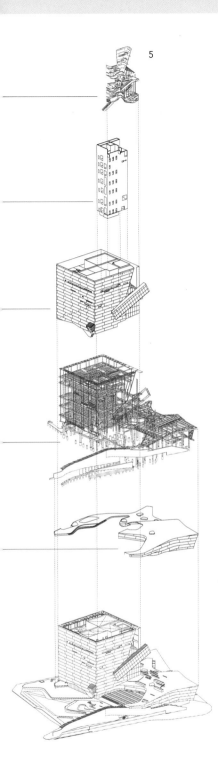

5

MicroStation®. This relationship has allowed designers from Morphosis to work with Bentley as beta testers, as was the case with GenerativeComponents™ (GC), the generative design suite that is now integrated with their BIM software. Morphosis continues to use GC as well as other parametric tools such as Grasshopper™ to study facade patterning, and generally the choice of tool is dictated by project staffing. For larger parametric design problems, such as the Phare Tower in Paris, the practice is more commonly using Gehry Technologies' Digital Project™.

PEROT MUSEUM OF NATURE AND SCIENCE, DESIGN AND CONTROL OF PRECAST PATTERNING

The design development of Morphosis's Perot Museum of Nature and Science brought up a series of interesting opportunities to use digital fabrication. The practice's design team worked with Dallas-based general contractor Balfour Beatty Construction, which understood the benefit of these tools. Morphosis's contract required the practice to complete construction documentation and detailing activities that constitute the formal submission, but the practice also suggested that the contractor build a building information model for all speciality areas within the building. This led the Balfour Beatty team to either produce the models themselves, or require each subcontractor to supply one to them for review. The efficiencies of BIM were well proven and schedule compression allowed the project to be completed one month ahead of schedule.

For the Perot Museum, the depth of information contained in the model and its use in design iteration was critical during the project's construction – BIM was used in both the design and construction phases of the project. The model was used for geometric rationalisation to perform such tasks as analysis, design coordination and clash detection, but also served as an important communication tool with the precast-concrete facade manufacturer, Gate Precast Concrete Systems. The design team created the three-dimensional model and then extracted two-dimensional data as per the architect's scope, but also used the model to test the way in which precast moulds could be fabricated for the facade and atrium space of the building. BIM was primarily used for steel coordination and precast panelling, and this portion of work was developed fully during the construction documentation phase. More specifically, BIM contained detailed information to actualise five key components of the building:

1   The *core*, which was cast-in-situ concrete
2   The *cube*, which was the building's precast exterior envelope
3   The *atrium*, which was the most geometrically complex precast concrete in the project
4   The *glazed facade* for the escalators and vertical circulation
5   The *plinth*, which was the third piece of the building that was built in precast concrete with some complex geometry.

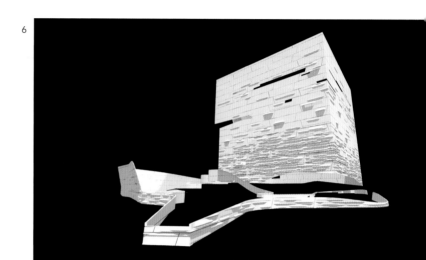

6

6 Morphosis, Perot Museum of Nature and Science, Dallas, Texas, 2010
An early design model for the Perot Museum of Nature and Science explored how a material transition, actualised in precast-concrete panels, could be achieved in an economic way.

7 Morphosis, Perot Museum of Nature and Science, Dallas, Texas, 2010
The Morphosis team went through many iterations of the museum's atrium, varying the geometry and studying the atrium forms both digitally and physically by creating 3-D printed models. This reliance on rapid prototyping happens during all phases of project design: scaled models during preliminary design stages, full-scale component mock-ups during construction documentation and actual component production during the construction phase.

7

Additionally, the Morphosis design team conducted an entire design-build session with Balfour Beatty (the project's contractor) and its subcontractors to ensure everyone understood how to control and make the formwork for the building's facade at an acceptable cost. While this would generally fall under the general contractor's scope, the relationship between the architect and general contractor was very important to the success of the project. The model was also used for surveying in the field to compare as-built conditions to the two-dimensional drawings. Scaled physical models, extracted from BIM, had a very large influence on design development. According to Brugger, 'At early phases of the design we might 3-D print three options every other day to sit down with Thom and the senior designer on a project to get their feedback for integration.'[2] Rapid prototyping is generally seen as something completely different from BIM; however, engaging in these technologies as part of the modelling process can translate a design from virtual geometry to the actualised data from the model for scaled physical models during design development, and increasingly for component fabrication during construction.

The Morphosis design team went through many iterations in studying the precast-concrete atrium geometry of the museum. The practice uses two Z Corporation 3-D printers to test digital models physically. These models help to drive geometric development – from formal geometry to component relationships and interior space. During the design development phase, full-scale mock-ups of joint details or facade connections are undertaken.

UTILISATION OF PRECAST CONCRETE AND SPECIFIC PANEL DEVELOPMENT AT THE PEROT MUSEUM

Panels of precast concrete were thought of as an ideal solution for the Perot Museum of Nature and Science as it materially engages both the *natural* and *scientific* aspects of the project. To achieve 'nature', the project geometries are meant to reflect the sedimentation of rock. BIM was used to explore the proper methods for developing precast formwork and for developing geometries that give the sense of the seeming randomness of nature. The 'science' aspect of the project is achieved through the design of a rock garden at ground level, and a stone garden at roof level which contains no planting, just a natural stone landscape that makes the transition to the striated precast facade and then to the lightweight concrete panels. This transition is meant to be poetic, expressive of the way a natural material is processed and synthesised by man.

Economics – project budgets and schedules – obviously affects all of the practice's projects. For Brugger, 'Each time we begin a project we tend to push the building's geometry, the building's envelope, and once the economic realities of the project take hold we end up having to reel the project back in. The projects in some instances become simplified; however, not at the expense

8

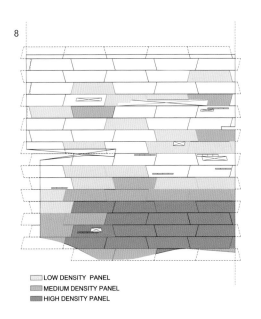

LOW DENSITY PANEL
MEDIUM DENSITY PANEL
HIGH DENSITY PANEL

(E3) EAST FACADE - PRECAST CONCRETE PANEL LAYOUT

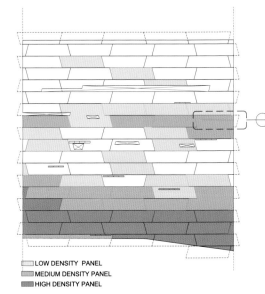

LOW DENSITY PANEL
MEDIUM DENSITY PANEL
HIGH DENSITY PANEL

(C3) NORTH FACADE - PRECAST CONCRETE PANEL LAYOUT

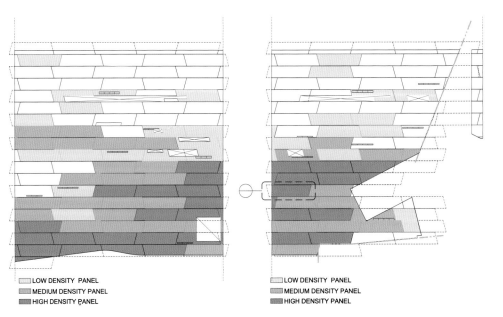

LOW DENSITY PANEL
MEDIUM DENSITY PANEL
HIGH DENSITY PANEL

(E1) WEST FACADE - PRECAST CONCRETE PANEL LAYOUT

LOW DENSITY PANEL
MEDIUM DENSITY PANEL
HIGH DENSITY PANEL

(C1) SOUTH FACADE - PRECAST CONCRETE PANEL LAYOUT

8 Morphosis, Perot Museum of Nature and Science, Dallas, Texas, 2010

The facade panel system was ultimately created as a *knowledge pattern* in Digital Project™. The atrium was designed with the same logic but as the geometry itself is more complex – it has both single- and double-curving surface geometry – that panel system required some additional formwork and had additional construction costs. Both the atrium and the plinth have curvatures that required secondary formwork, but this formwork was used much more intensively in the atrium to accommodate a wider range of radii in the panels and some additional curvature.

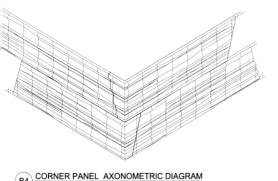

B4 — CORNER PANEL AXONOMETRIC DIAGRAM

of our initial design intent.'[3] The design team initially imagined CNC milling formwork for the building facade's precast-concrete panels, so used their router in the Culver City office to create full-scale mock-ups and variations and then investigated how those variations came together in plastic moulds. Following this exercise they engaged the precast manufacturer, Gate Precast, to better understand their working methods. The team was able to discuss different options for producing the panels and looked into ways to configure and reconfigure moulds, which from an efficiency standpoint was critical for panel production. The language of the facade panels ultimately emerged from a synthesis between the geometry of scaled prototypes and the production methods the precast manufacturer would employ in the creation of formwork.

Rubber models were used to produce the formwork, and the design team developed a simple logic to drive panel development – they created subdivisions of each precast form based on size capabilities. This process yielded three different types of geometry:

1 A piece that curves out at its base
2 A piece that meets the first panel at a midpoint to continue the geometry
3 A piece that will return the assembly back to flat geometry at the top and bottom.

The panels have four elevations, four different heights, and up to four segments of the initial panel subdivision. When combined, the design team realised the need to add a fourth type, which combined four different panels with two different heights. This work was done in Digital Project™, and ultimately yielded 39 geometric families that come together, with four panel geometries based on the angle and perimeter condition – two parallelogram-type panels, and two mirrored conditions of these that are combined. Basic layout of the geometry is tiled so that different formal variations can occur with a small number of actual panel types. The four panel types with 39 families are mated with a series of 24 triangular panel shapes that allow any of the panel types to come together. This ultimately created 13 different panel densities that were deployed on the facade. The use of triangular panels allowed any of these different densities to merge, forming continuity in the patterning on the facade.

Morphosis continued a long-standing relationship with Los Angeles-based John A Martin & Associates (JAMA), who provided structural engineering services. JAMA created and shared a building information model for the primary steel structure. Morphosis built one for the secondary steel for reference and coordinated this work with the structural team. Morphosis coordinated their work with the precast manufacturer, who developed all of the sizing requirements for the secondary steel, as it was supporting their panels.

Initial models were used in the fabrication of full CNC mock-ups of the precast panel types for the facade, and Morphosis

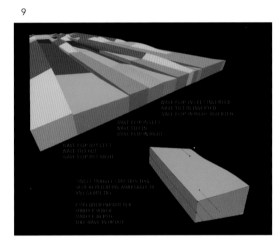

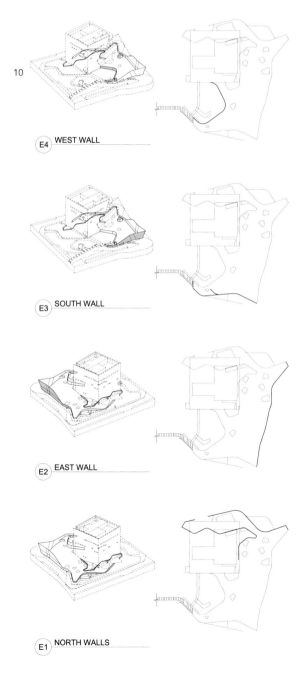

E4 WEST WALL

E3 SOUTH WALL

E2 EAST WALL

E1 NORTH WALLS

9 Morphosis, Perot Museum of Nature and
Science, Dallas, Texas, 2010
The design team created the facade geometry
by adding constraints to the virtual facade
model. By defining the parameters of module
width, module depth and the geometric flare,
which they refer to as 'max wave in or out', the
team created a variable system that gives the
facade a seeming randomness which likens it to
something that could occur naturally.

10 Morphosis, Perot Museum of Nature and
Science, Dallas, Texas, 2010
Once the plinth geometry was designed and
rationalised, a series of drawings were created
to show the north, south, east and west walls
three-dimensionally, in plan, and as 'unrolled' or
flattened surface geometry for fabrication.

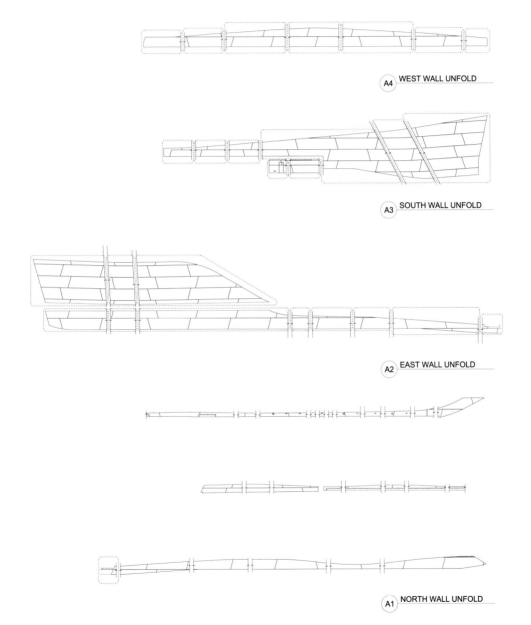

A4 WEST WALL UNFOLD

A3 SOUTH WALL UNFOLD

A2 EAST WALL UNFOLD

A1 NORTH WALL UNFOLD

11 Morphosis, Perot Museum of Nature and Science, Dallas, Texas, 2010
Once form-liners were produced, individual panels were poured at the Gate Precast facility in Texas. Panels were poured upside down to achieve the finish on the panel front. The process involved delivering concrete to the formwork via an overhead crane and then manually smoothing the panels with metal rakes.

12 Morphosis, Perot Museum of Nature and Science, Dallas, Texas, 2010
During design development, Morphosis used a three-axis computer numerically controlled router to create foam mock-ups of both the facade panels and the formwork that would ultimately be manufactured to form the actual panels.

11

12

13

offered to mill formwork negatives for the precast manufacturer. Ultimately, the precast manufacturer opted to create the formwork manually by saw-cutting plywood ribs and using Masonite® as sheathing and Bondo® to smooth seams. *This is an important aspect of the Morphosis process as the BIM can still be instructional, but allows manufacturers who are unable or unwilling to adopt direct-to-manufacture technologies to engage in complex part and assembly construction.* The precast manufacturer was located in Texas, and a team of designers worked directly with them at their production facility. Morphosis assisted with panel layout and created the nomenclature for each of the panel types, and ultimately created two additional sets of panels that further varied depth and projection. This addition required some bolting between panels, which again was specified by the precast manufacturer.

The formwork was constructed so that it could be taken apart and reassembled to create different panel types, so BIM allowed the designers and manufacturers to come to a library of standardised components that could be reassembled in different ways to produce variation. In general, the atrium panels have more curvature than those attached at the plinth, and serve to further the design intent to express the transition from the natural to the synthetic.

ADDITIONAL LEVERAGE OF BIM

This project was also the first venture for Morphosis in 'model as documentation', in which as-built conditions and input from contractors were incorporated in the building information model. For the interior ceiling in the atrium lobby, the design team developed a four-way directional clip, a ball and socket joint, with the interior ceiling manufacturer. The clip was used to attach the double-curving interior ceiling, constructed from metal mesh, to the steel above. The clip allowed Morphosis to move away from the standard rail systems used to hang mesh ceilings and thereby allowed for formal exploration within the ceiling. The use of a four-corner clamp allowed a wide array of geometric configurations to produce the complex curvature of the ceiling. The construction documentation simply contained a reflected ceiling plan and descriptions for each point at which the geometry changes direction, as well as a volumetric drawing, connection detail locations and a note to refer to the building information model for all information. Morphosis supplied the model for all of the documentation and construction of the ceiling.

Autodesk® Navisworks® was used for clash detection within the construction detailing activities phase, which generally falls under the general contractor's scope. Morphosis participated in this process by requiring the contractor to notify them about any conflicts discovered in the model, allowing them to protect design intent and be certain that no decisions adversely affected the architectural design of the project.

14 Morphosis, Perot Museum of Nature and Science, Dallas, Texas, 2010
With the general contractor, Balfour Beatty, Morphosis envisioned a prefabricated and modular mechanical system that would be craned into the museum and coordinated with facade panel installation.

15 Morphosis, Perot Museum of Nature and Science, Dallas, Texas, 2010
The museum is composed of several different building and programmatic components and is sited next to an elevated highway that separates it from downtown Dallas. Morphosis relied heavily on digital tools and worked closely with a precast-concrete manufacturer to achieve the undulating precast-concrete exterior of the 16,700-square-metre (180,000 ft^2) museum. © Iwan Baan

15

14

16 Morphosis, Perot Museum of Nature and Science, Dallas, Texas, 2010
The completed museum received an overall rating of 85 per cent on the Green Globes® rating scale and 100 per cent for its design and sustainable performance measures. Morphosis leveraged the design, visualisation and coordination efficiencies of BIM to ensure the building's success. Green Globes® ratings in the United States building industry are rare – only 12 out of 759 certified buildings have reached a four Globe (the highest) certification.

 16

Mechanical coordination was also included in the BIM scope, especially in clash detection as the mechanical system was largely prefabricated outside Dallas and craned into place. The cores demonstrate how well a solid model worked for the project. Morphosis modelled all the mechanical work in the core, including all of the ductwork, and all of the piping for sewage and domestic water supply.

At Morphosis, not all projects are necessarily computationally heavy or rely on parametric design to create solutions; however, the Perot Museum serves as an excellent example of the capabilities the practice has chosen to integrate into the design process. In the end, Morphosis still relies on logics that emerge from a process of design rationalisation and ordering. The design team remains the most important part of Morphosis' design process, and their robust use of digital tools allow them to move architecture forward and actualise their designs.

NOTES

1 Discussion with Cory Brugger in New York, 16 April 2013.
2 Ibid.
3 Ibid.

IMAGES

4 | NEW METHODS: NEW TOOLS

1 GRO Architects, MoC MoC Japanese restaurant, Princeton, New Jersey, 2009
For the interior design of MoC MoC, GRO Architects developed an infrastructural system of mahogany timber slats that modulate between horizontal and vertical components to organise the restaurant's interior spaces and building systems, including lighting, fire suppression and HVAC. Extensive BIM and, more specifically, digital fabrication technologies, were used to deliver the project.

OPERATIVE LINES AND MODELLING SOFTWARE

Traditional production tools (pencils, slide rules, triangles) have now substantially been superseded by the more streamlined and efficient ones embedded in computing software. However, the most basic constituents of design production, points and lines, still have abundant utility in the way the designer works with software. This is to say that traditional devices at the core of our profession are not abandoned, but subsumed and reconfigured by new design and production techniques. The writer and filmmaker Manuel DeLanda has suggested that the first problem in deploying a design methodology is how to represent its sequential process as a well-defined series of operations.[5]

In his article 'Representational Forms and Modes of Conception' written in 1985, architect Mark Hewitt writes that the historic idea of artistic conception 'involves the creation of a mental picture or idea, which may be represented in the form of drawings or model'.[1] Robin Evans notes that this is precisely how Le Corbusier speaks of his design for the Chapel of Ronchamp of 1956. It is 'the most celebrated and best documented example of design by sheer force of imagination. Creation is described as exclusively cerebral'.[2] However, in this project and others in which complex forms were constructed as ruled surfaces, it was the technical understanding of geometry and projection by André Maisonnier and others in Le Corbusier's office that led to the actualisation of the building. A straight line swept over a series of points to form a surface describes a ruled surface. The surface can curve in one direction, but is easily rationalised as straight in another. More specifically, it was the designer's ability to work operatively with lines, as opposed to understanding them as representational, that led to the production of the working drawings used in the construction of the chapel. Predating the introduction of 3-D modelling software in the design process, this technique demonstrates the necessary process of instilling measure and other attributes in the building's ruled surface geometry in order to build or actualise it.

Some writers have conceptualised these opportunities as a paradigm shift in the architectural production and delivery process. More specifically, they claim, we have moved from the old paradigm of the *possible to real*, to a more seamless one, the *virtual to actual*. In the introduction to his book *Architectures of Time: Toward a Theory of Event in Modernist Culture*, Sanford Kwinter makes the difference explicit: 'What is most important to understand here is that unlike in the previous schema where the possible had no reality (before emerging), here the virtual, though it may yet have no actuality, is nonetheless already real.'[3] This position advocates that form making is not a static practice based on memory or Hewitt's mental picture or idea.

PHILOSOPHIES OF DESIGN AFTER DELANDA

Manuel DeLanda poignantly reinforces this notion by differentiating between two distinct design methodologies. He contrasts a 'cerebral' methodology – one in which a form is generated as an immaterial thought process awaiting the application of a material – with one that at its essence takes into account a philosophy of materiality. DeLanda refers to Gilles Deleuze, who in developing a discourse around materiality writes, 'A philosophy like this assumes that the notion of the virtual stops being vague and indeterminate. In itself, it needs to have the highest degree of precision.'[4]

Animation and other temporal, or *time-based*, computer operations prevalent in the 1990s did little to placate similar formal speculation in architectural design; they in fact reinforced the notion of a static cerebral image – though arrived at through an entirely different means. A popular phrase of the time referred to the stopping problem of animate form, that is, how a designer chose to privilege one instance of a form (in a specific timeframe) over another was arbitrary, and generally such discussions fell into subjective aesthetic critiques. DeLanda seems critical of such a use of software when based on selecting a time subjectively, 'when one looks at current artistic results the most striking fact is that, once a few interesting forms have been generated, the evolutionary process seems to run out of possibilities. New forms do continue to emerge but they seem too close to the original ones, as if the space of possible designs which the process explores has been exhausted.'[5]

Another example of the use of a subjective, aesthetic process in digital architectural design is image mapping, in which representational criteria, as opposed to performance-based criteria, are used in the selection of an appropriate design proposal. Three-dimensional modelling programs were first implemented to simulate what a building would look like, with libraries of 'materials' (generally bitmapped images) that could be applied with relative ease to preconceived forms. These forms were primarily variations of non-eidetic geometry (planes, spheres, cubes) that had no relation or resistance to the representations of materials that they would receive. The outcome of such

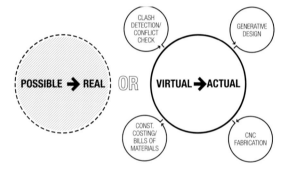

operations was largely deemed successful if the applied image maps were adequate in texture and scale – brick walls with clean 1:2 grout lines must be real. Whether brick was a suitable material choice for such a form, or the general appropriateness of masonry construction, was usually given far less consideration. This representation of reality further separated architects from the material process of building. When not linked to a database or library, the bitmapped brick (or grass, granite, or 'purple', for that matter) wall has no properties or attributes that architects must consider in constructing that wall. It has no weight, is not affected by its height to thickness, nor displays any resistance if another virtual object is placed on top of it. Consequently, it has no reference or attribute data to support whether it can sufficiently behave like a wall.

ATTRIBUTE DATA AND THE VIRTUAL LINE

The possibility to respond to material or geometric factors such as stress, weight, hardness, volume, area, or time-based concerns such as sequence, has allowed designers to apply attributes virtually that yield form, as opposed to specifying it cerebrally. For David J Andrews, in 'considering what would be required in a new methodology for the design of large and complex systems, it is instructive to draw a distinction between procedures that have been adopted to manage the process of design and ways of describing how the design process actually occurs'.[6] While BIM applications allow a certain amount of customisation in terms of how a designer actually wants to work – say beginning in a virtual sketch environment or creating three-dimensional geometry by

2 GRO Architects, the virtual to actual, 2012
The virtual to actual paradigm, a material-based process which involves the 'becoming' or virtual development of a form into an actual (physical) object.

3 GRO Architects, deformation of a plane over time, 2012
Deformation over time can be tracked with parametric software. The location of points at time A can be measured with respect to location of points at time D.

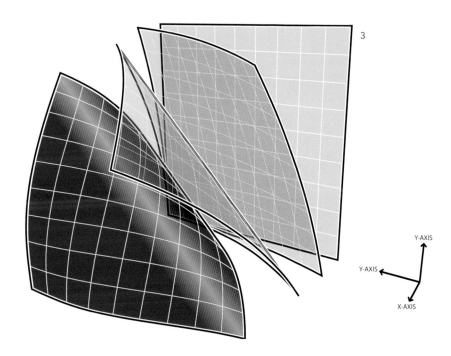

Y-AXIS

Y-AXIS

X-AXIS

ETABS

4 (0,2,0)

5

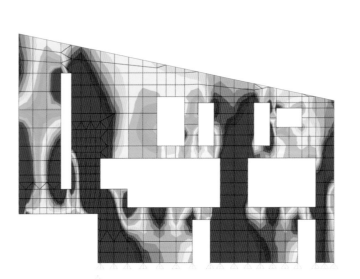

| -15.0 | -12.7 | -10.4 | -8.1 | -5.8 | -3.5 | -1.2 | 1.2 | 3.5 | 5.8 | 8.1 | 10.4 | 12.7 | 15.0 |

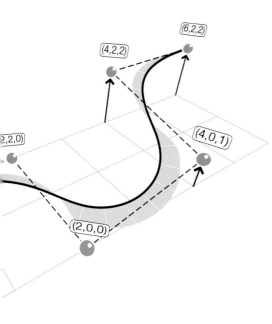

(6,2,2)
(4,2,2)
(2,2,0)
(4,0,1)
(2,0,0)

4 GRO Architects, spline curve, 2012
A spline curve in Cartesian space, location
of points is noted and referenced from
an origin. The grey fill indicates curvature
analysis, which measures the direction
and magnitude of curvature. The point at
which the fill crosses the spline represents a
change in curvature, or point of inflection.

5 GRO Architects, SKN House,
Skaneateles, New York, 2005
Buro Happold worked with GRO Architects
to produce a finite element analysis (FEA)
model showing axial forces in a wall for
a house in upstate New York. The stress
patterns show forces generally increase
around openings, where they must move
laterally or diagonally before being
transferred to foundations or footings.

scanning a physical study model – they necessarily require that the designer address procedurally how she/he will manage the development process itself. For instance, which aspects of a design must be constrained while others can more loosely develop?

As BIM software is based on computer graphics and the development of data-driven and infused geometry, it is helpful to understand as the essence of this process the development and management of the *virtual line*. The term is used in two ways here: first, literally as a geometric connection between two or more points that are developed into more complex geometry such as surfaces and solids; second, more importantly, as a process of varied translation between virtual modes of production. In its most basic form a line is described as a one-degree curve, defined by two vertices in Cartesian space. Digital tools allow us to operate with more complex lines called splines. A spline is a three-degree curve, receiving its shape from the placement of three or more points in Cartesian space, connected by a smooth vector. This vector can be embedded with information or attributes, such as coordinate points or minima and maxima measures of curvature, or even optimal orientations and exposures. By embedding the line with attributes that yield form, as opposed to specifying it, we can procedurally trace the development of a virtual design proposal.

Both the diagram and constraint geometry are useful in establishing design goals and the optimisation of these goals through simulation. Issues such as solar orientation and projected energy consumption based on siting, as well as structural or material testing through finite element analysis (FEA), are possible through the extrusion or surfacing of line geometry that is set within a metric, or constrained, relationship to such criteria via a linked database. Such simulation allows the earlier and potentially more iterative or nuanced relationship between energy efficiency, structure and programming at the level of schematic design.

In following this logic, the line, on its transformation from the virtual to the actual, is held constant as measurable geometry through the design process. It acts as diagram, constraint geometry, profile and simulation in the execution of design proposals, developing a more exact materiality while allowing construction or fabrication sequences to be tested. This multi-dimensional concept of organisation speaks less to a reductive or scalar process (say, the extrusion of planar lines to create an elevation or the jump in scale to a jamb detail once a door is located in plan) than to one in which familiarity with the translation and communication of data is paramount. If these different 'states' of line can be understood as both organisational and inherently linked to technique (execution), we can avoid the rote responses typically garnered by the '*just because I can*' formalism often associated with computing in design.

Lars Spuybroek, in an interview called 'The Aesthetics of Variation' also speaks of the line as a device of continual becoming through a procedural method of removing memory and a priori static-ness from the vocabulary of a form. 'Let's put all the forms between solid and liquid on line. Solid is on one side. That's how architects generally understand form: idealized, crystallized, a priori, archetypical. No dynamics, no contingency, only memory. I think the first one after solid form going in the direction of liquid is structure: it's more open, not necessarily Platonic. It's not the dead clay of Platonism; there are forces, points and lines involved … Then we have configuration; it's the word some of the Gestaltists used for form. There is going back and forth between actual perceptions and virtual memories; it's much more dynamic than structure. Next to configuration, we have the modern notion of pattern, which is sort of between information and form; it is generally considered fully emergent … All patterns that were single forms or formulas a hundred years ago are now very complex patterns, full of "imperfections" and irregularities. Then, I guess, closest to completely liquid, we have Deleuze's rhythm, his continuous variation and modulation.'[7]

STATES OF LINE

In the MoC MoC (pronounced *moshi moshi*), 220-square-metre (2,400 ft²) two-storey interior renovation of an existing commercial space into a full service restaurant, sushi bar and kitchen, the line becomes an actualised material construct that both organises interior space and situates building systems. The project is useful in demonstrating how architects can develop and transform the virtual line using BIM.

Diagram: Unlike a static drawing, such as a two-dimensional line drawing in Cartesian space, the diagram can be understood as a set of notational directions that dictate relationships between parts and assemblies both formally and temporally. Stan Allen suggests the diagram 'is a graphic assemblage that specifies relationships between activity and form'.[8] Diagrams are not representational, but anticipate new assemblies or organisations. In fact, many new software packages speak to this literally as they are written so that the designer can work in a local 'part' environment, at mid-scale in an 'assembly' environment, and then globally at the scale of product or building. As a diagram, the line organises formal relationships, sets up systems of measure, and can order procedural relationships.

The interior organisation of MoC MoC was originally conceived as a thickened 2-D mat, and studied as a series of two- and three-dimensional virtual sketches, which sought in plan to subdivide the space into three more intimate dining areas and a sushi bar. Ceiling height within the space was low so the slat system would need to be layered in such a way as to promote this space-within-a-space concept while still leaving enough headroom to exceed code and comfort limitations. From these sketches, a three-dimensional diagram was created using Rhinoceros® to study the transition from horizontal component (ceiling) to vertical component (wall). At this point a series of organisational options were shared with the owner so a final seat count could be

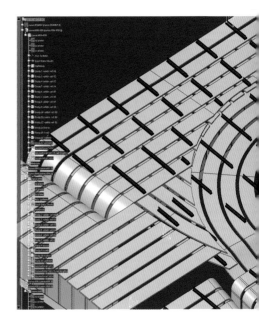

6 GRO Architects, Mo C Mo C Japanese Restaurant, Princeton, New Jersey, 2009 Using Digital Project™, GRO Architects was able to query the complex interior form of the MoC MoC thickened 2-D mat and link the information model to an Excel spreadsheet to obtain a precise cost estimate of the project. By doing so, the firm was able to engage the general contractors bidding on the project – all were well over the project budget – and work with them to revise their costs. Once the use of CNC output for the slat system became apparent, two of the five contractors that originally bid on the project became comfortable with the proposed construction process.

ascertained given the proposed layouts. The final developmental diagram contained a series of polylines and arcs, which, acting at different levels in elevation, conveyed a smooth and layered space that was scaled to occupancy. During this time, a kitchen layout in the basement space was designed and integrated with the design decisions occurring on the floor above. It was decided that the armature would be fabricated from 18-millimetre (¾") finish-grade mahogany plywood.

Constraint geometry: Engineers in the automotive, shipbuilding and aerospace industries have applied parametric constraints to virtual models for some time. Parametric constraints such as parallelism, position, length, radius, coincidence and tangency allow for the automatic updating of overall geometry as local decisions are made or changed. Wherever possible, a series of macro- and micro-numerical constraints were virtually added to MoC MoC to reflect the actual material and fabrication conditions and to anticipate detail and finish of the mahogany sheets.

Macro-numerical constraints:

- Each level of the armature needed to be subdivided so that each component could be nested on and cut from a 1,200 x 2,400 millimetre (4'–0" x 8'–0") sheet of plywood. The optimisation of nested components will be discussed later;
- The elevation change between layers of slats was set to 50 millimetres (2", which would still allow for a 2,150-millimetre (7'–2") clearance at the lowest point of the project's interior armature.

Micro-numerical constraints:

- Bending radii were constrained between 150 and 300 millimetres (6" and 1'–0") for all horizontal to vertical transitions assuming 18-millimetre (¾") stock material;
- Slat width was set to 225 millimetres (9") with a 50-millimetre (2") gap intended to maintain a linear expression of components. This was achieved by adding virtual planes within the model to which different levels of geometry were referenced over a series of nine reflected ceiling plans.

Such a rule-based process can also be scripted in programming language. Several modelling packages now come with script editors and native file types sympathetic to established programming languages such as C++™, Python or VisualBasic®. Still newer plug-ins to conventional CAD modelling packages such as Grasshopper™ for Rhinoceros® allow users to script through a fairly intuitive graphic user interface.

Numerically driving geometry creation within software is very similar to the generating of code to numerically control a piece of hardware such as a router – a set of coordinates and sequencing of operations is encoded to the hardware, or controlled, to literally tell it what to do.

7 GRO Architects, toolpath simulation, 2008
The two-dimensional computer graphic simulation of a toolpath, or space-filling continuous curve, is projected over material stock of a given length, width and depth.

8 GRO Architects, horizontal profile, 2012
Projecting a one-degree curve onto a three-dimensional shape generates a two-dimensional profile. Such an operation is useful in the generation of architectural plans or sections from a three-dimensional virtual model.

7

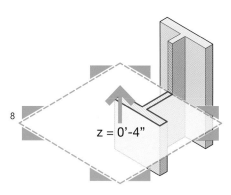

z = 0'-4"

8

Profile: The profile in architectural representation has traditionally been a horizontal or vertical cut through space that images the plan and section. Flattened profiles in the development of MoC MoC were important not only in the generation of two-dimensional detail sections which were reviewed by building department officials, but also in the generation of unfolded geometry and toolpaths for the fabrication of the armature. For the former, armature geometry and interior and exterior walls were generated from the virtual model and then coordinated with the two-dimensional drawing files of consultants, including a mechanical, electrical and plumbing engineer, kitchen designer, and audio/video installer.

A useful technique for quickly generating two-dimensional profiles is through projection. By specifying a three-dimensional shape, a projection curve and a view or projection direction, an image of the three-dimensional shape will be projected onto a *planar surface*. Projection has been used for centuries in technical drawing, not only to generate two-dimensional representations such as plans and sections, but also two-dimensional perspectives of three-dimensional views, where lines converge towards one or two points in space. Methods for perspectival projection were developed in the early Renaissance by, among others, both Alberti and Brunelleschi.

Toolpath: The toolpath is the Cartesian rationalisation of material distribution or subtraction to form a three-dimensional shape executed by a CNC machine; as such it is a space-filling curve after the work of the 19th-century mathematician Giuseppe Peano (1858–1932). The path can have encoded into it instructions for two-dimensional cuts such as profile cuts, pocket cuts or subtractive holing (drilling); or instructions for three-dimensional cuts such as contouring or surfacing through parallel and horizontal roughing and finishing. The toolpath is generated through a software interface on a CNC machine – it can also be manually generated from Cartesian coordinates – by mapping the total movement required by the tool, or interface, which physically forms the material such as a router bit, over a given volume (x, y and z dimension) of material. Total movement refers to all travel required by the tool including engagement, retraction, cutting and clean-up passes. When multiple parts are being machined from a single piece of stock material, a cut-transfer is specified. The cut-transfer allows the forming tool to temporarily leave the stock to move to another area and form the next part. These moves collectively form the toolpath, which is visualised as a continuous curve that moves two-dimensionally, as a plane curve, or three-dimensionally, as a space curve, within the limits of the stock.

To generate toolpaths for the CNC cutting of each slat, the *unfold* command was used in Digital Project™ so that the rolled surfaces, which allowed the armature to translate between horizontal ceiling and vertical wall, were flattened to a construction plane. Using projection, the software creates a planar surface of the rolled shape. Typically, parameters that allow the designer to specify

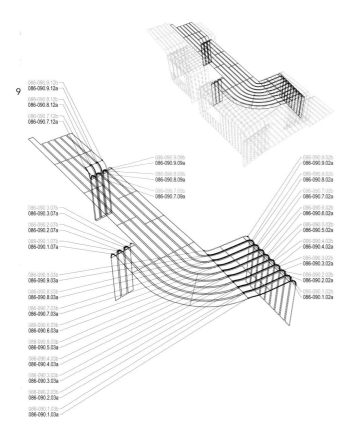

9

9 GRO Architects, MoC MoC Japanese restaurant, Princeton, New Jersey, 2009
GRO produced an assembly drawing for each slat family based at a particular datum from the Digital Project™ model for efficient assembly of all CNC-cut parts on the project site. Of critical importance was the size and orientation of the non-flat curving slats, which in most cases had a larger offset on the top side and a smaller one on the lower side. Reversal of these would prevent the overall armature from fitting together. This sketch illustrates wood slat layers 086–090 in detail, coordinated with the prefabricated precision-cut mahogany slats and their distinct 'sushicons', which graphically link the drawings and component parts.

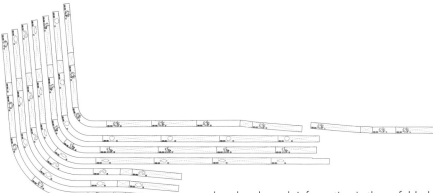

10 GRO Architects, MoC MoC Japanese restaurant, Princeton, New Jersey, 2009
The armature was further codified by the use of sushi icons and a numbering system, which sought to ease installation of the complex assembly. These 'sushicons' are graphically linked to the construction documents, indicating to the contractor the sequencing of the slats. Each slat on every layer of the armature was unfolded in Digital Project™ so they could be nested onto a virtual material sheet, in this case 19-millimetre (¾") mahogany plywood. While many of the slats themselves were flat and at 90-degree angles, they were joined to one another by more irregularly shaped pieces that were used to make the transition between datums within the horizontal assembly and also from the horizontal ceiling to vertical walls. The flattened panel geometry was then brought back into Rhinoceros® where a plug-in called RhinoCAM® allowed for toolpaths to be created. This process was undertaken with architecture students at the New Jersey Institute of Technology.

bend and punch information in the unfolded shape are used so that manufacturing drawings can be developed. The geometric term for a surface that can be unfolded is a *developable surface*, meaning it can be flattened onto a plane without distortion. The unfold operation was critical as these pieces when unrolled formed a parallelogram as opposed to a rectangle – there was found to be a slight skew of the overall armature geometry. The spatial organisation of MoC MoC's interior required slight rotation to be taken up within these rolled transition pieces. If it were assumed that the flattened pieces were rectangles, as it could be in a manual fabrication process, the armature would not have fit together in actuality as it did virtually.

At this point two distinct but interrelated operations took place. First, all planar geometry was exported into Rhinoceros® so that a plug-in called RhinoCAM® could be used to generate toolpaths for each piece of the armature. Prior to toolpath generation, each piece needed to be nested onto a virtual 1,200 x 2,400-millimetre (4'–0" x 8'–0") sheet of mahogany plywood. There exist plug-ins that use algorithms to nest pieces in efficient ways, and we will see examples of this, however, for MoC MoC, GRO nested each piece manually on sheets of plywood for digital fabrication. RhinoCAM® and other toolpath and g-code generators allow the designer to simulate the cut virtually, prior to actual fabrication.

CONCLUSION: CONFRONTING ABSTRACTION

Perhaps the most interesting aspect of information modelling as a new paradigm that replaces both construction documents and shop drawings is the way we as designers *confront abstraction*. Though attribute data is more precisely managed within the virtual model, designers may still rely on intuition and past experience to evaluate the appropriateness of a design. Aspects of design, such as proportion, organisation and order can easily be scripted and explored through the information modelling environment; however, in understanding the role of novelty in architectural design it should again be asserted that information modelling would not replace the desire of the author-architect. Referring to Stan Allen's essay 'Terminal Velocities', 'design does not operate on the basis of resemblance, but on the basis of abstract codes and a complex instrumentality'.[9] For Allen, using abstraction the designer can organise internal relationships of a project without

being encumbered in early design stages by the material reality of buildings. This notion both supports and distances itself from the operations being discussed here when considering that the virtual already exists as something that is *real*. Above all the reader should not suppose working abstractly is synonymous with working in an imprecise way.

Through the digital transformation of the vector, we can understand the development of an information model, from an initial sketch idea to a fully formed and simulated virtual building referred to on the construction site. Throughout this transformation as decisions are made, geometry is embedded with data leading to a fully formed information model. In this sense, the relationships between components within an information model are made less abstract as the model develops; however, because the working methods advocated here are iterative and nonlinear, the diagram – the organiser of potential relationships within the model – is not lost, but a device against which the desired development of an information model can be checked.

NOTES

1 Mark Hewitt, 'Representational Forms and Modes of Conception: An Approach to the History of Architectural Drawing', *Journal of Architectural Education*, Vol 39, No 2 (Winter 1985), pp 2–9.
2 Robin Evans, *The Projective Cast: Architecture and Its Three Geometries*, MIT Press (Cambridge, MA), 2000, p 272.
3 Sanford Kwinter, *Architectures of Time: Toward a Theory of the Event in Modernist Culture*, MIT Press (Cambridge, MA), 2002.
4 Gilles Deleuze, *Bergsonism*, Zone Books (New York), 1991, p 94.
5 Manuel DeLanda, 'Philosophies of Design: The Case of Modeling Software', Alejandro Zaera-Polo and Jorge Wagensberg (eds), *Verb: Architecture Boogazine*, Actar (Barcelona), 2002.
6 DJ Andrews, 'A Comprehensive Methodology for the Design of Ships (and Other Complex Systems)', *Proceedings of the Royal Society: Mathematical, Physical and Engineering Sciences*, Vol 454, No 1968 (January 1998), p 190.
7 Lars Spuybroek, 'The Aesthetics of Variation', *NOX: Machining Architecture*, Thames & Hudson (London), 2004.
8 Stan Allen, 'Diagrams Matter', in *ANY 23: Diagram Work: Data Mechanics for a Topological Age*, Anyone Corporation (New York), 1998.
9 Stan Allen, *Practice: Architecture, Technique and Representation*, G+B Arts International (Amsterdam), 2000, p 149.

IMAGES

pp 88–89 © Fabian Birgfeld, pp 90, 91, 93, 97 (t) © GRO Architects, PLLC, image by Scott Corey; p 92 © Buro Happold; pp 94–95, 96–97, 98–99, 100 © GRO Architects, PLLC.

11 GRO Architects, MoC MoC Japanese restaurant, Princeton, New Jersey, 2009
The slat system, or armature, for MoC MoC is used to subdivide individual dining spaces within the small restaurant interior. The continuity achieved by the system, highlighted by white 'racing stripes', allows your eye to follow the multiple paths and outcomes of each slat, calling attention to different spaces within the restaurant and to the transition from horizontal to vertical through the various radii of the slats themselves.

POPULOUS

CURVILINEAR
WORKFLOWS

AVIVA STADIUM

1 Populous, Aviva Stadium, Dublin, Ireland, 2005–10
The Aviva Stadium, completed by Populous in 2010, is a football and rugby stadium in the Ballsbridge suburb of Dublin, Ireland, with a seating capacity of 51,700. Extensive shadow and solar simulations were undertaken to develop the stadium's exterior geometry, which was prohibited from casting shadows on the nearby community of single-family houses.

Populous was newly founded in 2009 from the group known as HOK Sport, which existed between 2000 and 2009, originating with the Sydney Olympics in 2000. Previously, from the mid-1970s, the firm had its roots as Lobb Sports Architecture. The firm, under David Hines – an Associate who leads the firm's parametric geometry group – has been using Rhinoceros® intensively on their stadium projects since 2005, with the initiation of the Aviva Stadium design. Populous established in their practice three items considering computation with regard to sports facility design, which were all defined through the delivery of the Aviva Stadium. A 51,700 seat stadium in Dublin, Ireland, it measures approximately 180 metres (580'–0") long and 140 metres (460'–0") wide. The firm articulated these items in a recent article in *AD*:[1]

1   The Aviva Stadium, which was the firm's first significant project, used BIM extensively. The project employed an immersive parametric design schema and was effectively delivered as a BIM building.
2   The Silverstone track circuit design was established as a parametric track analysis model used to design crash barrier distances and safe spectator seating arrangements. According to Hines, 'This was a combination of a simulator, which is already in use by F1 drivers, track design, and model to test assumptions of safe crash distances.'[2]
3   The Aviva geometry and bowl design would be generated by a large and heavily mathematical piece of script that computed views with respect to barriers, other seating and exterior geometry of the facility itself. This is the most processor-intensive piece of script the firm has ever created.

AVIVA: BUILDING SITE AND DESIGN

The location of the building is historic; it was the site of the first international rugby game in 1876 and it was important to keep the footprint of the stadium on the site. To the north, in Havelock Square small houses have a right to natural light, so shadow-casting studies of the stadium's shape were intensively reviewed, leading to the stadium dipping to the north. The building form was designed so it will never cast shadows on these northern buildings, encroaching, at most, into gardens and open space within the community but not onto building facades. Owing to the organisation of surrounding roads and parking, 50,000 spectators was to be a fixed limit and Populous's scheme ultimately provided seating for 51,700 spectators. The site was used by the Lansdowne Road stadium prior to Aviva, with similar capacity; however, about half was for standing spectators. The goal of providing a seat for each spectator was crucial to the Aviva Stadium design. The overall form of the stadium was arrived at quickly, however, the materiality and cladding would be developed intensively over a period of time. Hines, who was based on site for the final year of stadium construction, refers to the stadium as 'site responsive'[3] in the way it fits into its surroundings and does not overshadow the adjacent small-scale neighbourhood.

2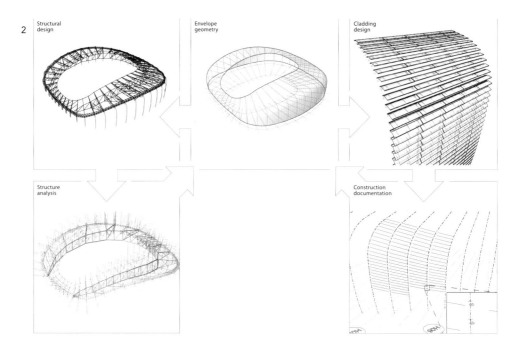

Structural
design

Envelope
geometry

Cladding
design

Structure
analysis

Construction
documentation

3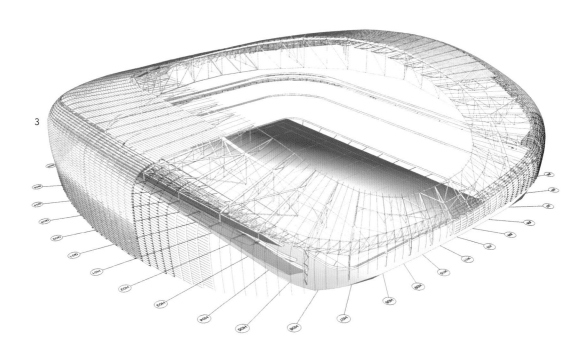

The solution of polycarbonate cladding for the facade and its continuity on the roof was selected for its translucency and reflectivity, so that it would not have an unfavourable impact on the surrounding houses. This gives the large stadium a literal transparency that makes it seem quite light. In describing the building's facade, Hines uses the example of Foster + Partners' Swiss Re Headquarters, referred to as 'the Gherkin', in London; he states, 'the closer you get to it the more round it looks in appearance',[4] suggesting you never read the eves and roofline and that the building's form effectively changes as you approach it. This was a crucial understanding to the way the design team wanted the stadium to be *perceived*. Maintaining the illusion of curvature around the building and the reflection of the sky makes it very smooth and lessens its impact on its surroundings.

STADIUM DEVELOPMENT

The stadium was developed through a combination of Rhinoceros® and Bentley's GenerativeComponents™ (GC), working closely with the latter under the guidance of Robert Aish, formerly of Bentley, who now works at Autodesk. At the time, the firm had a series of design models initiated in Rhinoceros® that were brought into GC to examine comprehensively the stadium's geometry and structural elements, and their detail. According to the design team, 'Design intent in terms of the form of the envelope was determined by manipulating the control curves to sculpt the shape'.[5] Through this process, the firm enjoyed a collaborative relationship with Buro Happold, and the two developed a shared model environment through a basic script and a Microsoft Excel® document. This model delineated Populous's responsibility for the secondary steel, facade cladding elements and their assembly, and Happold's responsibility for the primary steel elements that would support them. The model shared the same *skin*, which was a lofted surface without thickness that set geometric constraints from which each firm worked. The design process was truly iterative. As each firm's work developed, it would be compared with the original surface geometry articulated by the script. The team could then locate deviation from the constraining surface and discuss the merit of such deviation. The initial script allowed for updating of the shared building model semi-automatically, based on decisions made by the design team.

This process, according to Hines, was a 'game changer'[6] for Populous as it allowed the team to work with their engineer consultants for what amounted to an intense year while never having to specifically review a drawing. The team generally understood that the relationship between Populous and Buro Happold was, at its essence, established in the three-dimensional protocols they set at the initiation of the stadium design. Hines suggests, 'We were doing what we were doing and they were doing what they were doing' in that specific scopes and the level of detail required to achieve them were already established, so tender documents were easily extracted from the model at specific points in project development. By sharing information natively

2 Populous, Aviva Stadium, Dublin, Ireland, 2005–10
Populous created a BIM workflow for the Aviva Stadium by linking exterior envelope geometry to the structural and exterior cladding design through the delineation of a series of structural centre-lines and the edge of the stadium's concrete base. Populous and structural consultant Buro Happold developed the model using Bentley's GenerativeComponents™. The centre-lines in the envelope geometry located the series of tubular elements that tied the exterior cladding to the building's primary steel truss system and served as a point of reference for all design development. In addition to GenerativeComponents™, some structural modelling was completed in SolidWorks® and detailing in AutoCAD®.

3 Populous, Aviva Stadium, Dublin, Ireland, 2005–10
Populous imported all geometry into Rhinoceros® to study the coordination of building components with the building centre-lines they originally set, and the model illustrates the development of the stadium's exterior cladding system that was coordinated with Buro Happold's primary structure design. Orange curves illustrate vertical anodised aluminium tubes that translate horizontally to form the stadium's roof. Dark blue curves illustrate the centre-line of each cladding panel axis that attaches to double arm brackets. Light blue geometry illustrates the polycarbonate surface cladding, and the green interior curves illustrate the edges of the concrete tiered seating.

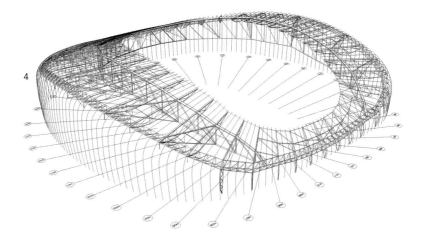

4

all the information contained in the model was updated via the scripting process itself. Hines believes this collaboration remains unique in the delivery of construction information.

Once the general contractor was chosen, it became apparent that different firms would deliver the steel and cladding design packages, but the level of detail and coordination was more than sufficient to lay out an initial radial column scheme to millimetre accuracy that would be the basis for the stadium's construction in its entirety.

From this virtual success, the Populous team took on a design process with the cladding subcontractor to refine this existing data so that very local, small element modifications necessary to deliver the stadium facade could be undertaken without disrupting the development of the overall constraint geometry. The team's building information model and spreadsheet data was then reissued so that the cladding subcontractor could import this information into SolidWorks®, ultimately giving them the ability to manufacture the stadium's component parts.

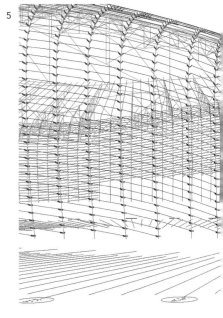

5

All BIM data was coordinated directly by Hines, who was responsible for compiling data from a team of up to five subconsultants, who were each producing a variety of information pertaining to the on-site construction of the stadium, and the coordination of individual scopes. Today, Aviva remains the firm's largest parametric success.

Since Aviva, Populous has adopted a full Revit® environment, which continues to be supported by Rhinoceros® and

Grasshopper™, as well as plug-ins that allow for the import of live geometry from Rhinoceros® into Revit®. Populous has seen in their work, too, more requests and contractual requirements for building information to be delivered to contracting teams in a digital model format. The firm has also adopted Autodesk's Navisworks® construction review and simulation software.

The building typology of stadiums clearly pushed Populous to digital packages that were biased towards curvilinearity. Hines believes the three-dimensional tools they use allow them to 'push the boundaries'[7] of what they can do. Prior to Aviva, the firm did work in a three-dimensional environment, but it was not as adaptable as the parametric environment, which allows a high level of detailed information and coordination and ultimately led to a workflow change within Populous's design methods. Once a model was built and established, the parameters allowed the team to make changes to the overall shape of the building without having to manually update everything that went with it.

DIGITAL CONTRACT RESPONSIBILITIES

Aviva was based on a conventional owner-architect-contractor agreement, and Populous managed and coordinated the model. Hines credits such a contract with giving the architect more of a final say on design of the building. Populous decided that it would be beneficial to all parties if they were in control of the digital model and the various data sources from others that were merged into it. The general contractor, John Sisk & Son, felt that Populous had the level of expertise required to coordinate a digital model of such a complex building. To coordinate the amount of information contained within the model, Populous established a working method with each subcontractor in which they designed the interface between the digital scopes of all parties involved. These interfaces, and Populous's data that supported them – like centre-line geometry – had points of reference that each consultant could work to. In this way, the subconsultants could develop between each other the amount of movement and expansion and general tolerances of each scope of construction information. When actual components were brought to site, these movements could be taken into account from other contractors.

The team did get to a point very early on where they were able to bring different packages, such as the steelwork or cladding, into their model. These tended to be very heavy and were not in their native format. For instance, steelwork was detailed in AVEVA Bocad Steel™ and cladding was detailed in SolidWorks®, and when these were brought into Populous's Rhinoceros® environment the polygonisation would prove difficult to handle, especially since the steel model included very localised information such as bolting details. The team realised they needed only to partially import this data based on the scope of work being coordinated; or they would simply use their own centre-line information, which was the basis of all subconsultant work, and establish what limited amount of geometry would be sent back for inclusion in Populous's model.

4 Populous, Aviva Stadium, Dublin, Ireland, 2005–10
Buro Happold's primary steelwork was transmitted digitally to Populous with actual thickness of primary steel trusses. Rhinoceros® was used to compile each of the discrete digital models from the structural design team. Buro Happold developed the structural design in Bentley's GenerativeComponents™ and linked their GC model to Autodesk's Robot™ Structural Analysis software for virtual simulation and analysis.

5 Populous, Aviva Stadium, Dublin, Ireland, 2005–10
Cladding mullions are tied back to the primary steelwork with a triangulated edge truss, shown in green. Through the process of laying cladding geometry onto the overall envelope, the design team made a conscious decision that the exterior louvres would sit in front of the facade's secondary structure, as opposed to within it. This established the flow along the facade so the louvres appear to be curving up and down the building. These brackets needed to be rotated to achieve the intended flow of the louvres, which were made of straight polycarbonate sections. The panels could not be properly 'fitted' to the stadium's exterior geometry without rotation.

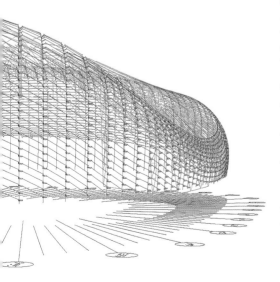

6 Populous, Aviva Stadium, Dublin, Ireland, 2005–10
The primary steel and cladding systems came together to create a warped roofline that dips to the north to prevent shadow casting on the adjacent neighbourhood. According to David Hines, 'It was difficult to capture what it feels like to be inside as the whole object is so encompassing.'[8]

STRUCTURAL DESIGN AND COORDINATION

Buildings the size of the Aviva Stadium tend to move significantly, especially when the individual movements of 50,000 spectators are taken into account. Pieces of specialised primary steel, such as the giant horseshoe truss that allows the stadium to dip to the small-scale houses nearby, can move up to 250 millimetres (10"). Since the cladding is hung from secondary steel, which is hung from the primary trusses, it is also susceptible to such movements within the building that needed to be accounted for in the detailing and movement joints for all of these building systems.

The largest coordination occurred with the exterior cladding contractor, Williaam Cox, a large Irish curtain wall manufacturer, and its detail team at Clad Engineering, a Basel-based facade company. The steelwork contractor was the Italian firm Cimolai, and Buro Happold worked with them on the structural engineering. John Sisk & Son had the responsibility of bringing all subcontractors together in the building's construction. Populous was able to review each subconsultant and report back to Sisk, but ultimately the decision to enter into contract was Sisk's alone. To facilitate coordination, Populous hosted fortnightly meetings in their offices with Sisk, as well as subcontractors responsible for steel and concrete work. These all-day workshops tested the extent of digital knowledge of each participant, and allowed for a fairly analogue exchange of ideas and information that could then be implemented digitally. Populous would bring highly detailed three-dimensional models and two-dimensional drawings extracted from them to these sessions, and the majority of detailing and coordination of tolerance discussions emerged at these meetings, where multiple consultants from the construction team were present. The meetings ultimately led the design and construction team to propose solutions with little or no curvature that could be put together in a way to imply curvature on the building's facade, through the development of an adjustable rotating double-arm bracket. John Sisk & Son, as the general contractor, was very much in favour of such a workflow, with both the analogue work sessions and the high level of digital articulation of the project models. Hines joked that the process became papal, and the team at several points asked, 'Can we see the white smoke yet?'[9]

This method of working is quite different from how many contractors will work, where the control of information flows only from them. That model, similar to 20th-century practice, minimises communication between the architects and subconsultants as a way of controlling risk and exposure. Still questions of the transmission of geometric models and information exchange were considered, as were questions of model ownership. Populous defined a point in time for this to occur, but this was well after Sisk had hired subconsultants and the analogue work sessions had occurred. At about four months into the process, Populous decided that their model was robust enough to anticipate the degree of tolerance and movement required for *mock-ups* to

7 Populous, Aviva Stadium, Dublin, Ireland, 2005–10
A double-arm bracket was developed to attach the stadium's louvre system to the secondary structure, which was constrained at a constant dimension of 430 millimetres (1'–5¼") from the centre-line of aluminium tube to horizontal centre-line of each bracket arm. The bracket is made of two cast aluminium elements: the 'V-shaped' vertical louvre attachment and the 'U-shaped' component that ties the louvre back to the secondary tubular structure.

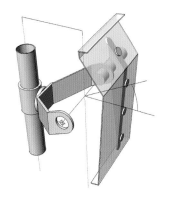

Perspective

Panel Rotation Angle

Values between   0-20 degrees   Values between   20-45 degrees   Values between
0-20 degrees

Cells used for panels
Cells not used for panels

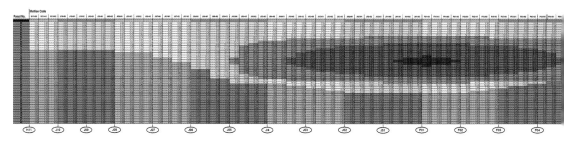

Panel Rotation Data ACW H11 - F11   01

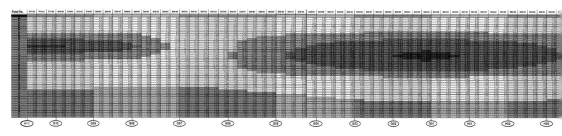

Panel Rotation Data ACW F11 - H11   02

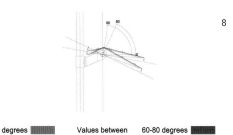

8

degrees ▨▨▨   Values between   60-80 degrees ▨▨▨

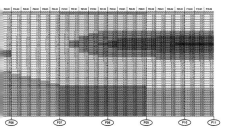

8 Populous, Aviva Stadium, Dublin, Ireland, 2005–10
Rotation data of the exterior louvres was compiled in
an Excel® file, literally unfolding the building facade
with rotational data for the mullions. Excel was used
to drive the panel rotation in the building information
model – as opposed to the extraction of data from
BIM to Excel – and accounted for natural ventilation
requirements. The grey portion of the spreadsheet is
not built, and the north edge of the stadium where it
dips to prevent shadow casting – shown in yellow – is
only 11 panels high. As the louvre system rounds the
facade, the number of panels and degree of rotation
increases. The spreadsheet codes the amount of
rotation by changing the colour of cells, whereby
red cells have the highest degree of rotation where
the panels approach the horizontal, between 60 and
80 degrees. The spreadsheet also used anticipated
wind-driven rain data to set distances between panel
faces in relation to their position on the building.

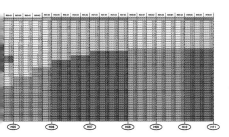

9 Populous, Aviva Stadium, Dublin, Ireland, 2005–10
A BIM model that constrained cladding centre-lines
was developed by the Populous team and was
shared with Buro Happold, who assisted the facade
contractor in the development of the mullions and
polycarbonate exterior louvres. The cladding model
was coordinated with the geometric envelope
model that originally defined all secondary
structure centre-lines.

10 Populous, Aviva Stadium, Dublin, Ireland, 2005–10
While the double-arm brackets are the same all over the
building's facade, they are set to different angles, which
yielded 4,114 unique panel positions on the building.
Brackets can rotate (1) horizontally about the secondary
structural tube or (2) vertically around the 'U-shaped'
component. Within that family there are 52 different
louvre-panel widths, each varied by a distance of 30
millimetres (1¼") – the largest difference being 52 x 30
millimetres or 1,560 millimetres (5'–2").

Architectural Building Information Model

9

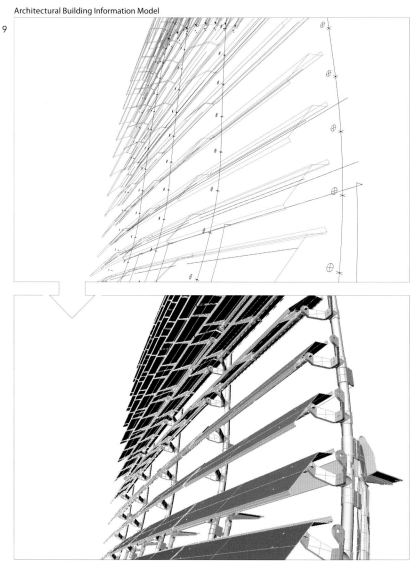

Construction Building Information Model

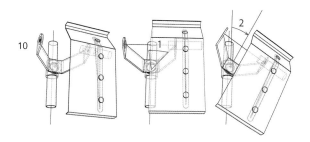

10

1

2

9

11

11 Populous, Aviva Stadium, Dublin, Ireland, 2005–10
A facade mock-up of the louvre panels and their rotation was produced for the Dublin City Council and Planning Department. Populous selected Sabic® Innovative Plastics, who cold-formed each 6-millimetre (¼") thick polycarbonate louvre using a Lexan® Exell® D sheet product. The louvre material has proprietary UV protection on both sides, which provides excellent weathering properties as well as impact resistance. The gutter detail was also produced as part of the mock-up. Panels are fixed on one side and pinned on the other to accommodate any building movement.

12 Populous, Aviva Stadium, Dublin, Ireland, 2005–10
Panel height was fixed at 1 metre (3'–3⅜"), but the rotation of the double-arm brackets created a family of 52 different panel widths. The louvre is fixed at four vertical points on the bracket and the bracket is fixed to a horizontal axle that connects to the double-arm bracket – the double arm holds the panel on one side and pins it on the other to allow for movement. The second row of panels shows a flipped tab, which the design team developed into a gutter system. While the gutter is not readily discernible on the building's facade, a series of drainpipes are seen on the building's exterior. The Populous team located points where these pipes could be tied into the concrete foundation of the building.

proceed and delivered their BIM model, still based on centre-line geometry, to Williaam Cox. The Cox team worked in both SolidWorks® and AutoCAD® to complete the detailed design.

SHOP DRAWING REVIEW PROCESS

Populous had decided to divide the stadium up into bays along structural centre-lines, and issued three-dimensional models of each bay and the parts that constitute them. Each bay model would contain information for four specific assemblies and their coordination: the roof, the primary steel, the secondary steel and facade cladding. As a secondary check, Populous would also request key building sections at areas where the building's structure and cladding would change direction. These were issued as dimensioned two-dimensional AutoCAD drawings, which would also be reviewed and signed off. Essentially, the building is defined by the geometric centre-lines of the radial grid, which also form the vertical mullions that take the building's cladding, so the two-dimensional sections taken at each of those centre-lines could be drawn and were true – they could be overlaid onto the three-dimensional model for additional verification.

CONCLUSION

Construction began on the stadium in 2006 and was completed in 2010. Its parametrically constrained facade is an iconic addition to the city of Dublin and acts as a national symbol of modern Ireland.[10] Since Aviva opened, Populous has expanded its use of BIM in stadium design. The firm delivered the London 2012 Olympic Stadium and is currently working on Eden Park in New Zealand; Casement Park in Belfast, Northern Ireland – both delivered in BIM through construction – and the Datong Stadium in Datong, China.

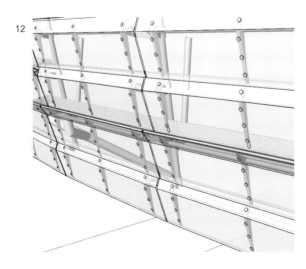

12

13 Populous, Aviva Stadium, Dublin, Ireland, 2005–10
The north-west side of the Aviva Stadium dips so as to
not impose shadows on the surrounding community.
This makes the stadium's iconic shape more striking,
especially during evening events.

NOTES

1 David Hines, 'Interoperability in Sports Design', *Architectural Design* (AD) Vol 83, Issue 2, John Wiley & Sons, Academy Editions, March/April 2013, pp 70–3.
2 Discussion with David Hines, 10 September 2013.
3 Hines, 10 September 2013.
4 Hines, 'Interoperability in Sports Design'.
5 Roly Hudson, Paul Shepherd and David Hines, 'Aviva Stadium: A Case Study in Integrated Parametric Design', *International Journal of Architectural Computing* (IJAC), Vol 9, Issue 2, p 191.
6 Hines, 10 September 2013.
7 Hines, 'Interoperability in Sports Design'.
8 Hines, 13 September 2013.
9 Hines, 10 September 2013.
10 See http://populous.com/project/aviva-stadium/

14 Populous, Aviva Stadium, Dublin, Ireland, 2005–10
Both the primary steel truss structure and the secondary aluminium tubes and clips are exposed and visible from the support spaces around the playing field. These systems, as well as the lighting and sprinkler systems, were all coordinated virtually and checked for conflicts by the Populous team. The louvre system is nearly clear, and allows an abundance of natural light into the spaces organised around the field.

5 | THE DIGITAL STATES AND INFORMATION MODELLING

AN ITERATIVE DESIGN PROCESS

In the years prior to the more wide use of information modelling systems, many architects were drawn to the computer for digital experimentation that was afforded by three-dimensional modelling tools. This opened yet another divergence in the codification of computing with respect to architectural design – while some were content adopting managerial efficiencies to projects through these new tools; others, in effect, were creating new problems through the generation of new and novel forms with the computer. As such, these early adopters of computing in architectural design – like Greg Lynn in Los Angeles, Alejandro Zaera-Polo in London, and Jesse Reiser and Nanako Umemoto in New York – began to redefine the authorial or creative act of designing with new tools whose broad application to architectural design had not previously been considered. The novelty of such projects as the Yokohama Port Terminal by Foreign Office Architects and the Presbyterian Church of New York by a team of Lynn, Michael McInturf and Douglas Garofalo gained notoriety as new architecture using digital design techniques that promised to change what this new architecture *looked like*.

Interestingly, in terms of information modelling it is not what these practitioners, then in their late thirties and early forties, visually produced that is the most exciting. As more design proposals were generated using the computer, it became increasingly clear that the most challenging problem was not to create the most novel geometric form, but rather how such forms could be rationalised and understood so they could ultimately be built. This task was generally given to a younger generation of architects and designers who assisted in the generation of these forms and shape grammars. Again, it was the profile, in the form of an orthographic virtual projection, that would allow for construction documents to be produced.

1

1 Greg Lynn, Michael McInturf, Douglas Garofalo, Presbyterian Church of New York, Queens, NY, 1996
The animation environment of AliasSTUDIO® was used to study and develop geometry for the main sanctuary space of the church. Initially, a range of shape grammars were studied, each deformed over a specified period of time. Ultimately such practices, which were precise geometrically, gave way to other means of testing and iterating the overall form and organisation of architectural projects through information modelling.

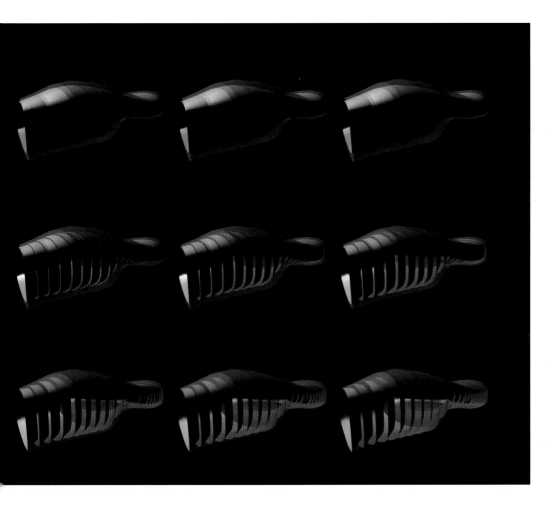

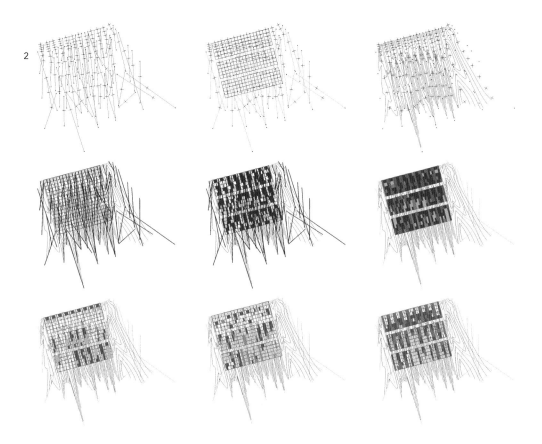

2

In the 1990s, software like CATIA® by Dassault Systèmes – a staple in the aeronautical and space industries for some time – began to be adopted, perhaps most famously for the complex documentation of projects such as the Guggenheim Museum in Bilbao, Spain. At the same time, Lynn and others were developing a series of digital techniques to deliver construction information about complex geometry to builders.

The Presbyterian Church of New York was developed primarily as surface geometry using the automotive design software AliasSTUDIO®. Now owned by Autodesk® and marketed to industrial designers, Alias is a surface modeller that has the ability to precisely generate double-curving surface geometry as NURBS and trim surfaces. Alias also has an animation environment that allowed for a range of iterations of the surface geometry that would become the project. While animation capacities are less prevalent in the information modelling packages in use today, with the exception of construction sequencing, the notion of 'ranges' figures prominently.

After modelling the existing masonry structure the church sits atop, and the surface geometry of the main sanctuary and adjacent spaces of the church, horizontal and vertical profiles through orthographic projection were sliced in much the same

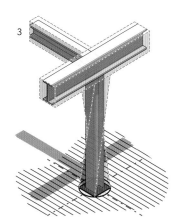

3

BEAM OPTION 1

BEAM OPTION 2

BEAM OPTION 3

way the stonemason worked manually with templates to describe complex shapes some 500 years earlier. These profiles – virtual lines that existed as two-dimensional planar geometry – were then exported to MicroStation®, a two-dimensional drafting package in which the building plans and sections were developed and details were drafted. During this period, 1996–99, two- and three-dimensional information was transferred between Lynn's office, first in Hoboken and then in Venice, California to McInturf's in Cincinnati and Garofalo's in Chicago, where remote teams each contributed to the development of a two-dimensional representational set of drawings.

While this project was designed and constructed prior to the phrase 'building information modelling', it is a sort of pre-BIM and its story illustrates the importance of design ambition and *novelty* in this discussion. The term novelty also finds utility in the automated ship design industry, where the *spectrum of novelty*[1] was often used as a measure in the modification or further development of radical configurations of hull forms to allow for moderate or high speeds. Such ships would be 'technically revolutionary and their design process is more akin to those which are used in aerospace practice, where the process would call for massive expenditure on novel research, including prototypes'.[2] While most BIM packages come with robust three-dimensional catalogues of building components from doors and windows to structural members and typical wall, floor and roof assemblies, they do not have the capacity to propose anything beyond generic and precedent building forms. The conceptual ambitions of the designer-author who uses information modelling tools still cannot be replaced. As information modelling activities promise to most radically affect the design process at the outset of a project, it follows that new design tools should allow the designer to work technically through important aspects of a project's development from *initial sizing and formal organisation* to *parametric relationships between building form and components* to *an architectural and engineering optimisation of building systems*. These will be further elaborated in Chapter 7. The following are a series of core modelling and simulation operations within the information modelling environment that can guide the preconstruction development of a project precisely and seamlessly.

GENERATIVE DESIGN

The term generative design, or algorithmic design, has been used variously to describe virtual geometric processes that are highly numerically controlled and constrained parametrically. Originally rooted in the mathematics of patterns, generative design allows the designer to input a series of relationships that are applied to a component, or series of components, to generate form, or to simplify modelling processes by automating a series of commands. Generative design activities are generally understood as novel as it would be very difficult for architects and designers to arrive at such shape grammars without the computational power of information modelling packages.

2 Richard Garber, Sebastian Khourian and Rajeev Thakker, Event/Infra/Structure, Barcelona, 1998
Use of digital tools in the design studio, especially at the graduate level, became prominent in the early 1990s. While there was originally much interest in geometric development, the parametric capabilities of digital tools soon led to the production of more measured yet novel solutions that were constrained diagrammatically early in project design. By being able to more precisely and three-dimensionally understand project sites and area constraints, designers could move away from more conventional starting points, such as tracing or making simple plan linkages, while still addressing very real problems. Here geometric development of a proposal by Richard Garber, Sebastian Khourian and Rajeev Thakker in Stan Allen's Event/Infra/Structure Advanced Studio VI, given in the spring of 1998 at the Columbia University Graduate School of Architecture, Planning, and Preservation, used existing topography and road geometry to propose a new three-dimensional infrastructural system on reclaimed land off the coast of Barcelona for a variety of programmes.

3 GRO Architects, generative design, 2013
Generative design is an increasingly used capability of information modelling software. By setting parametric or algorithmic relationships between parts or conditions, form-finding operations can yield a range of options that can be further studied by the designer.

Software applications were originally created as digital analogues for what designers do – Autodesk's popular AutoCAD® application allowed the draftsperson to draw in the computer much like they would with a pencil on Mylar® – however, this had a limited, if any, impact on challenging conventional design processes. In generative design, digital computation allows designers to write and use algorithms to generate geometric form, in effect, creating a rule-based environment for designs to virtually develop. An advantage of such processes is that they are controlled by numbers – they are inherently *parametric*. Changes can be applied to this system of geometry automatically so the designer no longer has to manually update aspects of the design. For instance, by numerically changing the size of a window once in a parametric model, the size of that window will change wherever within the model an instance of that window exists. Designers change their work by changing their design rules.

Many software packages now contain scripting environments that allow a program to drive a series of operations within the three-dimensional environment. This is not unlike a computer programmer generating 'code' to control a computing application. For instance, AutoLISP® is a fairly simple scripting language that can be used to drive AutoCAD, and a modified version of VisualBasic® can be used to drive Rhinoceros®. While these two applications aren't explicitly BIM packages, in that they do not have all of the special capacities described here, plug-ins are increasingly allowing static modelling packages to become more 'BIM-like' in that they have new suites of tools for more automated design operations. Such operations might be used to perform a command repeatedly, like rotating a series of panels to the XY plane for measure or comparison; or more interestingly to generate surface geometry through the lofting between a number of curves that have a length and rotational relationship to one another. Further, a designer could quickly generate a series, or *range*, of massings and determine which is the most appropriate for a given site or set of conditions.

Here there is a clear relationship between design processes using animation software in the 1990s and information modelling packages today: that the idea of a timescale has been replaced by the concept of a *range*. As already described, ranges are useful in considering design options and can be generated very easily through scripting.

SPATIAL CONFLICT CHECKING

As previously described, coordination of various trades within the construction documents and on the building site can be complex. The architect is generally responsible for such coordination during design phases, and would circulate two-dimensional design information required for engineers and technical consultants to perform their design services. Conventional documentation by various consultants, such as a mechanical engineer, would not necessarily be transmitted to another, such as a structural

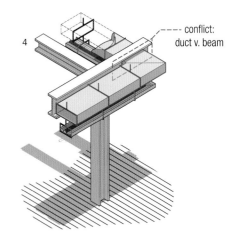

4   conflict: duct v. beam

consultant. This would at times lead to physical conflicts between building components during construction. For instance, a duct might have been designed to be routed through the same physical space as a structural beam, causing change orders on the project site and revisions to both the mechanical and structural documents. This cause and effect situation could also lead to revisions to other work including architectural and plumbing. Recall that the various trades – who execute the work done virtually by various consultants (structural, plumbing, etc) – are scheduled on project sites at different times, structural steel would be erected prior to plumbing risers, so virtual coordination of the construction sequence within an information model could prevent change orders in the field.

With information modelling packages, such conflicts can be investigated virtually, prior to the start of construction. Spatial conflict checking allows for real-time reporting of clashes between building components and equipment within the information model. Reports, in the form of XML documents, can be circulated to the entire design team so parties can take appropriate action to remediate any problems virtually. Such iterations encourage collaboration between the design team and generally make more expansive design operations prior to building, as opposed to positioning them in the field where errors are costly in terms of expenditure and time.

BILLS OF QUANTITIES

Prior to modelling packages, cost estimations were undertaken by the general contractor or cost estimator measuring the two-dimensional size of materials as an area, reported in square metres or feet, and applied to a unit cost of a material and cost of installation. As such, areas were broken down into rectangular or triangular shapes as best estimates being measured from a printed drawing set. Complex or curving shapes were difficult to estimate; and because specific costs of materials were based on the experience and local knowledge of the contractor that was reviewing the architectural drawings, estimates could vary widely.

As information modelling packages are object-oriented, individual components can be queried for material and performance data, as well as cost. Such data can be organised and output within a spreadsheet program like Microsoft Excel® so materials can be sourced and costs compared. By generating automated bills of quantities, the often difficult task of costing a building project is greatly simplified. Hyperlinks to web addresses could link virtual geometry to products or equipment from manufacturers or suppliers. Further, companies such as RSMeans publish an online database of construction and square-foot costs that is updated quarterly. The database includes open shop or union labour costs, is formatted to the Construction Specifications Institute (CSI) and is adjusted for cost differences per US geographical region. Hyperlinking between an information model and such a database could allow for the real-time updating of a cost estimate within the

4 GRO Architects, spatial conflict checking, 2013
Spatial conflict checking within the information modelling environment allows the designer to study the physical integration of building systems such as structural members and mechanical ducting, and ensure each does not interfere with the other.

5 GRO Architects, bills of quantities, 2013
Within the information modelling environment, the designer can query specific assemblies and generate bills of quantities that can be linked to database or web-based cost information.

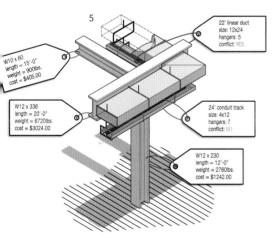

software environment, allowing all members of the design team access to such data, and enabling more effective decision-making on the development of a design within a given budget.

COMPUTER NUMERICALLY CONTROLLED FABRICATION

Computer numerically controlled (CNC) fabrication involves the direct translation of data from a software package to a piece of hardware which forms an actual material by processes of addition or subtraction. Architects such as Lynn, and later SHoP and many others from that generation, found initial interest in early information modelling packages through the ability to produce CNC models or mock-ups of their work. While the types of machines that have numerically controlled capabilities continue to grow, the concept of CNC machines is simple: virtual geometry is prepared for fabrication and usually exported through third-party software to the CNC hardware from the modelling package. The hardware then prepares the cutting or forming tool, and follows a *toolpath* to generate the part. Stan Allen writes about the possibilities of this exchange in 1998,

> … in architecture, the computer gets much more
> interesting at the moment it is hooked up to any
> device that allows it to produce something other than
> image. This includes such obvious examples as output
> devices – the everyday exchange between the screen
> and the plotter or printer, where the specific power
> of the computer as a drawing machine becomes
> evident. But it also includes rapid prototyping (the
> generation of three-dimensional models directly from
> computer files) as well as the use of computer milling
> and fabrication in the construction process itself. A
> consideration of these operations allows the discussion
> of the computer in architecture to enter into complex
> questions of implementation and realization, and
> opens up potentially important possibilities for the
> revision of practice.[3]

While Allen was specifically writing about the use of the computer, or digital technologies, in the design studios of architecture schools, the ramifications of CNC fabrication have gone far beyond the production of scaled models; and now full-scale building components can be fabricated. Indeed this discussion has lent itself to the revision of practice in terms of new methods for shop drawing review and component fabrication. This aspect of information models also directly links the virtual to actual conceptual design paradigm, as developed by DeLanda and others, to these processes.

Export to a CNC machine involves the translation of the data into numbers, coordinates specifically, which the hardware follows to form the material. While some machines continue to use proprietary methods of import and export – such as Z Corporation's line of three-dimensional plaster printers – a relatively standard machine code language called G and M codes has been in existence for almost 50 years. Initially developed so machinists could input numeric data by hand at a controller attached to a machine, this programming language took on greater operability as CNC machines were developed. While a full explanation of the language is beyond this scope, G codes allow for the actual positioning, changing and use of tools to form materials. These codes are engaged at the initiation and through the execution of a *toolpath*, while M codes (machine codes) manage the overall CNC machine, turning spindles on and off as well as controlling visual displays. As building parts are increasingly custom-cut or formed, many have linked this emerging interest in high-tech manufacturing with a new rise in the US manufacturing economy, which in turn has led to new federally funded research centres such as the National Additive Manufacturing Innovation Institute in Latrobe, Pennsylvania. The institute connects regional manufacturers with top universities and technical experts from the government, allowing would-be manufacturing entrepreneurs to 'buy the devices and begin turning out high-tech metal parts for aerospace, automotive and other industries at lower cost and higher quality faster than offshore suppliers'.[4]

SHOP DRAWINGS

One of the aspects of the traditional design and delivery sequence that promises to change radically with the adoption of information modelling practices is the checking and procurement of shop drawings. According to attorney Jeffrey S Wertman, shop drawings are 'the drawings, diagrams, illustrations, schedules, catalog cutouts (cut sheets), manufacturer's installation pamphlets, and other data or information which are specifically prepared or assembled by or for a contractor and submitted by a contractor to illustrate some portion of the work on a project'.[5] This usually requires a specialty subcontractor to prepare fabrication drawings that are reviewed by the general contractor and then by the architect prior to the fabrication of specialty components such as built-in furniture, cabinets or specialised mechanical parts, as well as mixes for concrete and structural steel detailing. The architect, or sometimes engineer, will check the shop drawing to ensure that the fabricator is meeting the architect's design intent, as well as cost,[6] materials and components, ultimately using professional judgement as to the appropriateness of the shop drawing component and its coordination with other project components.

This aspect of project construction exposes the architect and others to liability that is outside the scope of services normally included in contract documentation, and though the architect's responsibility in the checking of shop drawings is described in AIA contract A201 'General Conditions of the Contract for Construction' – an agreement between owner and general contractor – shop drawings are not part of the contract documents, generally because they are not prepared by the architect. The checking and coordination process requires that multiple paper copies are distributed with hand notations, and seals and

6   GRO Architects, three-axis CNC router, 2011
As digital tools in related design and manufacturing fields – such as the shipbuilding industry – developed, opportunities to automate the manufacturing and fabrication process became desirable for their precision and cost savings in labour and production. Many material manufacturers to the building industry have adopted computer numerically controlled (CNC) technologies and can produce material assemblies directly from the designers' information models.

signatures recorded as each construction professional reviews the work. As such, coordination problems are encountered similar to those in construction drawings described earlier.

The promise of attribute data being attached to geometric components in the information model can collapse the expansive review process significantly, with comments made within the shared virtual model. Again, it is not the efficiency of information modelling that is being described here, but the impact of information modelling on the design process itself. Consider four features that play an important role in the expansion of design processes through information modelling: spatial conflict checking, bills of quantities, generative design and computer numerically controlled (CNC) fabrication. These have been demonstrated and used in the performative design of ships, where simulation and fabrication are common elements in the delivery of a yacht or sailing boat.

CONCLUSION: BIM AND ITERATION FROM DESIGN THROUGH CONSTRUCTION

Through the work of Greg Lynn and others mentioned here, a new notion of design, and ultimately *craft* is arising in contemporary design practice. Lynn has said craft is no longer produced by tradesmen – their work producing manual tectonic effects in works of architecture. On the contrary, he suggests a new notion of craft in design arises in the *toolpath*, and a new generation of craftsmen is being trained in a completely virtual environment. This makes new designers digitally predisposed to work with virtual materials and materiality. That design practice today is a *material practice* is rooted in the belief that matter is at the base of the architect's operations: that the base of ideas and processes used by the architect today is inherently material as opposed to being rooted in language or sign. The (especially virtual) models, diagrams and drawings of the architect move away from the space of representation and become part of the material construction of the building itself.

Implied in the development of an information model is the ability for the designer to work iteratively, which is, working through repetition with *difference* on the development of a design. With the advent of parametric capabilities in modelling, the designer need not work in a linear fashion. Changes can occur at any point of a project's development, with developments following that change updating automatically.

NOTES

1 DJ Andrews, 'A Comprehensive Methodology for the Design of Ships (and Other Complex Systems)', *Proceedings of the Royal Society: Mathematical, Physical and Engineering Sciences*, Vol 454, No 1968 (8 January 1998), pp 198.
2 Ibid.
3 Stan Allen, *Practice: Architecture, Technique, and*

7

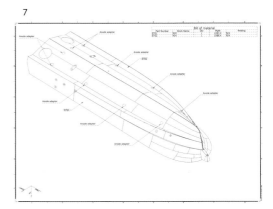

7 Vripack, large yacht engineering department, 2013
Once hull geometry is rationalised, information modelling packages can automatically generate bills of quantities for surface parts, as seen here in a boat hull.

8 Vripack, large yacht engineering department, 2013
It has become increasingly difficult not to use CNC fabrication in the shipbuilding industry's design and construction process. Modelling packages for direct-to-manufacture output in ship design have been broadly adopted by ship designers and the same virtual model used in the development and performance simulation of ship geometry is ultimately used for the actual fabrication of the ship's hull. Production packages, which show how assemblies of CNC-produced parts are assembled to form a hull, are like instructions in assembling a puzzle, and are commonly allowing licensed welders to enter the ship construction industry without any previous training.

Bill of material

Part Number	Stock Name	Qty	Wght	Nesting
01-HL-32	Al.PL 05 H321	1	75.4	6818-PL5 -5083 H321-36
01-HL-33	Al.PL 05 H321	1	70.5	6818-PL5 -5083 H321-43
01-HL-34	Al.PL 05 H321	1	83.6	6818-PL5 -5083 H321-31
01-HL-35	Al.PL 05 H321	1	80.7	6818-PL5 -5083 H321-33
01-HL-36	Al.PL 05 H321	1	51.5	6818-PL5 -5083 H321-39
01-HL-37	Al.PL 05 H321	1	42.2	6818-PL5 -5083 H321-41
01-HL-38	Al.PL 05 H321	1	20	6818-PL5 -5083 H321-42
01-HL-39	Al.PL 05 H321	1	23.4	6818-PL5 -5083 H321-37
01-HL-40	Al.PL 05 H321	1	22.8	6818-PL5 -5083 H321-40
01-HL-41	Al.PL 08 H321	1	67	6818-PL8 -5083 H321-09
01-HL-42	Al.PL 08 H321	1	66.5	6818-PL8 -5083 H321-08
01-HL-43	Al.PL 08 H321	1	28.4	6818-PL8 -5083 H321-09
01-HL-44	Al.PL 08 H321	1	6.2	6818-PL8 -5083 H321-09
01-HL-45	Al.PL 05 H321	1	114.5	6818-PL5 -5083 H321-29
01-HL-46	Al.PL 05 H321	1	43	6818-PL5 -5083 H321-30
01-HL-47	Al.PL 05 H321	1	82	6818-PL5 -5083 H321-34
01-HL-48	Al.PL 05 H321	1	38.4	6818-PL5 -5083 H321-32
01-HL-49	Al.PL 05 H321	1	48.3	6818-PL5 -5083 H321-40
01-HL-50	Al.PL 05 H321	1	31.5	6818-PL5 -5083 H321-34
01-HL-51	Al.PL 05 H321	1	17.4	6818-PL5 -5083 H321-35
01-HL-52	Al.PL 05 H321	1	10	6818-PL5 -5083 H321-33
01-HL-53	Al.PL 05 H321	1	7.6	6818-PL5 -5083 H321-37
01-HL-55	Al.PL 05 H321	1	23.7	6818-PL5 -5083 H321-36
01-HL-56	Al.PL 05 H321	1	7.2	6818-PL5 -5083 H321-37
01-HL-57	Al.PL 05 H321	1	3.3	6818-PL5 -5083 H321-29
01-HL-58	Al.PL 05 H321	1	7.9	6818-PL5 -5083 H321-28
01-HL-59	Al.PL 05 H321	1	4.5	6818-PL5 -5083 H321-29
01-HL-60	Al.PL 05 H321	1	5.8	6818-PL5 -5083 H321-37

Representation, G+B Arts International (Amsterdam), 2000, p 153.

4 Rana Foroohar and Bill Saporito, 'Made in the USA', *TIME*, Vol 181, No 15, 22 April 2013, pp 22–9.

5 http://www.bergersingerman.com/newsletter/NewsletterPDF/WertmanSept08.pdf

6 Form B141, the 'Agreement between Owner and Architect' has since 1997 required architects to prepare a preliminary cost estimate as part of basic services, something that is made easier through information modelling.

IMAGES

GRO ARCHITECTS

JACKSON GREEN HOUSING

1

GRO Architects is a New York-based architectural firm that has, since 2006, completed a series of projects using digital design techniques and building information modelling, some of which have been used to illustrate concepts in this book. GRO first adopted BIM for a commissioned housing project that included the adaptive reuse and addition to an existing masonry building in 2006. Revit® was chosen to coordinate the new construction – which was primarily wood with some structural steel – with the masonry column structure and load-bearing brick exterior walls of the existing building.

The continued use of these technologies has allowed GRO to explore the seemingly disparate notions of design variability with novel but cost-effective construction practices. Led by partners Richard Garber and Nicole Robertson, the partners will at times initiate design projects by developing three-dimensional organisations of curves in a tool such as Rhinoceros®, based on hand sketches that are then shared and further articulated by a design team, following the idea that the virtual line is further developed through the addition of constraints.

Many of the firm's projects have significant budgetary constraints and increasingly they rely on digital tools to continuously test design solutions against cost. The notion that BIM tools can be used creatively, while integrating very pragmatic aspects of project development such as budget and schedule, is an important one for GRO. These variables are addressed very early in the design process, and shared among the project team as a way of driving efficient development.

This method of working allows for the input of environmental and other criteria in a way that makes GRO's projects expressive of their development process while defying a specific aesthetic,

1 GRO Architects, Jackson Green housing, Jersey City, New Jersey, 2012–14

The 22 units at Jackson Green are constructed using four stacked modular boxes that are 4.88 metres (16'–0") wide x 9.75 metres (32'–0") long on the first floor and increase in length to 10.36 metres (34'–0") on the second and third floors with a minimum 610-millimetre (2'–0") cantilever, creating a covered entrance for all the units. While most units have a 610- millimetre (2'–0") cantilever, units 08W–14W are shaped by a cantilever which varies from 2.44 metres (8'–0") at its longest on unit 8W back to 610 millimetres (2'–0") at 14W. This tapered cantilever follows an existing property line and a kink in Rose Avenue. The cost per square foot is $112 USD including site costs, meaning building construction costs were just over $72 USD per square foot. Modular construction is the only viable construction mode given these constraints.

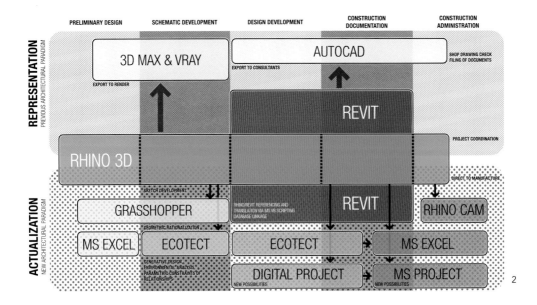

2 GRO Architects, 2013
Digital workflows at GRO are organised around BIM and digital fabrication tools and increasingly privilege simulation and actualisation of sustainable design ideas as opposed to representation. The transfer of data between geometric and numeric software allows for rigorous development of design ideas while controlling project constraints such as cost.

and supports the idea that sustainable design is increasingly becoming an integral part of smart and efficient project development, as opposed to a discrete way of working or additional service offered by architects.

As a rule, the firm follows three general concepts in the deployment of digital technology in the service of architectural design:

1 Routers are not only for topological cutting. *Increasingly architects are working directly with manufacturers to produce a series of parts that then fit together with low tolerances;*
2 Complex but economical assemblies are possible if interpretation is controlled. *As direct-to-manufacturing capabilities become more ubiquitous, the possibilities for novel architecture grow. But controlling data isn't everything, controlling interpretation is just as important so as to minimise human error;*
3 Parametric models extend our reach. *Parametric models allow architects to extend the reach of a design vision, making more responsive architecture possible for more people to enjoy.*

JACKSON GREEN: A NEW MODEL FOR MANUFACTURED HOUSING

The need to provide space for an increasing population while addressing the needs of sustainability and density has been an important driver of design explorations in both the academic and professional communities. As the global population increases, GRO believes density becomes paramount in finding a solution to a long-term sustainable housing design agenda. In the end, these solutions are resilient systems, robust enough to anticipate change

3 GRO Architects, Jackson Green housing, Jersey City, New Jersey, 2012–14
Jackson Green is the product of shared risks by a city redevelopment agency, a not-for-profit developer and the design team, which included GRO and a prefabricated housing manufacturer that agreed to hold liability on all building components except building foundations, facades and roof elements – in effect all of the items that could not be prefabricated.

over various environmental scales. In this sense, we are in a space race, not to mark new territories in our universe but to rethink density and use our space and resources on Earth in a sustainable and economically viable way. Solar energy has long been a focus of sustainable research and design objectives. In his 'Laws of General Economy', Georges Bataille speaks of the wealth of solar energy: 'Solar energy is the source of life's exuberant development. The origin and essence of our wealth are given in the radiation of the sun which dispenses energy – wealth – without any return.'[1]

Further, the infrastructure necessary to distribute resources, both natural and synthetic, can be made more efficient when it serves more densely populated areas. Density is closely linked to the viability, and sustainability, of buildings and urban areas and the opportunity to consider it within the process of design and construction of a building project allows the architect to consider their work in a larger and cooperative context. Prefabricated modular construction has become the key component of this rationale for GRO. By using a majority of standard modules and only strategic custom components, variation can be achieved economically.

At the time of writing, construction is nearing completion of a 22-unit modular housing project located in Jersey City, New Jersey. Named Jackson Green by the Jersey City Redevelopment Agency, the 3,700-square-metre (40,000 ft^2) project will be a prototype for affordable and workforce housing projects undertaken by the city. The units are organised along Rose Avenue in the Martin Luther King Jr Hub section of Jersey City, with 14 on the west side of the block and eight on the east. At the level of planning, density forms the basis of the architectural strategy with minimal building footprints, covered car port to create an elevated exterior space without the need for additional land, and a highly vertical living organisation of three floors plus roof deck for these attached single-family homes. There are several sustainable attributes deployed in the units, including a solar hot water system and insulated panelised walls, but more important is the manner in which the building was designed and transmitted to the modular prefabricator.

Passive design strategies were studied from the early phases of the design process. Autodesk® Ecotect® was utilised to understand such strategies and develop ideas about solar orientation, passive cooling and shadow casting. The building's mass was generated with these factors in mind, but also needed to take into account limitations in the factory of Custom Building Systems, the modular fabricator, as well as shipping logistics. For the base size of a unit GRO arrived at 4.8 metres (16'–0") wide by 10.2 metres (34'–0") deep. A drop deck trailer could easily transport a unit of this size without additional permitting fees. Variation is introduced to the project through modification of the standard module into two types that are fundamentally different in terms of programme organisation, and another level of variation is introduced to many of the units by a geometric modification based on site criteria.

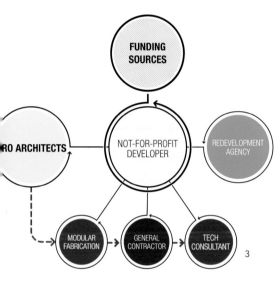

3

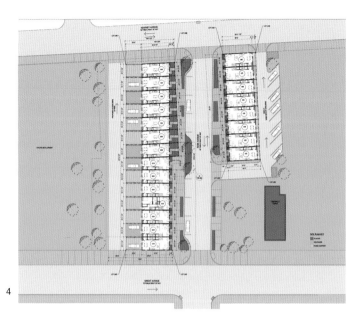

4

There are two aspects of the building's form of particular interest, that also challenge the modular design process. First, a specific site attribute – which is a kink in Rose Avenue mid-block between Ocean and Kearny Avenues – was exploited. While initial discussions with the city and civil engineering consultants pointed to straightening the street, it was ultimately decided that the kink could be used to add variety to some of the housing units. This kink in the street projects outward approximately 2.44 metres (8'–0") at mid-block and by the end of the block tapers down to 610 millimetres (2'–0"). By using the kink, the design team expanded interior space up to 11.6 square metres (125 ft^2) while providing shade for the entry level of the units. Ultimately, the shading benefits of this strategy led GRO to provide a minimum 610-millimetre (2'–0") cantilever on the remaining 16 units as well so each unit has a certain amount of solar control at its porch and entry.

The form of the roof also presented design opportunities. From the outset of the project GRO felt it was important, given the building's location in one of the largest cities in New Jersey, that the building's massing should exemplify an urban solution, as opposed to designing the 22 units to seem like attached but individual houses. To achieve this, the roof was conceived as a ruled surface that was developed three dimensionally. The ruled surface is an urban gesture that acknowledges the thoroughfare of Ocean Avenue by raising the height of the north-east corner of the building, and also allowed the firm to control views from each unit's upper roof deck, where residents could see in some instances New York Harbor and the Statue of Liberty.

4 GRO Architects, Jackson Green housing, Jersey City, New Jersey, 2012–14
While a dense mid-rise residential neighbourhood exists around the MLK Hub District, vacant lots deflate the potential success of this centre of transit and retail. The intention of the overall massing of these 22 units, comprised of 88 individual modular boxes, was to minimise the expression of the individual boxes and to unify the form so that it could work on an urban scale.

5 GRO Architects, Jackson Green housing, Jersey City, New Jersey, 2012–14
Wood or steel-concrete modular construction systems have become quite relevant in the efficient construction of larger scale multi-family residential projects. With BIM, not only the component parts such as wall and floor systems can be controlled, but also whole unit modules that are fully assembled and coordinated, achieving a level of precision – first through digital simulation – that is seen more in the shipbuilding industry and is now making design accessible to a broader population of people who want to live dense, sustainable, economically viable and better lives.

6 GRO Architects, Jackson Green housing, Jersey City, New Jersey, 2012–14
The modular box in its generic efficiency as a standard unit can be leveraged to yield higher degrees of variation. The economy of scale in producing multiples of the same unit allowed resources to be shifted to the production of difference and individuality of living units, a consequence that is specifically related to the density of the boxes which eases logistics and resource allocation. Variation occurs in section as well – double-height spaces are carved out to visually connect between floors, bringing in natural light and creating a sense of openness. Working with standard modules as the basis for the project there is an economy of scale that emerges in the replication and variation of the same 22 units across the site.

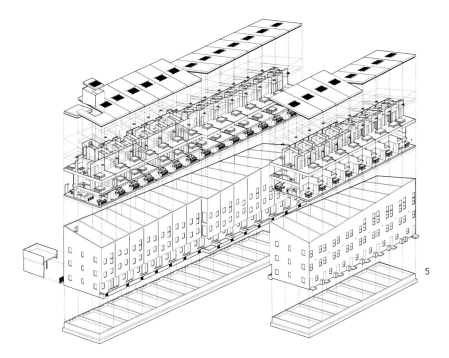

5

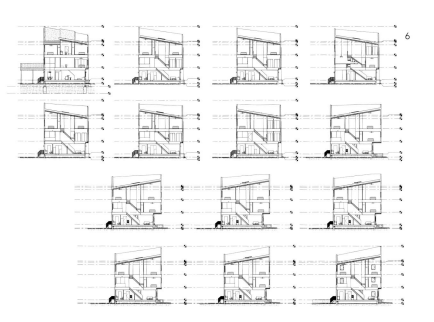

6

7 Custom Building Systems, Jackson Green housing, Jersey City, New Jersey, 2012–14
As part of their contractual agreement, modular prefabricator Custom Building Systems produced two-dimensional CAD drawings of each Jackson Green unit.

8 GRO Architects, Jackson Green housing, Jersey City, New Jersey, 2012–14
Conventional modular construction has been just as slow to accept digital tools as the conventional building industry. It is the integration of BIM technologies on both the design and fabrication side that makes the end product economically and environmentally sustainable. BIM was used to fully coordinate design intent with shop drawing production by the modular prefabricator. Instead of a time intensive and costly conventional shop drawing review process, two-dimensional CAD data was overlaid in GRO's Revit® model streamlining the design and fabrication process.

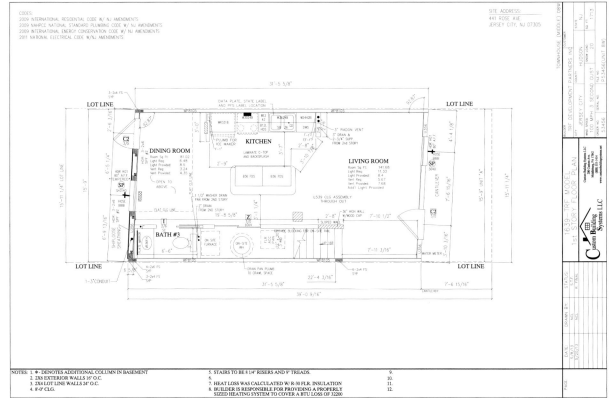

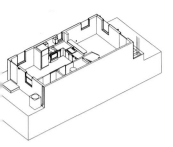
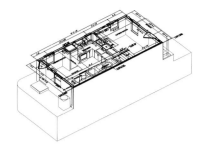

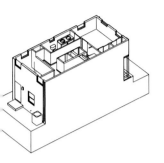
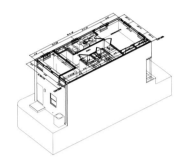
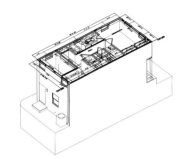

DATA TRANSMISSION TO THE MODULAR PREFABRICATOR

More important than the sustainable attributes imagined in Jackson Green, is the development of true variation in the units – of the 22, 14 are unique – as well as the data sharing process with the modular fabricator. From the outset, GRO was determined to minimise if not completely do away with the conventional shop drawing review process, which is tedious, time consuming and costly, as drawings are traditionally printed and shipped back and forth.

While the modular prefabricator was not willing to completely embrace a shift to a three-dimensional digital environment, they understood these working methods. The shop drawing review process in the end required GRO to receive CAD data produced by the modular prefabricator and overlay it onto the fully developed Revit® model to locate inconsistencies in the 2-D drawings. This saved greatly on time and shipping costs, and facilitated a sort of digital communication with the modular prefabricator they would eventually become comfortable with.

Variation was achieved in several ways, including building form, interior materials, unit layout and the option of additional items, such as car port and roof deck, while departing from a standard set of components common to each unit. When combined with a staggered window pattern on the facades and the roll of the ruled surface roof design, the units express both a sense of wholeness at an urban scale while still allowing prospective owners a degree of individuality.

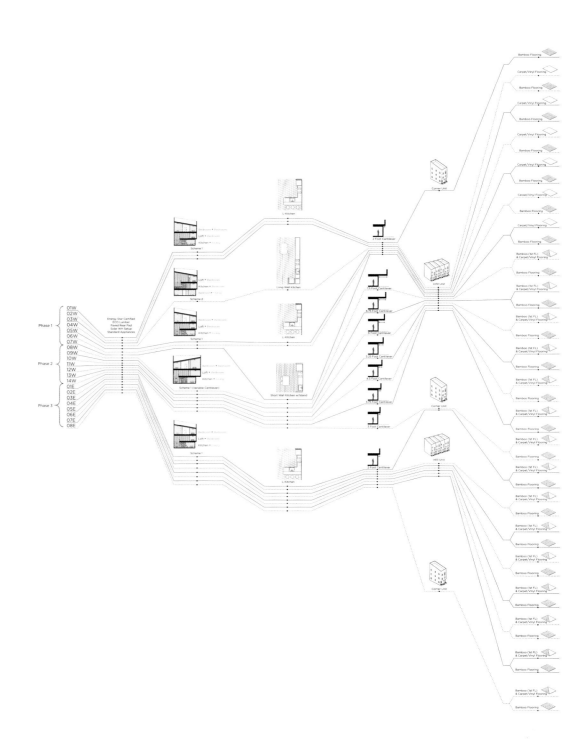

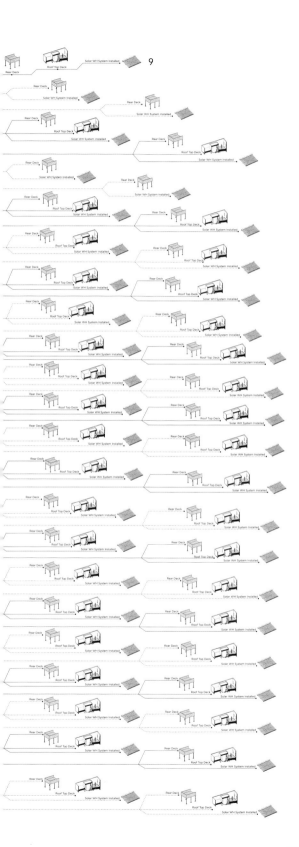

9

9 GRO Architects, Jackson Green housing, Jersey City, New Jersey, 2012–14

Of the 22 Jackson Green units, there are 14 different types – something that required the modular prefabricator to rethink their manufacturing processes and integrate with GRO's data for efficiency. This typology diagram groups units through similarities such as kitchen layout or cantilever length. All the units start with a common set of components including Energy Star certified appliances, a solar hot-water system set-up and the use of fire-retardant lumber. Variation is added through additional building options and amenities like rooftop or rear patios, and building configuration and orientation – such as southern orientation and being an infill or corner unit; and use of materials – including bamboo flooring or carpet. Such variation was contained as data in the BIM.

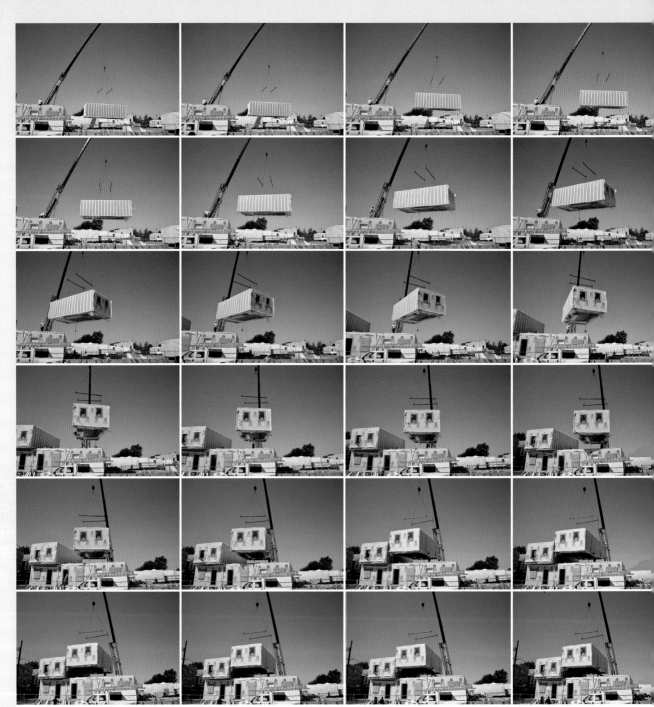

10 GRO Architects, Jackson Green housing,
Jersey City, New Jersey, 2012–14
The first four units of Jackson Green, comprised
12 modular boxes, craned into place over a
single day in February 2013. The units were
factory-produced over an eight-week period
prior to being shipped to the project site.

11 GRO Architects, Jackson Green housing,
Jersey City, New Jersey, 2012–14
A CNC-produced physical model was prepared
as a way to better understand how the modular
units at Jackson Green would fit together.
Custom Building Systems uses a proprietary
stacking method in which a 625-millimetre (2′–1″)
airspace exists between the framed finish
ceiling and the finish floor above.

11

12 GRO Architects, Jackson Green housing, Jersey City, New Jersey, 2012–14
At the time of writing, all 22 units have been completed and craned into place with site work in the process of being completed. While the majority of construction was achieved in the Custom Building Systems' factory, the on-site construction scope included the installation of Nichiha fibre-cement rainscreen and a latticework of Green Wall Cables by Greensulate® that will provide additional building shading as the lattice system matures. The project's ruled-surface roof is evident from this vantage point, and One World Trade Center can be seen in the distance.

Following the completion of the shop drawing review process of the eight eastern units, production commenced. The units were ultimately delivered to the site in two shipments of four units each in February and May 2013 and were assembled in a period of two days. Units were set on a prefabricated foundation system that was coordinated with a precast subcontractor located in southern New Jersey. The 14 units that make up the opposite side of the street have been delivered, and construction will be completed in Spring 2014.

NOTE

1 Bataille, Georges, *The Accursed Share: An Essay on the General Economy, Vol 1 Consumption*, trans Robert Hurley, Zone Books (New York), 1991, p 28.

IMAGES

6 | STRATEGIES FOR COMPONENT GENERATION

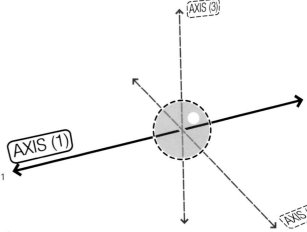

1

THE BOTTOM-UP OR TOP-DOWN APPROACH

Building information modelling allows computing techniques to surpass traditional architectural production tools most commonly associated with the drafting room. More precisely, information modelling allows for the creation of intelligent *components* that can be used to construct a building as an assembly. In contrast, computer-aided design (CAD) tools allowed architects to produce drawing sets within the computer offering better project management and coordination between consultants, via electronic data transfer, etc. CAD simply changed the medium of architectural production from a physical one to a virtual one. The lines spoken about in the previous chapter were vectors that had basic attribute data such as length, start and end point, and degree of curvature; with the potential to add additional attributes that specifically linked them to design or construction. Information modelling has allowed virtual geometry to become *smart* in that it shifts the virtual design environment from *class-oriented* to *object-oriented*. This distinction is important, as previous 2-D and 3-D software packages simply listed geometric objects as a type or class, some examples of this are lines and surfaces. Information modelling packages link objects through libraries or other groupings to contain more attribute data than simply geometric handles. This might include material properties like weight, or environmental properties such as solar exposure based on an orientation. From *Wikipedia*, 'An object contains encapsulated data and procedures grouped together to represent an entity. The "object interface", how the object can be interacted with, is also defined. An object-oriented program is described by the interaction of these objects. Object-oriented design is the discipline of defining the objects and their interactions to solve a problem that was identified and documented during object-oriented analysis.'[1]

1 GRO Architects, point plotting, 2013
Most information modelling geometry begins with a series of plotted points. Points are oriented in Cartesian space on the X, Y and Z coordinate axes, or can be oriented on a topological surface in U, V and W space.

Still, libraries contain common types of components, and many manufacturers of building products, such as windows, shopfronts and structural members, are increasingly creating virtual models of their products for use in building information models. But what if the designer desires to work with, and optimise, non-standard shapes? Most information modelling packages have the ability to build geometric components that can have more specific attribute data ascribed to them.

Any preliminary study of BIM needs to start with the creation of virtual geometry, and the *virtual to actual* paradigm will govern this description of geometry. It should be stated that curvilinear shape development is privileged here, as the majority of software programs that enabled geometric experimentation from the 1990s onwards were surface-based applications, and these shapes, when not conceptualised properly and rationalised tectonically in a building design, open themselves and those who use them up to criticism. In fact, in writing about the *turn* to digital design techniques in architecture, Mario Carpo has suggested, 'curves can express and even symbolize the formal possibilities of digital tectonics better than any other shape'.[2] These shapes, favoured by the automotive industry, were smooth and continuous but didn't account for the thickness of virtual architectural 'parts' necessary in virtual building. While shape developments are shown as discrete operations, such as the creation of a lofted surface, it is the combinatory nature of these processes that yields an actual organisation of building components and such non-eidetic form grammars should be encouraged only if they can be controlled by their authors.

The surface geometry that allowed for the generation of the Presbyterian Church of New York mentioned in Chapter 5, and several other projects, such as Lynn's competition projects for the Cardiff Bay Opera House (1994) and the Yokohama Port Terminal (1995), ultimately was parametric, in that it had a history (it was created by splines generated from plotted points that were then turned into lofted surface geometry); however, the form was not solid and object-oriented beyond 'handles' or numeric codes used by the software to identify each individual piece of geometry – each part.

SKETCHES

Most information modelling packages come with a mode that allows the designer to sketch within a two- or three-dimensional environment. Sketches are generally constrained to a world coordinate plan (XY, XZ or YZ) or some other geometry like a point in space. It is useful to think of the sketch environment as a boundless two-dimensional plane on which the designer draws. In most cases, the sketch environment can be re-entered and when changes are applied any surface or solid geometry developed from the sketch will *update* – this is a basic parametric function of information modelling packages. An example of this might be changing the rise/tread relationship of a stair due to code

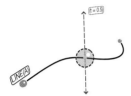

T - Space

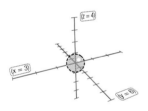

XYZ - Space

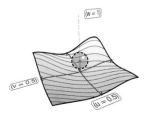

UVW - Space

STRATEGIES FOR COMPONENT GENERATION 146–147

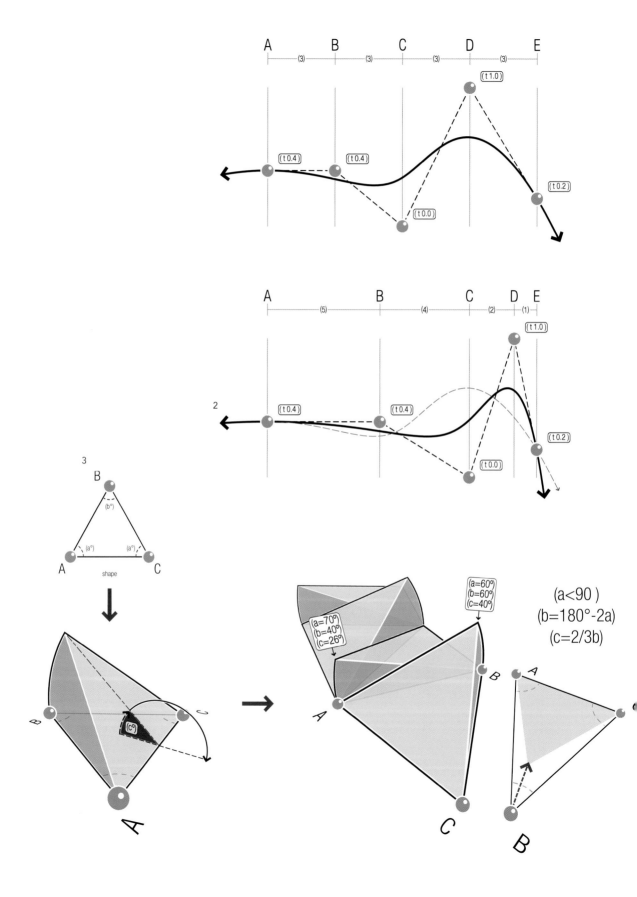

or field conditions – if the stair rise is changed from 150 to 175 millimetres (6" to 7") within the sketch environment, the solid stair geometry developed from the sketch would update to reflect this change. Whether the designer is making a standard building component, such as a stair, or something more novel, such as the undulating roof of a train station, the sketch is an initial profile or curve shape to which *constraints* can be applied. Geometric constraints applied to curves become attributes of those curves that can also be updated later. Basic constraints include *length, angle, distance, relative position, fixing/joining, coincidence, co-planarity, symmetry, parallelism and radius/diameter*. In more sophisticated packages, custom constraints can be scripted through programming languages. Interestingly, the term *sketch design* has also been used in the ship design industry to describe, 'the early design stages for naval ships', where the sketch was not simply a 'hasty pictorial impression'[3] but had implicit in it an initial formal organisation and sizing of a boat hull.

Interestingly, as we have seen with *sketches*, processes embedded within information modelling packages are based on some of the same manual production tools they have replaced. Most information modelling packages have different types of files that address the understanding that teams of designers and consultants will work collaboratively on information models remotely, so the need for changes in parts of the model to update automatically is paramount in decision making. We will refer to such a hierarchy as Shape > Part > Product development, though specific naming conventions for the files will vary with different IM packages:

A shape is a set of geometric objects that have a series of attributes and parametric constraints. Shapes can be combined into parts, which are smaller portions of a larger building or object. Finally, the larger building, or assembly, is contained within a product file. The product file is the most complex in that it contains the most comprehensive information about a building; however, this information is referenced into the product file so that products may contain very little actual geometry, it contains the image of geometry as referenced from a part file. This aspect of information modelling is important in considering file management – especially with large and complex building projects, it is important to keep file size as streamlined as possible.

SHAPES

Shape grammars are made from three basic geometric elements that also have a hierarchical relationship: points, lines and planes. From these elements nearly any type of geometry can be created. It is important at this point to outline the various types of lines, *curves*, planes or *surface geometries* and their attributes, to become familiar with the geometric generation used in information modelling. Ultimately the surface geometries created will be made *solid* for use in part models; however, it should be noted that many 3-D modelling packages were created based on solid

2 GRO Architects, spline parameters, 2013
A constrained curve in which points along the curve, corresponding to gridlines, are moved changing the overall shape of the curve. By setting gridlines, point locations are locked, but changing the dimension between gridlines can modify the curve.

3 GRO Architects, Shape > Part > Product, 2013
In information modelling packages, the designer has the opportunity to select predetermined parts or shapes – primitive geometries such as cubes, or cones – or, more interestingly, to build up geometry from the plotting of points, the surfacing of splines and the solidifying of surface geometry. This is referred to here as Shape > Part > Product development.

C - B - A

'primitives' that were acted upon, added to, subtracted from, etc, to create three-dimensional forms. These methods, now generally superseded in favour of the more controlled means of shape generation discussed here, have also been written about in a discussion of digital design philosophies by the theorist Manuel DeLanda. Recall that for DeLanda, primitive geometries such as spheres, boxes and *tori* exist as eidetic objects, that is, they are the most basic or common types of forms that have simple mathematical rules for generation.

On the contrary, the designer more specifically controls shapes that are built up from points, and can be either intuitively sculpted or plotted based on mathematical rationale. In Euclidean geometry, a *point* is the most fundamental mathematical object, perhaps best thought of as a dot existing within a virtual environment – an exact position within space. Points are defined by a limited set of attribute data that simply dictates position in three-dimensional space – X, Y and Z coordinates. Multiple points can be used to generate surface geometry when grouped into a *point-grid*, but most commonly are used in the creation of *curves*.

Curves might be understood as second-order geometry in information modelling. They have the following attributes: *length*, *degree* and *number of points*. Recall from Euclid that the simplest curve, the straight line, is a curve drawn between two points. The number of points within a curve and the curve's degree has a specific relationship, as this example of a simple line, a curve bound by two points, can only have one degree meaning it will always be straight. As more points are added, a designer's ability to create curves of higher magnitudes is possible. Generally, second-degree curves are arcs or circles, while we will refer to third-degree curves as *splines*.

It should be stated that a spline doesn't necessarily have three degrees at a minimum. A spline is a series of quadratic lines that maintain a degree of continuity. A spline with six points and degree one would be a basic polyline, but joined, and one object nonetheless. As you increase the degree it changes the amount of points taken into account while creating segments. A line with seven points and degree three has only five segments and uses four points in the generation of each segment (two at each endpoint). Splines do not need to be plotted within Cartesian space, they can also be plotted or projected onto surface geometry.

To plot a spline, a minimum of four points are needed, and the minimum number of points plotted, under four, will be the same as the degree of the curve. So, a one-degree curve or straight line has a minimum of two points; a two-degree curve or arc has a minimum of three points; and a three-degree curve or spline has a minimum of four points. Discussion of curves with higher degrees will be omitted as all shape grammars discussed here can be generated by curves of three degrees or less.

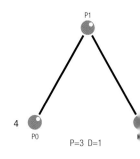

4

4 GRO Architects, degrees of curvature, 2013
Graphic of straight line, arc and spline as defined by points (three) and degree. In plotting a series of points to build up surface geometry, the designer will specify the type of curve and its degree of curvature. One-degree curves are straight lines, and multiple straight line segments joined at end points are polylines. Two-degree curves are arcs, and three-plus-degree curves are splines.

5 GRO Architects, NURBS curvature, 2013
Non-uniform rational basis spline curves (NURBS) are special types of splines. They are made up of a series of plotted points, through which a smooth, continuous curve passes. New segments are created when the smooth curve changes direction.

5

6 GRO Architects, spline manipulation, 2013
A sequence of spline manipulation by moving a single point around a series of grid points in Cartesian space.

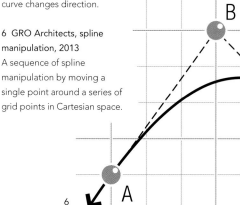

6

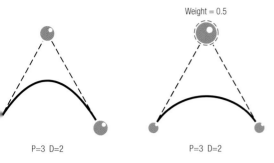

Weight = 0.5

P=3 D=2   P=3 D=2

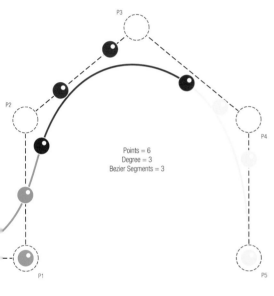

P3

P2

Points = 6
Degree = 3
Bezier Segments = 3

P4

P1   P5

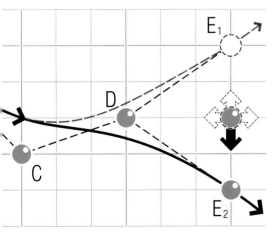

E₁

D

C

E₂

A distinction should also be made between splines and a special type of spline, a NURBS curve. A non-uniform rational basis spline (NURBS) is a curve that is plotted from a series of points and has smooth continuity, and is defined by its order or degree, control points which are weighted, and a knot vector. The weighted control points offer another parametric control – by applying a larger weight to a control point NURBS curve, the designer can more specifically control the shape of the curve with fewer points.

For DeLanda, splines are already *smarter* than their primitive counterparts as they allow the designer the opportunity for local manipulability – by moving a point along the length of the spline the designer can modify the curve's overall shape by changing the profile of two specific curve segments occurring on either side of the point; but also in that they have a virtual materiality. By this he is not suggesting conventional materiality like masonry or metal, but that splines offer a sort of *virtual-resistance* or weight through which the designer can control actual material attributes such as smoothness or rate of curvature:

> The first departure from the world of obedient polygons was represented by special flexible curves called 'splines'. These curves already contain a kind of singular behavior. In this case, singularity refers to the special points that define a curve, such as the inflection points at which a curved line changes direction. When curves are defined by their singular points (inflection, maxima and minima points) they become a little more 'alive', a little more plastic, since one curve can continuously be deformed into another and will count as the same curve so long as it deforms the same singularities.[4]

This distinction is an important means for understanding a basic premise of information modelling, which will be described in greater detail later; splines have a *history* of plotted points which makes the relationship between these points *parametric*. Thus, splines already have inherent in them a kind of information that allows for a streamlined shape – the designer need not plot every point along the curve to get the desired shape, but merely plant several key points that allow the virtual spline to be represented in the most streamlined way.

SURFACE GEOMETRY

Ultimately, our curve geometry, regardless of degree, needs to be developed into a surface and finally a solid, which will allow for the embedding of building information data beyond the types of attributes discussed here (length, degree of curvature, number of points, etc). Note this is a distinction from the part or product libraries many BIM packages include – these might be customisable doors and windows, or structural steel shapes. This chapter is primarily concerned with the generation of new types of shape grammars made possible with information modelling, which allow designers to create truly novel virtual forms and rationalise them for building.

In establishing the difference between surfaces and solids, a very simple distinction can be made: surfaces have no *thickness*; they are infinitely thin virtual representations of geometry within the computer. The BIM software Digital Project™ refers to surface operations as *Generative Shape Design*. A most basic way of creating surface geometry from splines is by *lofting*, or creating multi-section surfaces. A history of lofting describes the development of the term.

Lofting has been deployed as a technique in boatbuilding and early 20th-century aviation construction as a means to translate curvature in a scaled drawing to one that is full scale and can be used for the actual fabrication of a boat's hull or plane's wing. This manual process required numerous draftspeople and the use of battens or light wooden sticks that could be bent to the desired curvature. Lofting to create three-dimensional surfaces in the computer is a far easier process. As the surfaces are created from curve geometry, the same attributes can be input; however, with surface geometry we control these attributes in two directions – *U and V*. Though surfaces exist in Cartesian (X, Y and Z) space, it is general practice to list surface attributes in two directions. These directions, U and V, can be thought of as a deformed grid on which the surface exists, and are mapped to X, Y and Z coordinate space. If the surface is rectangular in silhouette, but deformed in its U and V directions, it is called a *patch*. Similar to DeLanda's ideas about splines taking the most streamlined shape from the curve sections in its make up, one can the imagine hundreds of points plotted to give a spline its desired shape as hundreds of related but varying sections. Lofts, however, generally take their three-dimensional shapes in the same way that splines do – they find the most streamlined way to virtually represent themselves based on the several points that define them. In this sense, we can think of computers and software as lazy – they find the simplest way to represent the virtual forms created within the three-dimensional environment. Perhaps this is a note that should be taken into consideration as we translate towards building.

THE LOFT IN SHIPBUILDING

Lofting emerged as a translation technique first for boat- and shipbuilders and then for those who built aircraft prior to advancements in manufacturing technology. The manual lofting process is in many ways similar to its virtual counterpart and a brief description is useful. It should be noted that the virtual process of lofting a boat hull is quite similar to its analogue counterpart.

The traditional technique of lofting itself is, in essence, a bridge between design and fabrication activities. The boatbuilder had to enlarge and translate the lines and offsets drawn by the naval architect to full scale, so that moulds could be cut for the boat hull. Lofted drawings should include information on deck elevation as well as different areas of curvature showing the volume distribution of the submerged section of the hull. A description in a boatbuilding manual calls for a 'smooth flat surface of sufficient

7 GRO Architects, lofted surface, 2013
A three-degree surface is created by lofting between three curves.

8 Blanchard Boat Company, lofting a boat hull, Seattle, WA, early 1950s
The creation of a plywood hull pattern based on the naval architect's full-scale lofted drawings.

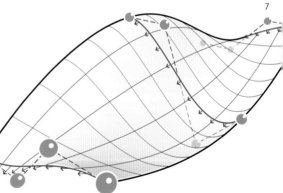

size'[5] to translate from scaled drawings to full-scale construction lines. This translation involves: the full-scale superimposition of all hull lines including plan (the *half breadth*); elevation (the *sheer plan*), in which the forward half and aft half are split by the centre-line; and cross section (the *body plan*). Similar to two-dimensional architectural drawings, a series of horizontal lines are first laid out noting several datum levels: the baseline for the construction, a series of waterlines and a series of 'butts' or horizontal lines that curves will pass through.

Next, a series of diagonals are laid from a centre-line in section or elevation to ensure that the curves of the hull are smooth and symmetrical along the long axis; and also allow the alignment and proper fairing of longitudinal and horizontal curves. Rabbet lines will sometimes be used to translate diagonal lines vertically in elevation to ensure alignment between sheer and body plans. The butt datum lines will serve as reference lines to the buttocks, which are lines of varying curvature that are shaped for the off-wind performance potential of a hull, and at the hull's stern their steepness will indicate how clean the boat's wake will be. Waterlines will be used to plot a series of contours on the half breadth, which is a reflected plan of the hull bottom. Of these curves, the *design waterline* will specify at which height the designer intends the boat to float. A series of offsets from these plotted lines and curves generally yield plank *thickness* of the hull's deck, framing and transom at the hull's rear.

The process of manual lofting was time consuming, and a large hull could take several weeks to properly translate for the making of profiles and moulds. Framing a boat from the full-size loft drawings required the creation of moulds or forms onto which smaller stock of wood or metal, called stringers, was pressed to achieve the shape of the hull. Once the stringers described the overall shape of the hull, finish material was applied to the outside of the hull, making it watertight. The designer needed to understand fully the thickness of stock used in these operations, and take them into account when describing offset dimensions either in tables or on the hull drawings themselves for proper lofting and construction.

OTHER SURFACE GENERATIONS

Though lofting as the primary means to move between curve plotting and the generation of solid geometry will be the focus in examples used in this book, a brief discussion on other types of surface generation is helpful to understand more fully the virtual modelling environment. Multiple other surface types can be easily created, including a *revolved surface* and a *swept surface*. Of the two, a revolved surface is the simpler: a profile curve is rotated around a point or curve in space, leading to a closed or partially closed shape. There are few parameters in the generation of revolved surfaces, but the designer will need to specify the degree of rotation – 360 degrees will lead to a closed shape as long as the top and bottom of the shape end at a point – as well as the

8

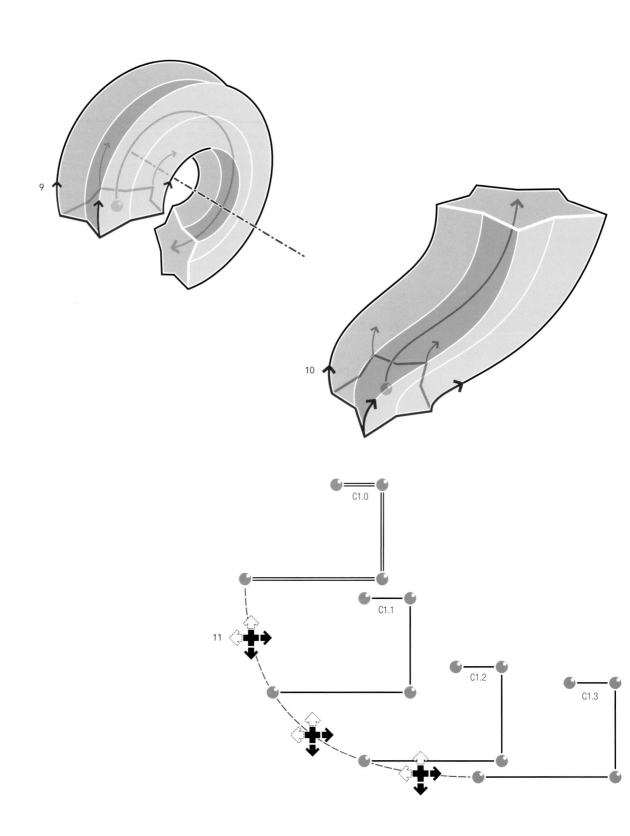

9

10

C1.0

C1.1

11

C1.2

C1.3

degree of surface curvature. A typical example of a revolve surface is a wine glass, where half of the symmetrical section of the glass – the profile curve – is revolved around the Z-axis at a base endpoint to create the shape.

A more complex type of surface related to the loft is the swept surface. To generate a sweep, the designer will specify a number of rail or guide curves and a cross-section curve. The cross-section is then plotted along the rail curve to create a surface. In essence, the cross-section curve need not be planar – it does not have to be a *profile*. If only one rail curve is selected, the cross-section is simply extruded along the rail path. If multiple rails are selected, the cross-section curve will deform, based on the spatial relationships between each. There are several subtypes of swept surfaces, including two rails and a radius, in which a surface is generated between two rails based on the numeric specification of the radius value; centre curve and radius, in which a surface is generated from a rail curve swept along a radius; and a rail and tangency surface, in which a surface is generated by a cross-section curve swept along a rail to the tangent limit of another surface. Each of these operations leads to one-, two- or three-degree surface geometry that lacks *thickness*.

TRANSLATORS AND SURFACE GEOMETRY

If lofting is understood as a linear, or step-by-step surfacing condition controlled by the ordered profiles of curves, then a discussion of the three basic translation tools available in both BIM packages as well as older CAD packages is worthwhile to understand other types of surfacing techniques. These are *move*, *rotate* and *scale*.

Moving is simply relocating geometry from one place in Cartesian space to another, *moving an instance* is *copying* that original geometry to a new location so multiple geometries exist from an original. Generally, a base point and an endpoint are needed to simply move or copy an object. This is an important concept in that generative design allows for the creation of iterations with *difference*, that is, multiple copies of an object that deform with respect to the objects before and after it. Rotating involves translating an object by an angular dimension as opposed to a linear one.

Generally, a base point and either an angle of rotation or a reference and endpoint are needed to rotate an object. Three-dimensional rotational techniques, including *unfolding* and *orienting* are used in rationalising geometry.

Scaling involves translating an object by a size factor. Generally, a base point and either numeric input, or two reference points, are necessary to scale an object. Scaling can be done in one, two or three dimensions. While three-dimensional scaling is most common with CAD packages, the ability to scale in one dimension (stretching) and two dimensions (fitting) are of use in geometry rationalisation.

9 GRO Architects, revolving a section, 2013
A revolve surface is created by rotating a profile curve around a point.

10 GRO Architects, sweeping a section, 2013
A swept surface is created by sweeping a curve along one or two rail curves.

11 GRO Architects, move and copy translations, 2013
Translating, or moving, a series of line segments by relocating points in Cartesian space. In the first instance, the line segments are moved from a point in space (x, y, and z) to a new location relative to the first (1, 1, 0).

C1~new~

C1~old~

relative+(1,1,0)

m (x,y,z)

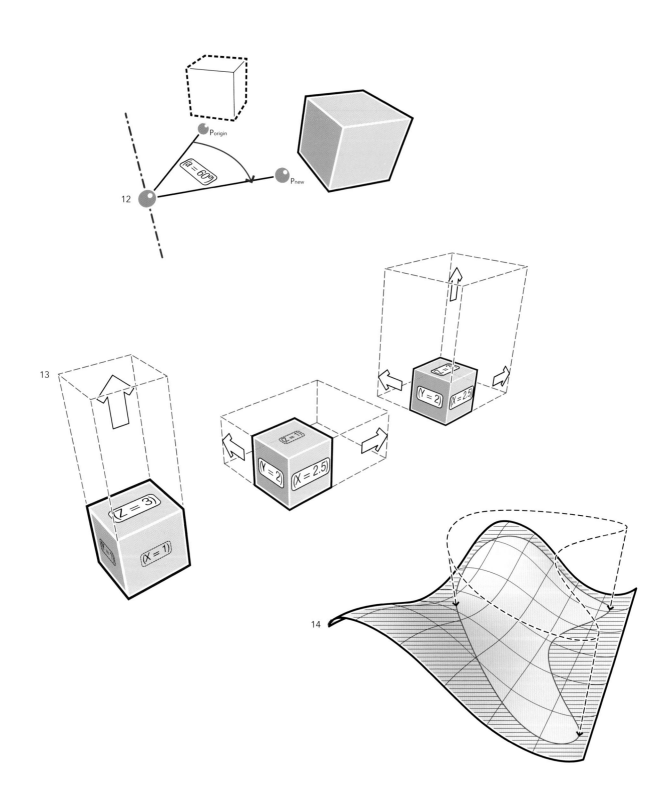

With an understanding of translation commands in three-dimensional modelling packages, several different types of developable surfaces are possible. The most basic of these is a *revolve surface*, which consists of a sectional curve being revolved around a point in space. Revolve surfaces can be closed if revolved 360 degrees – making them geometrically solid if they are closed about the point of revolution, but can also revolve to any angular attribute as specified by the user. *Swept surfaces* involve the translation of sectional curves along one or more other curves. The most simple of these, the sweeping of a profile curve along a one-degree curve (a straight line), is called an *extrusion*, in that the resultant surface does not vary along its length. More complex surfaces can be created by sweeping curves along two different curves, such as curves at the profile curve's two endpoints. By using two different curves to sweep (translate) along, a fair amount of variation can be achieved through this simple command.

The next group of surfaces involves the definition of surface geometry by the selection of regions of points or curve boundaries. The most simple of these is a surface from planar curves. These are closed curves that can be of one, two or three degrees, but only change direction in two dimensions, meaning they are flat on one axis and in effect they are *sections* or *profiles* – refer to Chapter 4 for a discussion on *profile* as a *state of line*. Planar surfaces are simply trimmed patches that fit within the boundary of the planar curve. Another type of patch surface can be developed through edge curves. These curves do not need to be planar nor adjacent curves coplanar; however, most information modelling packages require that the curves have coincident or tangent endpoints.

Additionally, surfaces can be developed by using a three-dimensional point field to locate U and V subdivisions and the boundary of a surface. In this case subdivisions or *isocurves* that geometrically define the surface itself are mapped to the points within the point field. The point field can be periodic, like a grid, or differentiated. Finally, polysurfaces are two or more surfaces, generated from any technique, joined together. An example of these might be a loft and a partial revolve surface that form the front panel and wheel well of a car.

THICKNESS

Fully formed components, whether developed from curves and surfaces as described above or selected from a catalogue within the information modelling package, need *thickness*, that is, they need to be recognised within the virtual environment as solid objects. As such they are *object-oriented* and can be tagged with a wholly new series of attributes beyond the primarily geometric ones described in the previous section. These might include manufacturer data, specifications and cost; more specific material data, such as section modules, moments of inertia or allowable deformation in the case of structural members; and even environmental data like capacity for solar gain based on orientation. Thickness is also a requirement for rapid prototyping scaled parts or architectural models as most three-dimensional printers require input data from fully closed solid models.

Additionally, fully developed – and solid – components are referenced into a different type of file, called a product or assembly file, which shows the physical relationship of each component with respect to the next. It is within the product or assembly file that some of the basic operations of information modelling packages, such as conflict or clash detection and the generation of schedules and bills of quantities, can be undertaken.

There are two simple ways in which surface, and even certain curve, geometry can be thickened: via *extruding* or *offsetting*. Extruding, which was originally introduced in the context of translating a curve along a line to form a surface, simply translates the surface along one of the three world axes to a user input length or coordinate. This is generally a simple calculation for a software package to perform and can be thought of through the following manual steps:

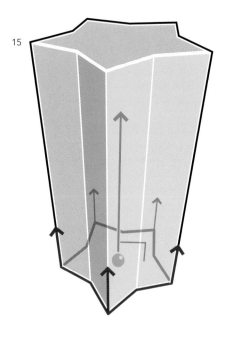

15

- Creating an instance (copy) of the surface geometry in a straight direction over some number of units;
- Lofting each surface edge of the original geometry to the corresponding surface edge of the instance;
- Joining each of these new lofts to the original surface geometry and its instance to form a closed, or solid, polysurface.

Offsetting a surface is a more mathematical procedure – recall the importance of offsetting in boat-hull lofting – for the software package as surface geometry is read as a series of points formed by the intersection of isocurves that are projected normal to, or perpendicular from, each point for a given distance. A surface normal is a vector that is perpendicular to that surface. The aspect of perpendicular projection from a discrete series of points allows for deformation to occur, so that the original surface geometry and offset surface geometry may be similar but not the same, therefore the offset geometry is not necessarily an *instance* of the original. Many information modelling packages allow for a solid to be automatically created by offsetting a surface; however, the same goal can be accomplished by simply lofting each surface edge to its corresponding one on the offset surface and then joining the series of surfaces together.

CONCLUSION: LIBRARIES, NOVEL FORMS AND DATA

Once a thickened surface is read as solid within the information modelling environment, a new series of digital operations can be undertaken. This chapter has been occupied with descriptions and techniques for developing geometric data from more primitive components such as points and lines, as such it is descriptive of many information modelling packages as well as three-dimensional modelling packages. The difference between these is that the former have the ability to add other sorts of information to the geometry so it can be better understood for the purposes of building – in effect removing some of the abstraction associated with three-dimensional geometry.

While there is a bias here towards creating one's own geometrical solutions for building problems, it should be stated at the time of writing that a number of building product suppliers have already made available libraries of products such as windows, doors and railings, most commonly in Autodesk® Revit® file format. This is not a new concept – many of these same companies previously made available their products as two-dimensional illustrations in the popular AutoCAD® or Drawing Exchange Format (DXF™) to use in computer-aided drafting. Such openness should be received with both caution and embrace – while the idea that architectural design can be reduced to the selection and organisation of pre-existing building components that effectively negates the authorial creativity being advocated here, the selected use of such products during the design process offers time savings and can streamline the development and specification process.

Generally, library products and symbols will contain information that built-up geometry will not, information such as cost, material specifications and assembly instruction. It is precisely the inclusion of this data as well as environmental and other criteria that can guide performance optimisation of an information model that will be explored in the next chapter.

NOTES

1 http://en.wikipedia.org/wiki/Object-oriented_design
2 Mario Carpo, 'Digital Style', *Log* 23, Fall 2011, p 48.
3 DJ Andrews, 'A Comprehensive Methodology for the Design of Ships (and Other Complex Systems)', *Proceedings of the Royal Society: Mathematical, Physical and Engineering Sciences*, Vol 454, No 1968 (8 January 1998), pp 196.
4 Manuel DeLanda, 'Philosophies of Design: The Case of Modeling Software', Alejandro Zaera-Polo and Jorge Wagensberg (eds), *Verb: Architecture Boogazine*, Actar (Barcelona), 2002, p 139.
5 Edwin Monk, *Modern Boat Building*, Charles Scribner's Sons (New York), 1973, p 25.

IMAGES

pp 146–147, 148, 150–151, 152, 154–155, 156, 158, 159 © GRO Architects, PLLC, image by Scott Corey; p 153 © Blanchard Boat Co. Collection, Museum of History & Industry.

15 GRO Architects, extrusion, 2013
The generation of a closed, three-dimensional solid by extruding a planar curve shape vertically along the z-axis.

16 GRO Architects, offsetting a surface by normal, 2013
By offsetting a surface based on normal and lofting between the original surface and the new, a solid is created.

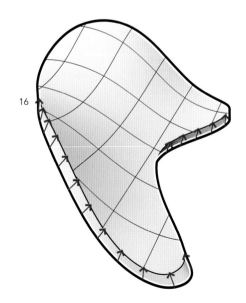
16

REISER + UMEMOTO

KAOHSIUNG PORT TERMINAL

For Jesse Reiser and Nanako Umemoto, partners at Reiser + Umemoto, RUR Architecture PC, there was never a clear line between digital technology, hand drawing and physical model making. They resisted ideologies about *the Digital*, which began in the 1990s. However, they also recognised early on that digital technology was not simply another 'tool' – in fact it is of paramount importance in the way Reiser + Umemoto works. According to Jesse Reiser, 'it makes possible things we could have never done through the manual work. This includes the speed at which things can happen in the digital environment.'[1]

Designing proposals for competitions in the 1990s was a critical aspect of the practice's growth. At that time it had achieved small built projects, but like most other architects was confronted by an economic downturn in 1992 that had a severe impact on the commissioning of architects and the construction of buildings. Competitions provided a means for the practice to test hypotheses it had been developing about programme, geometry and structure.

For Nanako Umemoto, 'the computer never particularly entranced us per se. It was always more of a question of how to get the computer to do what we were interested in materials doing, or what we thought materials could do'.[2] The design approach remains very authored and the partners are often critical of what software generates, suggesting they struggle against the inertia of automated production that digital tools allow. Reiser and Umemoto are specifically not interested in justifying their work by exposing the logic of the script, and they are probably more interested in ideas of craft than ideas of computation.

Reiser is increasingly happy that the computer is simply becoming 'part of the background',[3] believing the use of the computer has a dating effect on work. The pair does concede, however, that digital computation has advanced, suggesting that this resistance might be subsiding.

1 Reiser + Umemoto, RUR Architecture PC, Kaohsiung Port Terminal, Kaohsiung, Taiwan, 2012–16
The Kaohsiung Port Terminal is organised as a series of 'lobes' that support the various functions of the facility. The Ports Corporation Kaohsiung offices are located in the tower, which is a largely glazed and vertical portion of the terminal. The facade of the tower is made up of a flat glass curtain wall set behind an assembly of linear metal panels and structural steel tubes that support the glazing and span floor to floor. The main central lobe cantilevers slightly beyond a public boardwalk at the third level. The central lobe is adjacent to the departures area and serves as the main hall of the building. The smaller lower lobe cantilevers out over the road and serves as a VIP lounge that is accessed from the main hall. The lower lobe is for international arrivals and departures. Domestic arrivals and departures are wedged between the tower and the main lobe.

2 Reiser + Umemoto, RUR Architecture PC, Kaohsiung Port Terminal, Kaohsiung, Taiwan, 2012–16

The Reiser + Umemoto team developed a masterplan as part of the competition entry that engaged how the roads and boardwalk that run through the Port Terminal site connect to the larger harbour's edge. The team intended the boardwalk to extend beyond the eastern and western sides of the site to wrap this edge – the adjacent western site is for the Pop Music Center of Kaohsiung. The third-floor boardwalk would continue and create a pedestrian access to the other public projects around the Port Terminal. Working with a logistics team from Arup, gangways to board passenger boats were planned. Large cruise ships would use both gangways, but the south-western gangway is intended for international ships and the south-eastern gangway is for domestic ships. Arup also planned for the expansion of the boardwalk, which would include two additional gangways. Logistically, a ramped road goes up into the terminal for departure drop-offs, while a lower road serves as a pick-up location for arrivals directly under the departure hall. A smaller at-grade road for operational vehicles wraps around the site and is not publicly accessible. The drop-off area is at the north side of the building.

2

南

路

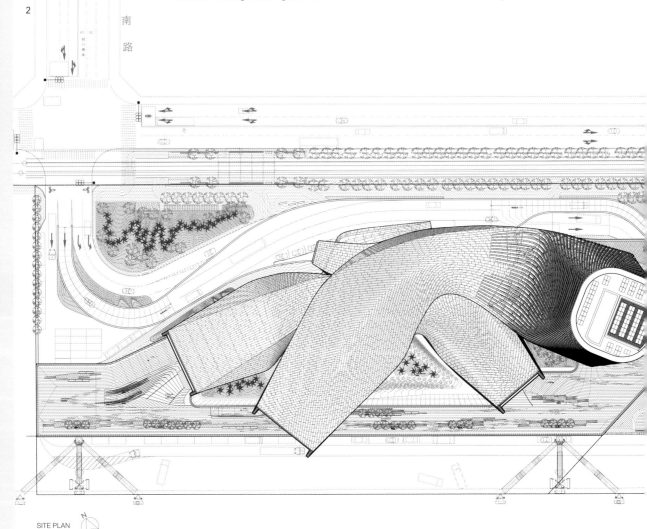

SITE PLAN

N

DESIGN PROCESS

The practice will typically start projects on several parallel tracks and begin by asking a generally pragmatic line of questions. This leads to the developing of all the volumetric and programmatic relationships so that a sense of overall mass can be determined. Programme will lead to a general building organisation and remains very important for the practice. For Reiser, speaking about the Kaohsiung Port Terminal, 'that project gets us into the relationship between infrastructure and landscape design as well, as there was an urban design component to the project which we brought in from the beginning'.[4]

The practice's earlier work was structurally expressive and examined how breaks in the regularity of structure could be opportunities for architectural novelty – both spatial and programmatic. In the practice's Yokohama Port Terminal competition entry, of 1994, the building form was very literally related to work Reiser and Umemoto saw on airship sheds – structures that house aircraft. That project developed typologically, starting with a shed, which was hybridised to show the way structure could be *mutated* to incorporate other programmes. In the current work, the port terminal in Kaohsiung, the structure came later, initially it was all conceived as *thickness* – how thick walls and other architectural components needed to be shaped to house certain programmes.

Reiser feels there is a consistency in the way they approach their work, and there are *traits* that are carried across projects. The pre-formal massing of functions and relationships is done on every project and is not particularly novel. At that point, design development is both analogue and virtual and some ideas about control within the design emerge as part of the medium. Having the ability to work well with the medium is a critical aspect of the use of digital tools for the practice.

Still, both Reiser and Umemoto have trouble with the current discourse of authorship. They feel it is difficult to see an author in remarkable buildings, creating an illusion of authorship. If a project becomes too individuated they feel it may not be very good, so they look for moments in their work that seem authorless – preferring to be objective witnesses who are very interested in understanding what is emerging in a design project. For Reiser, 'Architecture is not about the essence of a person; in fact most architecture is pretty selfless. Take the modern masters like Le Corbusier or Mies van der Rohe – if you set up certain parameters you are going to get that – it's not the essence of Mies van der Rohe or the essence of Le Corbusier, it is that the logics they were setting up would inevitably lead to their work.'[5]

3

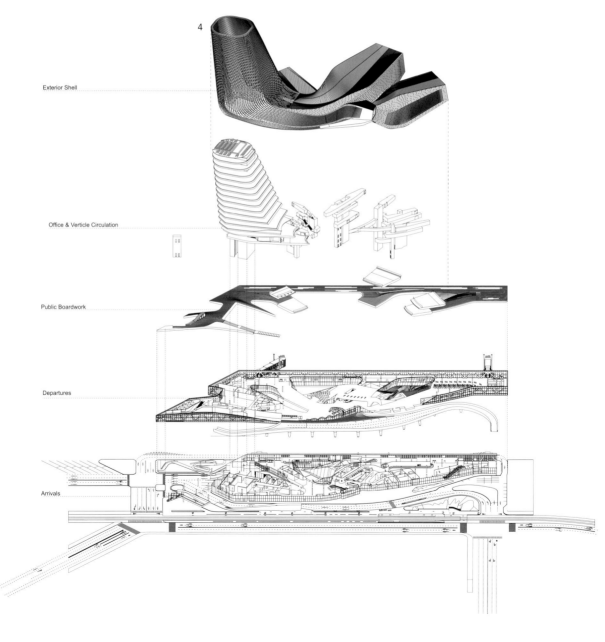

4

Exterior Shell

Office & Verticle Circulation

Public Boardwork

Departures

Arrivals

KAOHSIUNG PORT TERMINAL

Reiser + Umemoto won the design competition for the Kaohsiung Port Terminal in Kaohsiung City – one of the five special municipalities under the administration of Taiwan – and took the project through to construction documentation. The project broke ground in November 2013. The form of the building and its mass changed very little, though the project's design team had to revisit the design numerous times in development and the articulation of the envelope has changed greatly. The original competition renderings showed a smooth envelope that has given way to modulated panels that follow the building's exterior curvature. The envelope was originally conceived through a wax modelling process that was coordinated with the digital form-making process where the programmatic massing roughly dictated the volumetric constraints. These yielded quasi-typological groupings the practice calls 'lobes' as well as a more traditional architectural tower. These lobes persisted through the development of the whole project and define each of the programmatic halls called for in the competition brief. There was also a need to merge certain programmes. For instance, the tower component of the project was a requirement of the Ports Corporation of Kaohsiung Harbour, and it was necessary to connect the port authority programmes with the cruise ship terminal. In this regard, the arrival and departure venues for passengers were important and necessary to keep separate from the port authority office programmes.

For Umemoto, it was critical to tie these programmes to the urban planning idea of the *edge*. The team's ideological argument was that the problem the city had with reinventing the harbour's edge was that everything was understood only two-dimensionally – they had zoned blocks with different functions but had not considered opportunities to bring the public up and along the harbour. In fact, the city's original ambition was *not* to convert the harbour to public use, but to keep it functioning as a port and then add public uses and programmes to it. These constraints were not new to Reiser + Umemoto as they had been working with such concepts since their West Side Convergence proposal for New York in 1999, in which groups of users were defined, and programmes merged to include hotel and cultural areas combined with park and event spaces, retail shopping and commuter access to nearby rail lines. The team also looked at examples such as Carl Schurz Park on East End Avenue on the Upper East Side of Manhattan and specifically its connection to the Franklin D Roosevelt East River Drive, which slips under the park as the island of Manhattan bends to the north-west.

Recognising that the building would be sited on the edge of Kaohsiung harbour, Reiser + Umemoto decided to define the project architecturally, but also make it understood urbanistically as it extends along the whole edge of the city. It could simultaneously be an *iconic object* – something called for in the competition brief – but also be connected to a larger idea of developing the public infrastructure at the edge of the harbour.

3 Reiser + Umemoto, RUR Architecture PC, Kaohsiung Port Terminal, Kaohsiung, Taiwan, 2012–16
Visitors arriving in the main departure hall experience a panoramic view of the terminal, seeing into all three lobes, and the base of the Port Authority tower to the left of the entry. A tray within the tower houses an auditorium for Ports Corporation presentations to the public. The domestic departures lobe exists between tower and main lobe. The main departure hall serves as check-in for domestic and international ships. From the main hall is a vertical connection directly to the boardwalk on the third level, which serves public programmes such as restaurants. The white sinuous walls form the interior surface of the building's shell, behind which circulation and areas of refuge exist within the *poché*.

4 Reiser + Umemoto, RUR Architecture PC, Kaohsiung Port Terminal, Kaohsiung, Taiwan, 2012–16
An exploded axonometric reveals the Reiser + Umemoto team's organisational logic and design intent: (1) the building's exterior shell, (2) commercial floor slabs, and vertical circulation (the floating pieces are elevators, fire stairs, refuge areas and other *poché* between the exterior shell and interior finish) connect to (3) a third-level public boardwalk which includes a series of floor 'trays' that connect non-secured public programmes to the lobes above (4) a secure departures level and (5) a lower secure arrivals level.

5

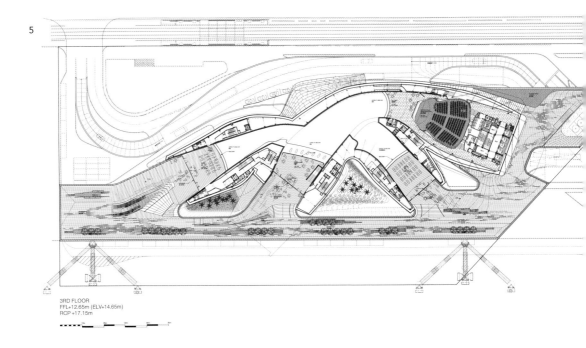

3RD FLOOR
FFL+12.65m (ELV+14.65m)
RCP +17.15m

5 Reiser + Umemoto, RUR Architecture
PC, Kaohsiung Port Terminal, Kaohsiung,
Taiwan, 2012–16
The terminal's third-floor plan reveals the
exterior boardwalk, which is a continuous public
space following the harbour that connects to
adjacent sites. The boardwalk connects to a
series of public 'trays' that lock into the building
lobes like fingers coming off the harbour. The
Ports Corporation will use the theatre at this
level for public presentations.

6 Reiser + Umemoto, RUR Architecture
PC, Kaohsiung Port Terminal, Kaohsiung,
Taiwan, 2012–16
Detail design for the terminal's canopy over the
main entrance for all departures, which is
located at the building's second level. Entering
under the canopy into the project's main hall,
passengers will experience a panoramic view of
the building's sweeping interior spaces. The
design team rationalised the building's geometry
so each piece of glazing is flat, but fits within
the structure to attain the facade's curvature.

6

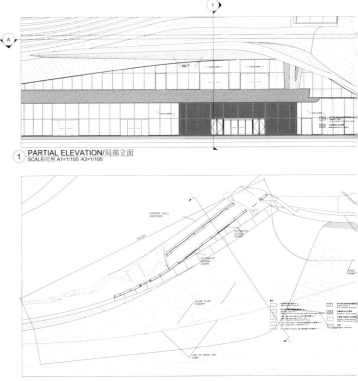

① PARTIAL ELEVATION/局部立面
SCALE/比例 A1=1/100 A3=1/100

SECTION/剖面 'A-A'

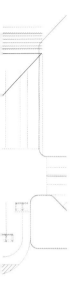

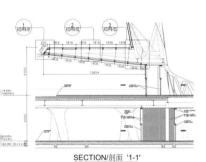

SECTION/剖面 '1-1'

圖例:

☐ 10mm單片強化玻璃 GL-1
10mm Tempered Glass GL-1

☐ 單片強化玻璃 (後側設置鋁板) GL-1
Spandrel Glass GL-1
Tempered Glass with painted aluminium backpan behind)

☐ 10mm+12mm argon+8mm Low-E中空強化玻璃 GL-2
8mm+12mm Argon+8mm FT IGU GL-2
Fully Tempered Insulated Low-E Glass

☐ 12FT+12Argon+8FT+1.52PVB+8FT強化膠合中空玻璃 GL-3
12FT+12Argon+8FT+1.52PVB+8FT GL-3

☐ 8+1.52PVB+8mm+12Argon+12mm 強化膠合中空玻璃 GL-4
8mm+1.52PVB+8mm+12Argon+12mm GL-4

▱ 8mmFT+12Argon+8mmFT 強化中空玻璃 GL-5
8mmFT+12Argon+8mmFT IGU GL-5

▨ 單片強化玻璃外側設置裝飾鋁金百葉
Spandrel Glass
with outboard decorative metal louvre

▨ 防暴雨鋁合金百葉窗
Rainproof Louver window

☐ 平開窗(安裝執手及多點鎖SS316)
Operable Window with handle, multilock and
SS316 friction stay restrictors.

▨ 鋁板
Painted aluminium

☐ 金屬屋面板
Corrugated Metal Panel

Tying these notions to the idea of three-dimensional zoning allowed the team to keep industrial functions at grade, the cruise ship terminal functions in the middle of the terminal and public functions and boardwalk at the uppermost levels. The original port terminal scheme was presented diagrammatically as a three-layered project, with the cruise terminal itself becoming architecturally similar to the organisation of an airport terminal. To that end, the team worked closely with the logistics group from Arup, arriving at a design in which passengers depart on an upper level and arrive circulating down to parking or public transport.

According to Umemoto, Kaohsiung was a first-stage open competition, but submissions were not anonymous as a way of ensuring selected design teams had relevant experience and could deliver the terminal building.[6] Part of the requirements of submission was including a portfolio of built work.

DIGITAL DESIGN AND DEVELOPMENT – BY REMOTE CONTROL

The design team had to go through a value engineering process as well as descriptive geometry exercises to show the contractors how such forms could be built – especially after an initial bid process that produced unachievable cost estimates. The design team had to indicate where curvature occurred in the project and where the facade could be built with flat panels and shared their work with Philip Fei of Fei & Cheng Associates – a Taiwan-based practice Reiser + Umemoto have partnered with to deliver the building. Fei and Cheng performed an initial cost estimate based on a process of applying more normative forms to the Reiser + Umemoto scheme. For Michael Overby, a project designer at RUR, 'Coordination of the various parts of a building would be a disaster on the large and complex projects that are under construction. The amount of control we can have of specific parts of a project at different times in the development process is important.'[7] Cost is something that can be controlled, especially with a more robust palette of tools, so the idea of cost as a constraint is an important one for any large, complex project.

There was one cycle of development with structural engineer Ysrael A Seinuk, PC in which the structural concept for the port terminal was developed. The structural design was ultimately handed over to a local engineering firm in Taiwan called Supertech Consultants International. The primary development occurred with facade consultants and with the logistics team at Arup. Arup Logistics interacted significantly with the client – there was less involvement with skin and structure – as the Port Authority would be running the cruise ship terminal and were particularly interested in specific functions of it, including baggage handling.

Through the process, Reiser + Umemoto maintained a boutique staff to develop the project with the team of consultants, a condition only possible through heavy reliance on digital technology. For Reiser, 'You no longer need an army of draftsmen.'[8]

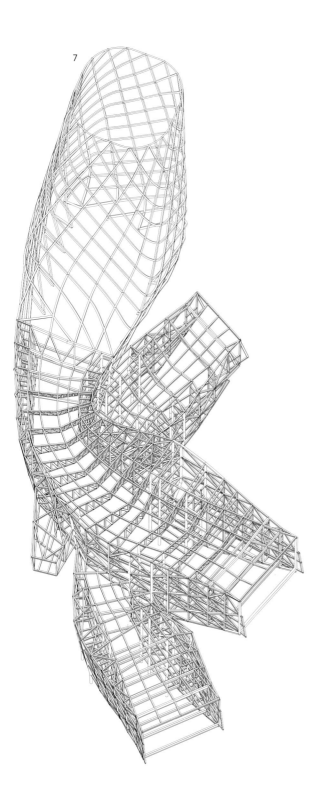

7

8

7 Reiser + Umemoto, RUR Architecture
PC, Kaohsiung Port Terminal, Kaohsiung,
Taiwan, 2012–16
The tower's structure consists of steel box-
beams of varied diameter that interconnect in
a lattice. As the tower transitions to the more
horizontal organisation of the terminal's lobes,
the structure becomes a bifurcated truss system
within which the design team planned all
vertical circulation and areas of refuge required
by Taiwan's strict health and safety guidelines.
By adding concavity to the roof of the main
lobe, the design team integrated a drainage
system into the terminal's geometry. The
terminal's structural system was developed by
initially exchanging three-dimensional centre-
line curves with Ysrael A Seinuk, PC in New
York, and later with the Taiwanese structural
consultant Supertech Consultants International.
Reiser + Umemoto modelled the final trusses
and box steel around the centre-line curves.

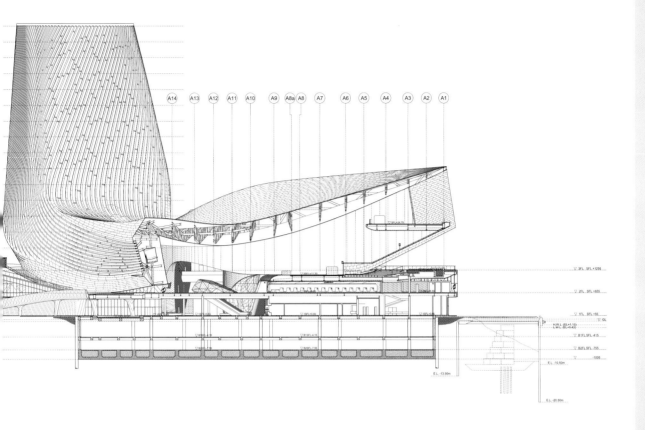

A14	A13	A12	A11	A10	A9	A8a A8	A7	A6	A5	A4	A3	A2	A1

8 Reiser + Umemoto, RUR Architecture
PC, Kaohsiung Port Terminal, Kaohsiung,
Taiwan, 2012–16
A building section through the terminal's
main departure lobe exposes the trays of
public programme and their connection to the
boardwalk below. An escalator, which takes
passengers from the first floor to the second
floor, is located under a large glass canopy that
artificially lights the main hall. An extension of
public space beneath the boardwalk containing
an elevator and stair allows for public access
to the boardwalk, so pedestrians can travel
from the ground level to the third floor without
entering secure areas of the building. There are
two levels of parking below grade.

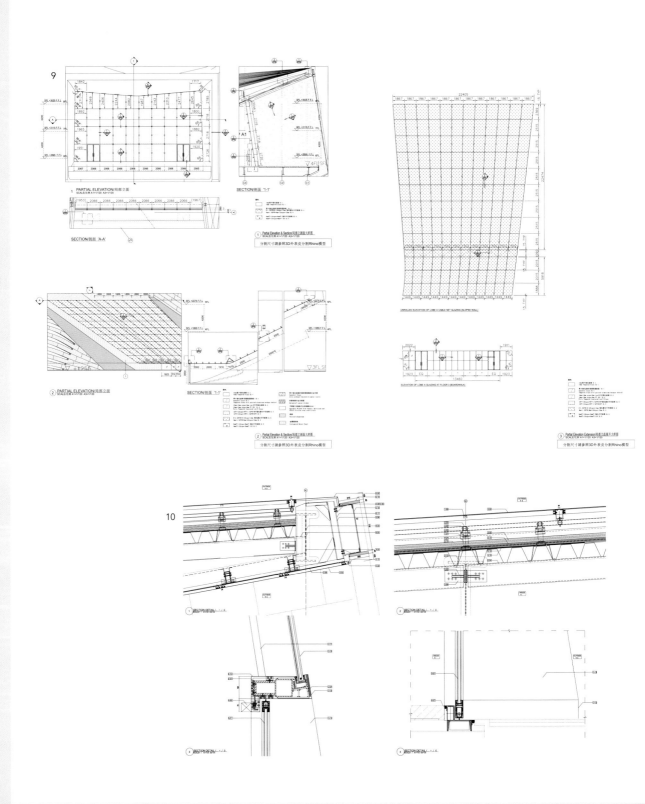

9 Reiser + Umemoto, RUR Architecture PC, Kaohsiung Port Terminal, Kaohsiung, Taiwan, 2012–16

The Reiser + Umemoto team used 'unroll surface' operations to determine the size and pattern of the large glazed area on the underside of the main lobe, which is hung with cable netting and exists between column grid A1 and A6. The team used Rhinoceros® to develop the geometry but were required to deliver a partial elevation of the glazing and cable net system (detail 1) and a two-dimensional unrolled glazing surface (detail 2).

10 Reiser + Umemoto, RUR Architecture PC, Kaohsiung Port Terminal, Kaohsiung, Taiwan, 2012–16

The design team delivered a series of two-dimensional details exported from their three-dimensional model, to describe lobe termination at various points of the terminal's exterior surface, in each instance deciding to set a curtain wall back from the edge of each lobe. The team also delivered two-dimensional details of the terminal's white metal panel soffit that terminates against the cable-net glazing system in the main lobe.

Coordination with the team of consultants was critical as was the resolution of the panelisation scheme. Overby coordinated structural design and its integration with the skin, engaging Taiwanese code consultants that came back to the design team with requirements for fire lobbies and zones of refuge, ultimately changing the project by increasing the size of the building cores. The building's volume and internal programmatic organisation were so highly resolved, a condition Reiser referred to as 'tight', that code constraints had to be highly managed during the construction documentation of the project. Ultimately the design team adopted a strategy of augmenting the cores and support spaces due to these requirements by expanding the building's *poché*. As soon as something new was added, it had an immediate impact on the structure and the skin, translating through all of the project's geometry.

In the end, the design team did not have a master model that linked this work, primarily as a result of the local architect having only two-dimensional capabilities, so it was decided that Rhinoceros® would be used to coordinate all geometric development and export two-dimensional design data to the team of consultants. This strategy was originally fraught with issues, as the Taiwan architects would make adjustments two dimensionally without fully comprehending the three-dimensional effects these would have on the overall building. For instance, the building's fire stairs weaved through the building *poché* and specifically did not engage the primary steel structure. The stairs did not stack in plan, and needed highly specific three-dimensional coordination, which included frequent trips to organise all consultant files based on the port terminal's geometry and the problems of geometrical construction. Supertech worked three-dimensionally so some structural coordination of the model was possible.

TO ACTUALISATION

The Reiser + Umemoto design team coordinated the construction document set with input from the consultants. Aluminium panel with a standing seam roof was decided on for the building's exterior cladding. The panelisation started at a basic subdivision that was primarily aesthetic and took into account limitations of panel sizes that were provided by the panel consultant. The facade consultant had a subconsultant called Lead Dao, a Taipei-based '3D advisor' who assisted in determining which panels needed curvature and which panels could be flat. The subconsultant worked in a three-dimensional format and in due time was able to send the Reiser + Umemoto team data to work with. The design team went through several versions of detailing the facade that were shared as a sequence of three-dimensional models with consultants and priced, until the current scheme of minimal curvature and the standing seam roof were determined. Fei and Cheng sent back sealed two-dimensional details based on the Rhinoceros® model. Several versions of the detail set and a sequence of the panelisation models went back and forth between the consultants. Ultimately very few panels had to be curved; only at crucial points in the building's envelope were curved panels necessary to achieve the design intent.

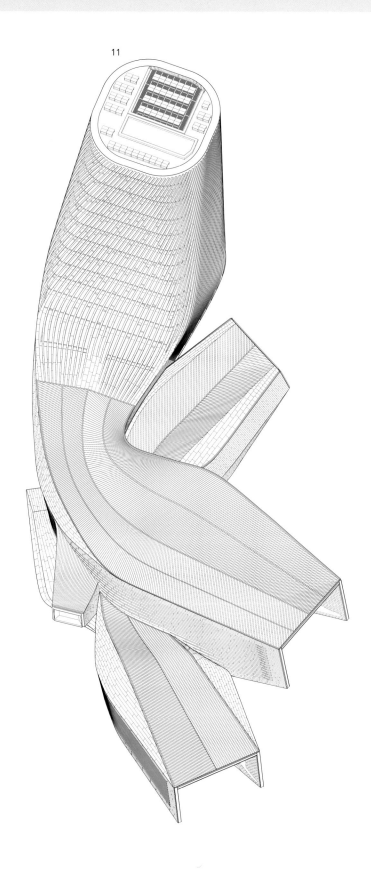

11 Reiser + Umemoto, RUR Architecture PC, Kaohsiung Port Terminal, Kaohsiung, Taiwan, 2012–16

During the cost estimation process, it was decided to use a standing seam aluminium roof over the terminal's three lobes, leaving the linear metal panel and glazing system for the tower and more vertically surfaced exterior portions of the other lobes. A series of steel tubes span floor-to-floor, following, according to Overby, a 'mostly vertical pattern' behind the skin system. A three-sided metal trough covers the tubes and accepts the exterior glazing.

12 Reiser + Umemoto, RUR Architecture PC, Kaohsiung Port Terminal, Kaohsiung, Taiwan, 2012–16

Working with a local Taiwanese architect of record Fei & Cheng, the Reiser + Umemoto team delivered two-dimensional details to describe the material transitions between the linear metal skin and glazing system and the long-rolled, standing seam aluminium roof. Specific geometric conditions were selected across the terminal's surface. These details integrate a drainage schema into each lobe's roof detailing, where a central gutter inset in the standing seam typically occurs where the lobes are dented along their length. The gutter in the main lobe connects back to the tower's drainage system.

12

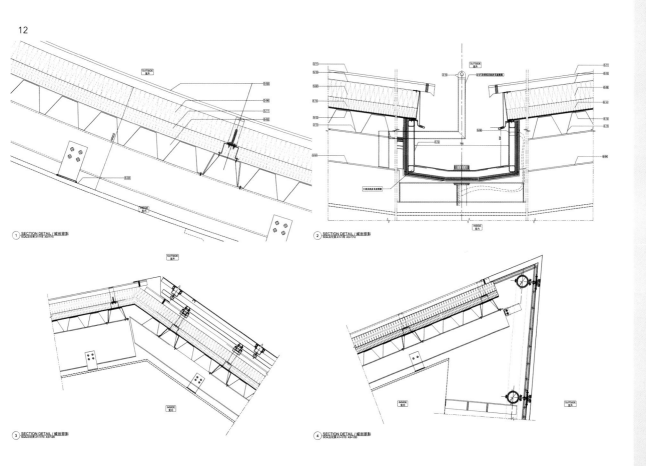

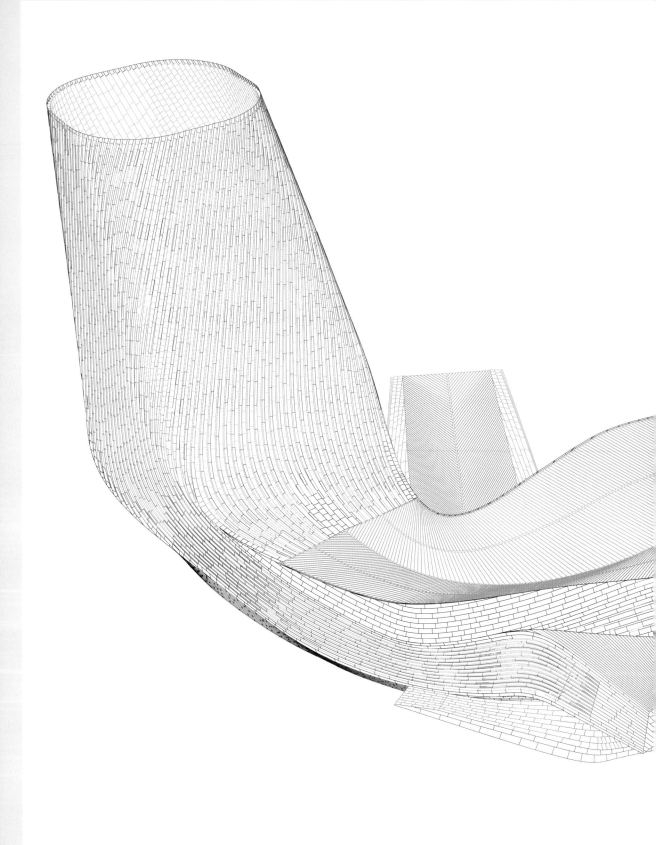

13 Reiser + Umemoto, RUR Architecture
PC, Kaohsiung Port Terminal, Kaohsiung,
Taiwan, 2012–16
The Reiser + Umemoto team exchanged
geometric data with Meinhardt Facade
Technology and Lead Dao to rationalise much
of the terminal's exterior skin into flat panels
while still achieving the building's design intent.
In the end, a colour-coded model was devised
to communicate the various panel types to the
facade manufacturer.

13

14 Reiser + Umemoto, RUR Architecture
PC, Kaohsiung Port Terminal, Kaohsiung,
Taiwan, 2012–16
The design team isolated various curved and
flat panels made of both metal and glass. The
graphic isolates (1) single-curved glazing; (2) flat
glazing, which covers the majority of the
building's exterior; (3) the thickness between the
glazing and the outer skin, which is a

450-millimetre (1'–6") depth – these are
normal to the outer surface and receive the
inset glass; (4) the standing seam aluminium
roof panels; (5) the curved cladding panels;
and (6) flat cladding panels. Magenta
panels in these images are panels that twist
– they are manufactured flat and then
pushed into place on site.

PANEL KEY

14 ▬▬▬ GLAZING - CURVED
▬▬▬ GLAZING - FLAT
▬▬▬ SIDE PANELS - BENT IN PLACE
▬▬▬ SIDE PANELS - TWISTED
▬▬▬ ROOF - STANDING SEAM
▬▬▬ GENERAL PANEL - SINGLE CURVED
▬▬▬ GENERAL PANEL - DOUBLE CURVED
▬▬▬ MEZZANINE PANEL - SINGLE CURVED
▬▬▬ CANOPY PANEL - SINGLE CURVED
▬▬▬ CANOPY PANEL - FLAT
▬▬▬ TOWER PANEL - FLAT
▬▬▬ LOBE A WALL PANEL - FLAT
▬▬▬ LOBE A INNER PANEL - FLAT
▬▬▬ LOBE A UNDERSIDE PANEL - FLAT
▬▬▬ LOBE B WALL PANEL - FLAT
▬▬▬ LOBE B ROOF PANEL - FLAT
▬▬▬ LOBE B INNER PANEL - FLAT
▬▬▬ LOBE B UNDERSIDE PANEL - FLAT
▬▬▬ LOBE C WALL PANEL - FLAT
▬▬▬ LOBE C INNER PANEL - FLAT
▬▬▬ LOBE C UNDERSIDE PANEL - FLAT
▬▬▬ LOBE D PANEL - FLAT
▬▬▬ SLOPED PANEL - SINGLE CURVED
▬▬▬ SLOPED SIDE PANEL - SINGLE CURVED

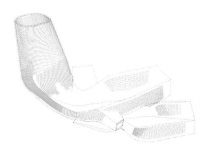

1. CURVED GLAZING

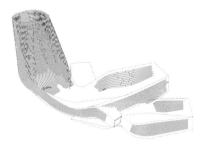

2. FLAT GLAZING

3. SIDE PANELS

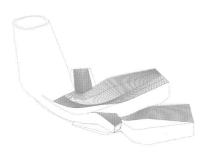

4. STANDING SEAM ROOF

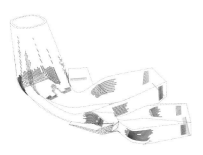

5. CURVED PANELS

6. FLAT PANELS

The project was taken through a second value engineering process while Reiser + Umemoto was developing their work. Fei and Cheng led this process, which was complicated by the 3-D to 2-D conversion necessary in transferring data files. The local consultants would send back suggestions on many parts of the building, including cladding systems, paving and landscape. There were aspects of the design intent that the Reiser + Umemoto team intensively worked on while their Taiwanese partners thought about reducing cost. There was a second round of cuts in the project due to a budget reduction to $90 million USD. The standing seam roof is terminated against the aluminium panels by a reveal that acts as a gutter, part of the value engineering process that Reiser believes improved the design, he prefers the continuity of the standing seam roofing, with fewer seams than the aluminium panels. The panelisation on the roof surface in turn takes on a herringbone appearance. There were construction issues with maintaining the depth of articulation, which is 500 millimetres (1'–4"), in the revealed sections of the tower that give the port terminal's forms their linear and sinuous expression. These reveals were an early candidate for the value engineering process, as it was believed constructing them in a shallow manner would allow the client to save money; however, the team was able to persuade the client that this depth was important, given the scale of the building, to register the desired effect. The curvature of the tower is achieved by incrementally rotating flat panels gradually along a seam, resulting in a small triangular gap. The glazing detail can skip each panel as can the external cap.

The Kaohsiung Port Terminal broke ground in November 2013 and construction is expected to take three years.

NOTES

1 Conversation with Jesse Reiser in New York, 28 August 2013.
2 Conversation with Nanako Umemoto in New York, 28 August 2013.
3 Reiser, 28 August 2013.
4 Reiser, 28 August 2013.
5 Reiser, 28 August 2013.
6 Umemoto, 28 August 2013.
7 Conversation with Michael Overby in New York, 24 September 2013.
8 Reiser, 28 August 2013.

IMAGES

7 | ASSEMBLIES AND THEIR SIMULATION

In the 1980s, alternative visions of computers and the future of design were expressed in competing views about programming. Some architects believed that designers needed to learn advanced programming. If designers did not understand how their tools were constructed, they would not only be dependent on computer experts but less likely to challenge screen realities. Other architects disagreed. They argued that, in the future, creativity would not depend on understanding one's tools but on using them with finesse; the less one got tied up in the technical details of software, the freer one would be to focus on design.[1]
Sherry Turkle, *Simulation and its Discontents*

Traditionally the driving issues at the beginning of the design process have been siting and environmental orientation, formal configuration, programmatic layout, and access and circulation. What if these could be paired with simulation operations such as environmental and solar performance, structural stability, natural and electronic lighting systems, and thermal analysis; how would this change the conventional workflow of design development? Coupled with notions of use and occupancy, the initial schematic design (information) model could test a large array of factors in design optimisation prior to later design stages involving large multi-disciplinary teams of consultants.

An assembly is defined as a series of components that are each linked to the assembly file, in the same manner that a series of CAD drawings can be referenced into a single file. Assembly files are generally small, enabling an ease of sharing among the project team in multiple locations. The ability to keep component files in a shared location so that various design team members and consultants can collaboratively develop and simulate a much smaller assembly file is desirable for aspects of workflow and speed. Additionally, an assembly would contain the work of different consultants to enable a real-time analysis of the integration of building systems such as structural, mechanical and plumbing systems within the architectural shell.

1 GRO Architects, PREttyFAB, Jersey City, New Jersey, 2007–09
PREttyFAB, a single-family house actualised in Jersey City, New Jersey, is a project in which GRO Architects synthesised simulation and fabrication technologies to deliver a 150- square-metre (1,600 ft²) building for the client at a total cost of $250,000 USD. For the project, GRO used a direct-to-fabrication process that involved shop drawing procurement in Autodesk® Inventor® with Northeast Precast, a precast-concrete company located in Millville, New Jersey, that produced the house's superstructure. Originally conceived as a prototype for affordable and energy-efficient urban infill housing, the house makes use of geometry to optimise solar collection, drainage and passive cooling. A flat portion of the roof contains a garden and a pitched section contains a 26-square-metre (280 ft²) solar array. These, plus insulated precast walls and radiant heating, make the home 30 per cent more energy efficient than typical construction.

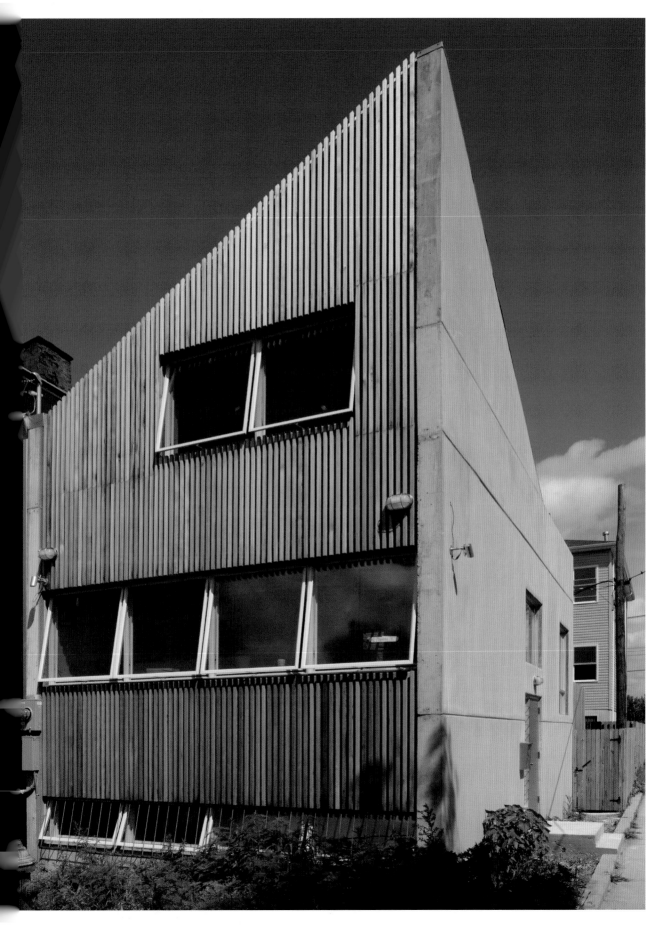

Simulation and analysis occurs within the assembly environment in information modelling packages, or in other software in direct communication with the building information model, and generally can include *numerical* and *architectural* descriptions of the design. Analysis conducted at the level of assemblies includes clash detection and conflict checking, as well as bills of quantities. Recall that all of these are efficiency-side aspects of BIM that promise to shift the current building paradigm of field errors and omissions to one that increases the iterative capacities of design through expanded responsibilities in the design phases, in an effort to make the construction process itself more efficient. In each case, data contained in the information model is *reported*, that is, the specific tasks of clash detection and listing material attributes attached to geometry are compiled in the form of an *extensible markup language* '.xml' or *comma separated value* '.csv' file, which can be opened in a web browser or spreadsheet program. These files can be used to make edits to part files, in the case of clashes by design team members, or transmitted to material suppliers or consultants for the development of cost estimates and material orders. In suggesting the benefits of digital simulations, Mario Carpo refers to them as an *additional treat* 'based on analytical tools, and the data they process, casual or statistical or other, must have been picked and ranked and their programs scripted, at some point by someone',[2] again reminding us of the changing state of authorship under the *digital*.

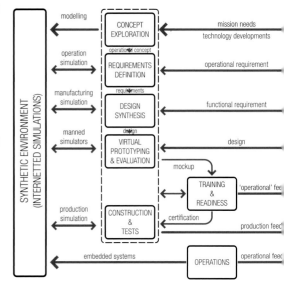

LESSONS FROM SHIPBUILDING

To better conceptualise information modelling processes and techniques in architectural design, a study of these technologies in another industry, specifically shipbuilding, is pertinent. Shipbuilding, and specifically the numerical and architectural descriptions of ships as complex systems, is chosen as the process is similar to buildings in that components and virtual data are customisable, but manufacturing processes to actualise ships need not be. This is unlike the design and manufacture of air- or spacecraft, in which production processes, at times, will need to be customised for novel or radical design. Beginning in the 1980s,

3

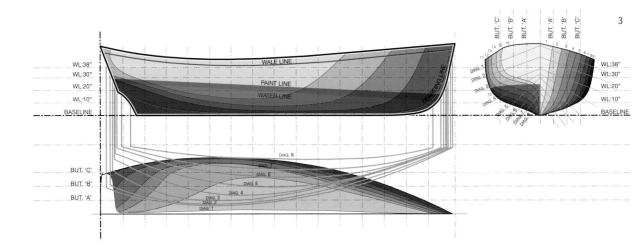

scholars and designers of watercraft began reconceptualising the design process to accommodate new computing technologies and found that such technologies had the most impact on the initial stages of design.[3] That is not to say that more downstream operations do not benefit from new technologies, but that the impact of new design processes, including form-finding and simulation, is greatest during the initial design stages, when both architectural and numerical descriptions can be generated prior to when large teams of designers and engineers are working on the system. For David J Andrews, '… because the eventual production process realizing the design product is the construction of the physical structure and the assembly within it of the multitude of interacting and interdependent subsystems, then ship construction (like ship design) has the closest parallels with large scale civil engineering and one off architectural buildings'.[4]

Interestingly, critical factors in the initiation of ship design are similar to those in architectural design, and in fact, it is possible through information modelling to expand the architectural field to include additional factors found in ship design, most notably *user interface*. Human factors in the operation of ships are as important as design issues such as structure, float, manoeuvring and hull form. As a way of including each of these, and others, in the initial design of a ship – or other complex system – Andrews proposes the use of building blocks, which are individual components that address specific *operational* or *performance* objectives of the complex system that are virtually aggregated into a 'Master Building Block', within a graphics environment.

The building block process has previously been outlined as a series of steps that the design would undergo, as opposed to a specific series of techniques and operations which would be personalised by each designer-author. If the design process is transformed through digital information models from a set of instructions using common components that lead to some preconceived solution to more of a procedural process, through which innovation and the creative development of custom components can be measured and managed, then the impact of information modelling on the initial process of design will lead to more comprehensive early solutions.

Andrews and others argue that the design of any complex system, the building block process at a 'technical level', consists of three vital and previously sequential sub-processes, after which are included terms specific to architectural design:

1 Initial sizing, where a gross size is obtained, *siting and programming*;
2 A parametric exploration, where principal dimensions and form are evolved, *generative form-making*;
3 The architectural and engineering synthesis, which is progressively performed within the constraints of the size and form previously determined, *systems performance and optimisation*.

2 GRO Architects, shipbuilding design and delivery, 2011
The shipbuilding design and delivery process, which is not unlike the architectural procurement of modular construction projects, has been codified as a continuous feedback loop – arranged here both vertically and horizontally – by Professor David Andrews. In a BIM environment, the ideas of concept exploration, evidenced in diagram development; requirements definition, evidenced in constraints; design synthesis, evidenced in profile generation, or two-dimensional document generation; and virtual prototyping and evaluation, as evidenced in toolpath generation; all follow a workflow that ultimately leads to construction and testing. This analogy is paramount to the adoption of BIM systems in the architectural design process.

3 GRO Architects, boat hull geometry, 2011
Naval architects typically produce line drawings of the longitudinal stringers for the bow and stern of watercraft. Here, the stringer lines of a sailboat are coordinated with the assumed stresses encountered while at plane. The diagram is expressive of the three points above.

ASSEMBLIES AND THEIR SIMULATION 180–181

These already lend themselves well to BIM activities, and each has embedded in its operations sub-processes that have existed within, and been challenged by, information modelling packages. First, the notion that these are sequential processes, as opposed to iterative ones, has been exhausted. Recall from Chapter 6 that information modelling packages have hierarchical histories that allow *geometric (architectural)* and *numeric* relationships to be changed at *any point* in the design process. The idea of working iteratively, especially when more comprehensive design can be achieved earlier in the design process, is fundamental to designing within an information modelling environment. Next, and relating to iterative design, is the measured parametric relationship in overall form. Adjustments to overall form and the internal relationships it organises can be constantly tested and finessed. Third, is the idea that systems optimisation is critical to the design process.

While the building block process outlined is specific to warship design, it is useful to understand the summarised objectives[5] as they relate to architectural design:

- A very broad intent and tentative outline requirement is identified and a design style proposed;
- A series of design building blocks are defined or selected (from a library or are newly created), containing geometric and tentative ship size and a set of hull dimensions postulated;
- The design building blocks are located as required within a prospective or speculative configuration space(s) and tentative hull form(s);
- Overall weight and space balance and performance (e.g. stability, powering) of the design are assessed, using the Paramarine™ naval architectural analysis routines;

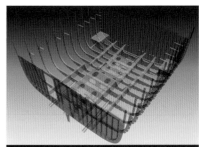

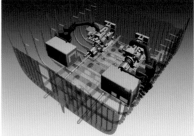

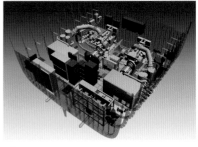

4

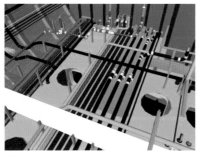

5

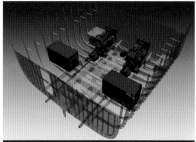

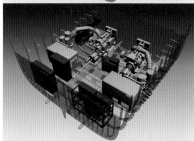

4 Vripack, large yacht engineering department, Sneek, the Netherlands, 2013
Vripack is changing the shipbuilding industry with its technological approach to construction. The virtual models are imagined as a 'kit of parts' that is simulated for bills of quantities, conflict checking and computer numerically controlled fabrication. Here a hull section is modelled with engines and mechanical piping prior to actual manufacturing.

5 Vripack, large yacht engineering department, Sneek, the Netherlands, 2013
Vripack digitally models and simulates all piping systems in the watercraft it designs. These models are shared with the fabricators and welders who are employed to route all physical piping in the boat hull. With this 'kit of parts' approach, any good welder can put the boats together – they do not need welders with experience in ship construction. These virtual simulation models are ultimately compared with the as-built condition for errors.

- The configuration is then manipulated until the designer is satisfied with both the configuration and the naval architectural balance;
- Decomposition of the design building blocks to ever-greater levels of detail is undertaken as required, and ship balance/performance maintained at the appropriate level.

Just as in the combination of individual parts (files) to form an assembly in an information model, each *building block* within the ship's design is a fundamental component within the design space, which contains all the information required of the particular part, and its function within the hierarchy of the 'master building block'. If we manipulate these six points to specifically respond to architectural design as it related to information modelling they might be:

- The development of preliminary programming and siting strategies for the design solution;
- A series of shape grammars within a given solution range, or the selection of components from a pre-existing part library, for preliminary formal solutions;
- The location and association of a selected tentative building form(s) with the site given previously outlined strategies; there is a *virtual immediacy* to site conditions through the model;
- A performance analysis of structural, material, environmental design, which includes day-lighting, shadow-casting studies, and resultant visualisations;
- The optimisation of the initial formal configuration(s) and performance analysis into a preliminary design proposal;
- The further refinement and integration of each part and assembly so that a greater level of detail and integration is achieved.

As suggested above, all items with the exception of further refinement of the preliminary design proposal can be done with a small team of designers at the beginning of the architectural design process. Therefore the information model developed has embedded in it a certain intelligence about the formal organisation of the whole, configuration of parts, function and level of performance of subsystems, prior to it being shared with the large and multi-disciplinary design team that will ultimately actualise the virtual design. As the design process articulated by Andrews suggests, the designer 'disposes the blocks as he or she chooses and then wraps round the blocks the necessary envelope'.[6] Readers might want to associate the Design Building Block approach with the process of manually arranging two-dimensional program blocks to generate an architectural plan; however, this would not be an accurate association. The process described herein is an integrated and iterative three-dimensional design process that leads to a *logical model*, which is simulated and optimised within the virtual environment. A programming exercise is simply two-dimensional space planning – the resultant organisation would not have a three-dimensional *formal resolution*.

VIRTUAL SIMULATION IN ARCHITECTURAL COMPUTING

Simulation has come to mean different things in architectural computing recently. Prior to the advent of attribute-based parametric information models, simulation primarily had to do with rendering and the notion that the computer image looks sufficiently like a real building, or could be experienced like a real building as in a walk- or fly-through. For Stan Allen, 'The unquestioned acceptance of the computer as a visualization tool is clearly market driven. It answers the client's need to predict what the building will look like before spending the money to build it. But the ideology of visualization is both naïve and somewhat duplicitous. Its trajectory is not from image to reality, but from image to image.'[7] This assumption lies in opposition to the development trajectory of an information model described here, specifically that a virtual diagram, with its abstraction of building organisation and systems, is something to be surmounted – that the best way to ensure a design is most fit for a building is how it is visualised in the computer.

The notion of simulation has historically been met with hostility and has divided many a faculty in schools of architecture. Sherry Turkle's quote that begins this chapter stands as testimony to the battle lines drawn in discussions about software adoption at the MIT Department of Architecture in the 1980s.

As information modelling was developing in the practice of architecture, simulation became common with computer numerically controlled (CNC) operations in which a virtual-scaled architectural model or building assembly is translated virtually to a piece of hardware such as a three-dimensional printer or milling machine (refer to Chapters 4 and 5). In keeping with the contracting notion of 'measuring twice and cutting once', most programs allowed architect-machinists to study such translations in a simulation environment where a piece of virtual material is formed based on the addition or subtraction process of the CNC hardware. While this did not guarantee the success of the machining operation – tool bits could break, printers could run out of memory – the designer could generally visually understand whether their intentions would be met during the *actualisation* of the model.

These processes of simulating part manufacture, still very much in use with the production of building components today and changing the *shop drawing review process*, are simple instances of more powerful simulation operations available through information modelling today. With the advent of information modelling tools, first in the engineering profession and then in architecture, designers use simulation to better test a set of assumptions on how their building will perform within specific criteria. This includes *environmental assessment*, such as how a building's orientation will affect natural lighting, solar collection, ventilation and shading. Such considerations can yield substantial differences in overall form, percentage of aperture within a building facade,

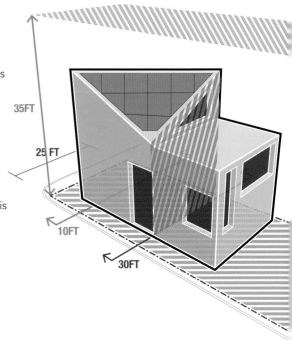

ORDINANCE	REQUIREMENT	PROPOSED
MINIMUM LOT SIZE	2,500SF	1,323 SF
MINIMUM LOT WIDTH	25 FT	22.45 FT
FRONT YARD SETBACK (MAX)	10 FT	6.0 FT
MINIMUM REAR YARD SETBACKS	30 FT	16.5 FT
MAXIMUM BUILDING HEIGHT	35 FT	25.75 FT

6

0 SF

6 GRO Architects, PREttyFAB, Jersey
City, New Jersey, 2013
The construction of PREttyFAB required GRO
Architects to obtain several variances from the
Jersey City Board of Adjustment. These
included variances for minimum lot size –
required was 230 square metres (2,500 ft²) and
proposed was 123 square metres (1,323 ft²);
minimum lot width – required was 7.6 metres
(25'–0") and proposed was 6.84 metres (22'–5");
minimum lot depth – required was 10.5 metres
(100'–0") and proposed was 17 metres (55'–9");
and rear yard setback – required was 9.1 metres
(30'–0") and proposed was 5 metres (16'–5").
The house was always conceived of as being
self-sufficient, so the simulation of solar
absorption based on orientation and
overall form was critical in obtaining the
necessary variances.

and amount of roof or wall space used for energy production
through evacuated solar tubes, for the production of hot water, or
photovoltaic panels, for the production of electricity. Construction
sequencing allows the designer to consider construction phasing
and schedule over time. In this process, a building site is modelled
to reflect a set of assumptions such as timing of trades, erection
of building components, use of cranes and the opening or closing
of routes. For Phillip Bernstein, 'building knowledge will reside in
information models with uses ranging from code and sustainability
analysis, fabrication, and assembly, to building performance
and management.'[8] Simulation need not follow component
generation per se. If types of simulation are considered among
the traditional design phases of Predesign, Schematic Design,
Design Development, Construction Documentation, and Bidding
and Construction it becomes clear that simulation has emerged as
an active and operative process that can guide the specific design
of components and assemblies. More specifically, as information
modelling allows more thorough design studies at the outset of a
project, aspects that determine the viability of large-scale products
including performance, quality, reliability and life-cycle costs
can be accurately measured without the work of a large multi-
disciplinary design team.[9]

PREDESIGN: PARAMETRIC BULK SIMULATION

Perhaps an under-considered use of the parametric capacities
of information models is in their ability to generate constrained
geometric configurations based on bulk requirements commonly
enacted by city planning departments; or the programme and
functional requirements of a facility owner. Bulk requirements
such as height, yard set-backs, building and lot coverage criteria,
and the angle of a sky exposure plane, generally dictate the
basic form of a building being planned for a specific site. These
requirements can be constrained in the same way that distance or
angular relationships are in component generation. This method
of simulation can quickly allow a developer to assess the size of a
planned building and therefore its development potential based
on the application of rule of thumb development costs.

There have been several recent attempts to standardise such a
practice, however, and numerous architects and designers have
quickly understood the utility of such parametric operations. Gehry
Technologies, the software and consulting company that emerged
from Gehry Partners and markets Digital Project™, have come up
with the concept of Gehry Technologies Return on Investment,
GTRoI, a consulting operation offered by the firm. By linking
hard cost data from a financial pro forma, geometric information
such as number of floors, floor area and building height can be
coordinated with building costs for different types of spaces, site
configurations and coverage requirements.

At Georgia Tech's AEC Integration Laboratory, Professor Charles
Eastman and his group of doctorate students are studying the
possibility of 'automated assessment' of conceptual designs

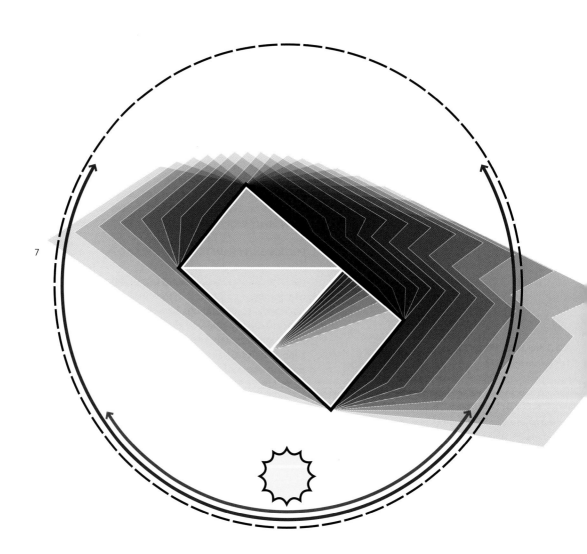

7

7 GRO Architects, PREttyFAB, Jersey
City, New Jersey, 2010
In a separate study, a shadow simulation of the
bulk model generated in the parametric bulk
analysis above is undertaken during the summer
solstice. The virtual model was exported from
the Rhinoceros® environment as a Drawing
Exchange Format (.dxf) file and imported into
Ecotect for the simulation.

8 GRO Architects, PREttyFAB, Jersey
City, New Jersey, 2010
Autodesk® Ecotect® Analysis graphic showing
total absorbed radiation (annually) on GRO
Architect's PREttyFAB prototype house. The
designers parameterised the location of a
south-facing roof, which received photovoltaic
panels. Ecotect was used to test the roof
orientation and tilt to ascertain its utility for
solar collection.

based on programme requirements. Though this process is akin
to intelligent space planning, and is less three-dimensional in
scope, the ability to automate critical relationships in building
design such as the adjacency of restricted defendant areas to
courtrooms in the design of a courthouse can greatly assist with
preliminary decision making.

SCHEMATIC DESIGN: ENVIRONMENTAL SIMULATION AND ENERGY USE

Recently, a series of programs and plug-ins have enabled
designers to visually assess how siting and building orientation
strategies respond to climatic and environmental data. While
these in many instances will reinforce the intuitive – a moderately
sloped south-facing roof is ideal for solar collection – these
tools nonetheless have allowed for an earlier awareness of
environmental criteria as they relate to design strategies and
formal solutions. Clearly the ability to make decisions based on
such criteria is inherently making design solutions that use these
tools more performance oriented.

Autodesk® Ecotect® Analysis is stand-alone software developed
by Dr Andrew Marsh that reads a variety of file types including the
standard Drawing Exchange Format (.dxf). The program accepts
imported geometry as three-dimensional solid or surface models
and links the model to a database of weather information based
on location. Currently most major US and international cities are
represented. The software simulates environmental criteria like
solar gain, shadow casting and reflection, effects of wind speed,
as well as thermal performance. Data is output both graphically
– it is simulated on the imported model – and numerically for
further calculation.

Additionally, environmental analysis can be accomplished
through scripts that can be run within information modelling
packages. A series of definitions published on the Web for the
Grasshopper™ plug-in for Rhinoceros® can also simulate sun
position and solar gain, based on an algorithm published by
the National Oceanic and Atmospheric Administration (NOAA).
Grasshopper, a plug-in and additional graphical user interface,
adds generative and parametric capabilities to Rhinoceros®. It
is a highly intuitive tool that is closely integrated with the robust
modelling environment of Rhinoceros®.

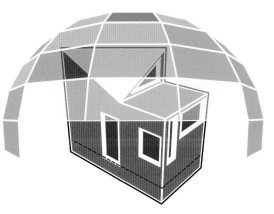

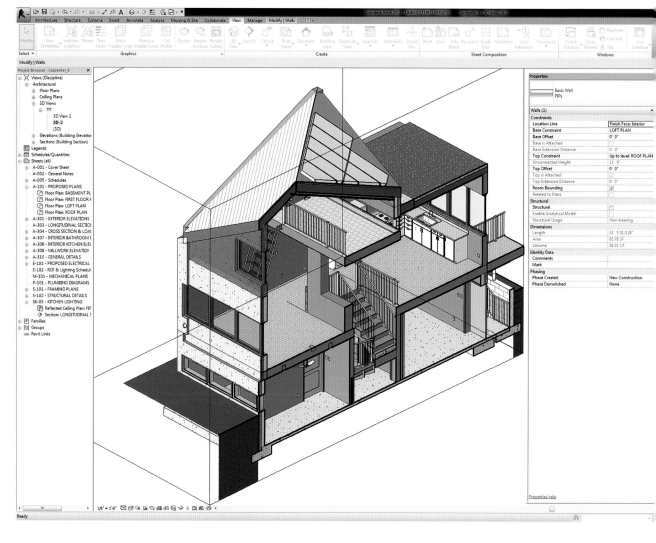

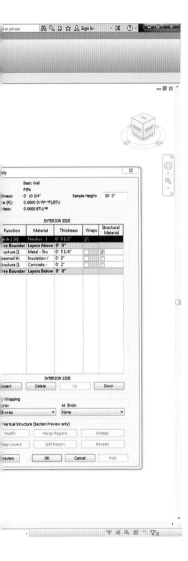

9 GRO Architects, PREttyFAB, Jersey
City, New Jersey, 2011
Autodesk® Revit® was used to coordinate and
develop all building components in PREttyFAB
including the precast-concrete walls, structural
steel, cedar rainscreen, exterior glazing, and
the photovoltaic and mechanical systems. In
addition to facilitating digital coordination
between the architects and precast fabricator,
a two-dimensional drawing set was extracted
from the building information model for
obtaining a construction permit.

DESIGN DEVELOPMENT AND CONSTRUCTION DOCUMENTATION: STRUCTURAL AND MECHANICAL SIMULATION

Increasingly, the analysis and simulation capacities of BIM are
being used in advanced structural and mechanical engineering
design. By adding such performance analysis, designers can better
understand how building proposals will transfer structural loads as
well as understand air flows, which is critical for good ventilation
and fire protection practices. While it is becoming increasingly
possible to perform such analyses within information modelling
packages, at the time of printing, third party plug-ins are still in
use in engineering firms that have adopted information modelling
technologies; however, these are communicating with standard
BIM platforms in more seamless ways.

SHOP DRAWINGS *REDUX*: PREPARING GEOMETRY FOR PHYSICAL OUTPUT

If whole building form, systems integration and construction
sequencing are now possible through information modelling,
then what becomes of the review processes in conventional
20th-century design practice as described in Chapter 3? As the
information modelling process now allows for an iterated and
complete virtual assemblage of parts of a system, the way in which
designers are working with fabricators and manufacturers has
radically changed.

10-16-2008 11-17-22 AM.JPG   10-16-2008 11-20-42 AM.JPG   10-16-2008 11-21-05 AM.JPG   10-16-2008 11-21-09 AM.JPG   10-16-2008 11-55-55 AM.

10-24-2008 1-20-07 PM.JPG   10-24-2008 1-21-56 PM.JPG   10-24-2008 1-22-11 PM.JPG   10-24-2008 12-24-24 PM.JPG   10-24-2008 12-24-52 PM.

10-24-2008 12-50-25 PM.JPG   10-24-2008 12-56-35 PM.JPG   10-24-2008 1-32-17 PM.JPG   10-24-2008 1-33-46 PM.JPG   10-24-2008 1-41-00 PM.J

11-11-2008 11-11-32 AM.JPG   11-11-2008 11-15-28 AM.JPG   11-11-2008 1-42-37 PM.JPG   11-11-2008 2-20-48 PM.JPG   11-11-2008 2-21-06 PM.J

11-11-2008 2-55-39 PM.JPG   11-11-2008 3-17-12 PM.JPG   11-11-2008 3-17-40 PM.JPG   11-11-2008 3-36-04 PM.JPG   11-11-2008 3-51-18 PM.JI

11-11-2008 4-53-59 PM.JPG   11-11-2008 5-10-04 PM.JPG   11-11-2008 5-29-30 PM.JPG   11-11-2008 5-30-09 PM.JPG   11-11-2008 5-33-32 PM.JI

4-2008 11-36-59 AM.JPG   10-24-2008 11-37-25 AM.JPG   10-24-2008 11-40-50 AM.JPG

10 GRO Architects, PREttyFAB, Jersey City, New Jersey, 2008

The 18 unique concrete panels that make up PREttyFAB's superstructure were craned into place over a three-day period. The wall panels were tied together by field-welded connections between stainless-steel plates that were cast into each panel in the factory. The roof panels were tied together with a steel beam and the foundation was tied together with a site-poured concrete slab.

4-2008 12-25-32 PM.JPG   10-24-2008 1-23-33 PM.JPG   10-24-2008 12-49-10 PM.JPG

24-2008 3-38-41 PM.JPG   10-24-2008 3-39-03 PM.JPG   10-24-2008 3-40-10 PM.JPG

11-2008 2-44-40 PM.JPG   11-11-2008 2-53-24 PM.JPG   11-11-2008 2-53-57 PM.JPG

11-2008 3-51-51 PM.JPG   11-11-2008 3-55-50 PM.JPG   11-11-2008 4-52-45 PM.JPG

12-2008 5-04-11 PM.JPG   11-12-2008 5-35-58 PM.JPG   11-15-2008 2-15-38 PM.JPG

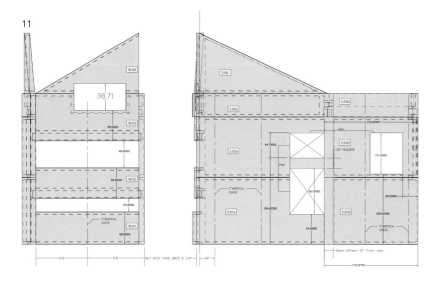

11 GRO Architects, PREttyFAB, Jersey City, New Jersey, 2008
Geometric data for the precast-concrete wall panels in GRO Architects' PREttyFAB house was extracted from Autodesk® Revit® and transmitted electronically to the precast fabricator, Northeast Precast. The fabricator further rationalised each wall panel using Autodesk® Inventor®, a solid modelling program, and sent two-dimensional shop drawings back to GRO to be overlaid back into the Revit® model for checking. Errors located in these virtual panels were noted and sent back to the precast fabricator for further coordination. In the end, 18 unique panels that formed the superstructure of the house were manufactured in this way.

12 GRO Architects, PREttyFAB, Jersey City, New Jersey, 2009
By transmitting three-dimensional data directly to the precast fabricator, GRO was able to ensure that panels were produced with minimal tolerances and the house fit together like a puzzle, set over the course of three days. The house ultimately performed as simulated, and was well received by the owner, the city and the public, receiving a Jersey City Green Award in 2010 and a Merit Award from AIA New Jersey in 2009.

NOTES

1 Sherry Turkle, *Simulation and its Discontents*, MIT Press (Cambridge, MA and London), 2009, p 19.

2 Mario Carpo, 'Digital Darwinism: Mass Collaboration, Form-Finding, and the Dissolution of Authorship', *Log* 26, Spring 2013, p 102.

3 DJ Andrews, 'Simulation and the Design Building Block Approach in the Design of Ships and Other Complex Systems', *Proceedings of the Royal Society: Mathematical, Physical and Engineering Sciences*, Vol 462, No 2075 (November 2006), p 3408.

4 Ibid, p 3410.

5 Ibid, p 3420.

6 DJ Andrews, 'A Comprehensive Methodology for the Design of Ships (and Other Complex Systems)', *Proceedings of the Royal Society: Mathematical, Physical and Engineering Sciences*, Vol 454, No 1968 (8 January 1998), pp 202.

7 Stan Allen, *Practice: Architecture, Technique, and Representation*, G+B Arts International (Amsterdam), 2000, p 153.

8 Phillip G Bernstein, 'Digital Representation and Process Change in the Building Industry', *Perspecta*, Vol 35, Building Codes, MIT Press (Cambridge, MA), 2004.

9 Andrews, 'A Comprehensive Methodology for the Design of Ships', p 188.

IMAGES

13 GRO Architects, PREttyFAB, Jersey City, New Jersey, 2009
The house's interior spaces follow the exterior form of the house, which was coordinated for performance through energy producing solar panels and the increased insulation capacity of 300-millimetre (1'–0") thick precast wall panels. A green roof was also installed over the kitchen space, which is accessed from a small mezzanine.

SHANGHAI TOWER

1

The prevailing reputation of Gensler as a practice that primarily executes corporate interiors is based on the work of its New York office, which is predominantly interiors oriented, but there is a wide diversity to what the practice does and certain offices tend towards specific types of projects. Gensler Shanghai, for instance, has focused over 80 per cent of the practice on architectural design, and specifically high-rise design. Gensler is a global practice, so offices from within the US support a certain amount of that work. When viewed from outside the New York lens, it is possible to understand the genuine diversity of Gensler's practice.

Gensler designed and delivered a successful mixed-use tower for PNC in downtown Pittsburgh in 2009. This work led to both a second Pittsburgh tower for PNC – the Tower at PNC Plaza – which is slated to be the greenest tower in the world, and the 21st- Century Tower in Pudong, very close to the Shanghai Tower. The practice has been increasingly engaging in high-rise work. The towers recently and currently being undertaken by the practice are non-standard, despite the fact that Gensler does not have the precedents and completed work that many practices engaging in high-rise design can claim. Design teams are expected to respond to environmental criteria and develop their own logics of material, structural and energy efficiency. Gensler attracts a diverse body of work, bringing a variety of expertise from its global staff to the specific design aspirations of each project. This reliance on such expertise means that the practice does not need to approach new work through precedents. Within the practice there are technical experts who understand how high-rise buildings are constructed, allowing the design teams to think about how different aspects of the building will perform in terms of structure and energy, but also in terms of interior workplace efficiencies and comfort levels – something the practice may be better known for. This approach and project diversity also introduces its own set of challenges, but the practice chooses to see these as productive.

1 Gensler, Shanghai Tower,
Shanghai, China, 2008–14
The Shanghai Tower will be the
tallest building in Asia upon its
completion in 2014.

2

GENSLER IN CHINA

The Gensler strategy in China has been to make a large commitment to having a local presence there, as opposed to setting up a small satellite office and sending the work back to the United States, which is a prevalent model. In the latter, all of the expertise stays in one or two groups in US offices. Gensler's model of establishing a local presence ensures expertise remains in the city in which they are building. The Shanghai office is currently staffed by 140 people, and a significant reason why the practice received the Shanghai Tower commission is that it has the capacity to deliver the project from the Shanghai Office, with support from a small group of US-based staff. The practice's Chinese clients receive both a local Chinese architect who understands the building culture of the country and the expertise of an international *brand* practice.

The tower design has been executed by a large team in Shanghai under Benedict Tranel, a Senior Associate and one of three firm-wide Technical Directors at Gensler. His role on the Shanghai Tower has been to assist with the development of the building's high-performance double facade, work that has been informed by a previous post at Heintges & Associates, a prominent curtain wall and facade consultant in New York City. As Technical Director, Tranel brings together expertise in design and construction, as well as specific software implementation as it relates to problems of facade design. Information modelling at Gensler has traditionally been about the integration of a suite of tools, and there is no single technology or software that fits any one project. Tranel feels there is a certain seduction in believing that everything will be on one platform and design will become 'easier', but it seems that different digital tools offer access to different information and as such the suite is critical for building success at Gensler – information modelling sets up exciting relationships between digital design techniques and what one is 'able to know' as an architect.[1] So building information modelling is seen as a software tool that, through parametric design, is empirically able to 'know' more data and detail about a building part or assembly than a human brain can. How that information is used is something else, and that is where the user interface – the intent of architect or designer – comes into play.

THE DESIGN PROCESS AND DIGITAL TECHNOLOGY AT GENSLER

At Gensler, the practice of architecture has the potential to be much more informed than it has been in the past. The firm always had an intuitive approach to design problems, but the computer can articulate why one solution is better than another, and how much better it is. Now much more complex calculations and simulations can be undertaken. Initially, these may still be based on intuition, but the computer is able, through parameters, to produce real results in near real-time. The new role of the architect at Gensler involves the studying and establishing of project parameters, which can be embedded in the model itself.

2 Gensler, Shanghai Tower, Shanghai, China, 2008–14
The Shanghai Tower twists at 120 degrees creating an interior core and exterior skin which allows for programmatic opportunities within the space created between these zones.

3 Gensler, Shanghai Tower, Shanghai, China, 2008–14
The Shanghai Tower boasts a six-level retail podium that also includes garden spaces. The podium is distinctively horizontal, to contrast with the tower's verticality and uses forms and materials that are more consistent with traditional Chinese culture. The podium also contains a conference centre adjacent to the retail programmes.

4 Gensler, Shanghai Tower,
Shanghai, China, 2008–14
Light pollution created by reflections
from the tower's facade and nearby
towers is limited by local Shanghai
building codes. Reflectance off the
tower's curtain wall was simulated
virtually and had an impact on the
guided design decisions as the
facade was developed.

4

For Tranel, 'the end game, from a technology standpoint, arrives when processing power will be such that all parameters, codes, everything that is necessary to construct a building will exist within the virtual model'.[2] The architect will still work within these parameters to ensure that design intent is maintained. Right now the architect's role involves setting these parameters, but architecture will remain an artistic endeavour through establishing the design intent that is supported and developed as more information is embedded in the model.

Within the context of Gensler, because of the practice's history and workplace legacy, projects are executed quickly. In the San Francisco Bay area especially, technology companies share this mode of operation. Deliberateness in this context might seem at odds with the culture, but given that digital technology does have the capacity to speed up design processes, perhaps it is a deliberate kind of decision making that the architect, as author, needs to retain.

For the last several years, Gensler has been exploring the use of supercomputers created by San Francisco Bay technology companies to render in real-time in a three-dimensional view as one walks through a building. These will ultimately augment an already wide range of modelling and imaging tools that were used in the design of the Shanghai Tower including Autodesk® Revit® and Ecotect® Analysis. The team has adopted a hybridised analogue and digital method – designers will still sketch design intent manually, but they will also generate parameters that will be used in an information model, such as maximum and minimum dimensional tolerances and other criteria for building components. The design process involves the creation of solutions for a range of difference, as opposed to detailing every single condition.

SHANGHAI TOWER: SIMULATION OF THE INFORMATION MODEL, THE DOUBLE FACADE

Since winning an invited multi-stage competition in 2008, Gensler has been working on what will be the tallest building in Asia, the Shanghai Tower. Simulation was used to gauge the overall performance of the building in terms of lateral resistance to wind speed, but also how the overall design and form of the building evolved due to lateral loading and other factors such as light reflectance. The building was conceived as a tapering, twisting box, but these early digital models did not respond well to wind loading in the computer. Tranel described the design at this point as 'not feeling quite right',[3] but the issues were far more specific in terms of building performance – the building was failing in simulations of *vortex shedding*. The building ultimately evolved with the vertical box form as the core and with the most efficient shape for the floor plates around it being a circle. The building was then enclosed by a double skin that circumscribed the circular floor plates with a series of triangles to account for the twisting the design team had originally intended for the tower. This allowed for a well-organised core, which is a nine-square grid, surrounded

5

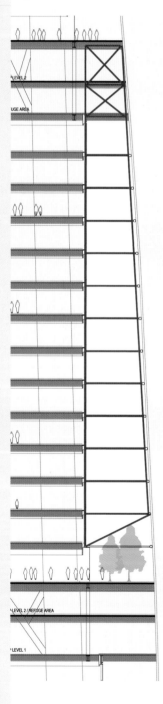

5 Gensler, Shanghai Tower, Shanghai, China, 2008–14
The design team conceived of the tower as an internal cylindrical core that would allow for similarity between floors for building systems, and an exterior curtain wall that is tied back into the core with rods that support an outrigger bell truss at the facade, resembling a bicycle wheel in plan. While the floor plates are varied through rotation from floor to floor, some standardisation is achieved through the cylindrical core design. The three-dimensional image shows the variation achieved by circumscribing the circular core with the building's triangular curtain wall. The dimension between the outer skin and inner core varies constantly in plan and section and is recorded and made physical by the rods, or 'spokes' of the wheel.

6 Gensler, Shanghai Tower, Shanghai, China, 2008–14
As Shanghai is an active seismic zone, the mitigation of earthquakes on a super-high-rise tower was of paramount importance. The design team deployed tuned mass dampers in the building to reduce the amplitude of vibrations caused by seismic activity. The dampers stabilise the inner core, which is tied structurally to the outer, varied, curtain wall.

7 Gensler, Shanghai Tower, Shanghai, China, 2008–14
As accurate computational fluid dynamics (CFD) results proved elusive given the size and complexity of the tower's curtain wall system, the design team resorted to a 16-metre (52'–5") physical model that was physically tested for its lateral stability in both wind and seismic loading. The tower as designed can withstand earthquakes up to 7.5 on the Richter scale.

5

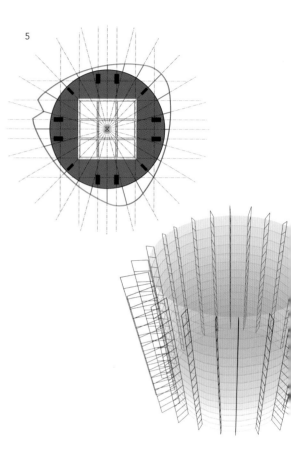

6

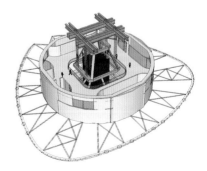

by a highly efficient circular floor plate. All of the geometric expressiveness of the form is achieved through the second layer of facade. While the twist allows for variation in each of the floor plates as they stack up the building, the actual floor plans within the tower are similar for each of a series of 14-storey zones. These ideas were generated through tandem processes, which included both modelling and simulation within the computer and wind tunnel testing of physical models.

The geometry became so complex it defied hand sketching, it was only possible to visualise it with digital tools, which brought another question to the design team – *how much twisting was too much*? The team returned to the concept of *vortex shedding*, understanding that there would be structural benefits to a geometric configuration that shed wind efficiently. Wind forces are by far the largest magnitude forces on the structure of a tower, and when winds hit the facade of the building they tend to accelerate to move around the perimeter. Through this acceleration, the air molecules that go around the building arrive on the leeward side of the tower at the same time as the air molecules that bypass the building. Once this acceleration reaches a certain speed, they begin to peel away from the surface of the building facade, creating large suction forces. Since the air speeds up, wind forces are often stronger on the leeward side of the building than the windward side, which can magnify the force to be greater than the wind speed itself.

The design team settled on approximately one degree of twist per floor, so over the original 121 floors – five additional floors were later added to create an observation deck – there is about 120 degrees of rotation in the building elevation. A wind tunnel lab ran tests for a series of different models that were three-dimensionally printed from the information model the team was developing to see which shape responded best. The wind tunnel testing was critical to the building development as a sufficient level of computational fluid dynamics (CFD) simulation at the scale of the tower proved elusive, even with an abundant amount of computing power. There were initial attempts to simulate wind testing within the computer, but most CFD simulation occurs for discrete portions of buildings, as in an atrium or other interior space. The desire to understand at a precise level how the building would respond laterally required the team to resort to the testing of scaled models. Physical simulation paid off, not only were wind loads reduced by 24 per cent, the structural steel in the building was reduced by 25 per cent, or an estimated cost saving of $58 million USD.

The team maintained an energy performance model of the entire tower as it was important to also understand how air would move between the double curtain wall of the facade, especially at heights where wind speed is a factor. The team took data generated from the wind tunnel testing and input this into the model, generating specific wind behaviours for specific times of day and year, both at and behind the exterior facade. This was

8

8 Gensler, Shanghai Tower,
Shanghai, China, 2008–14
As the building is in a high wind
zone, much of the development
of the facade involved the study
of vortex shedding to improve the
building's lateral wind resistance
through its formal configuration.
Capitalising on this problem, the
design team imagined outfitting the
building with rows of wind turbines
integrated into the curtain wall at
the tower's upper levels. These will
produce clean energy used by the
tower, thereby lessening its reliance
on conventional energy sources.

9

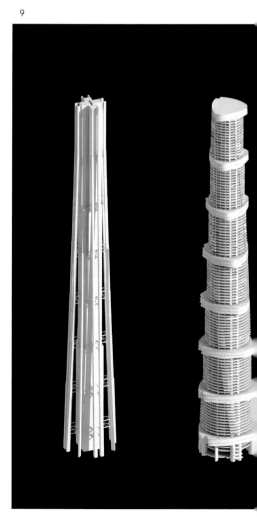

9 Gensler, Shanghai Tower,
Shanghai, China, 2008–14
The tower is composed of a series
of structural layers, including the
concrete core that is connected
horizontally to a series of outriggers
and a series of super-columns.

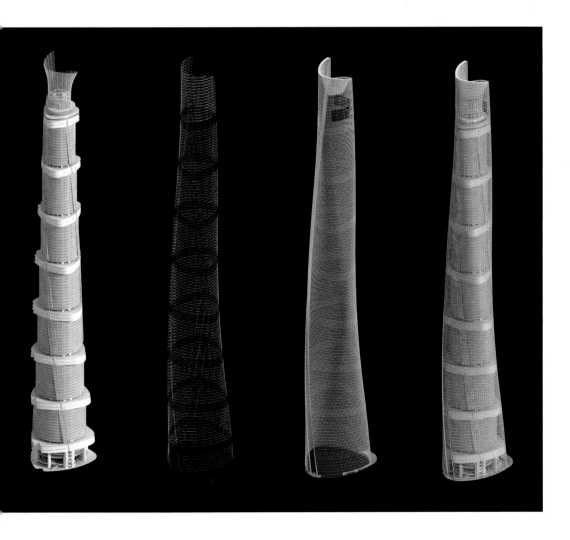

integrated with a simulated stack affect within the building to more fully understand what kind of air changes and flows were occurring within the cavity of the double facade. This process of inputting data into a building information model from other sources attests to a model's robustness in its ability to accept parameters from other forms of testing – the wind tunnel tests – and simulation.

The double facade's curtain wall ties together the standardised floor plates while also responding to wind forces at different elevations. It also helps to mitigate solar heat gain by recapturing and reusing heat and thereby reduces the heat load in the interior commercial spaces. By having this slot, or layer, of space as a part of the building's 'arrival' sequence, the double facade serves as an important Chinese cultural reference as opposed to a more Western notion of a plane of glass separating the interior and exterior.

Several interesting aspects of the tower design have been amalgamated into the building's actualisation. First, fire code in China is quite strict, requiring that there are floors of refuge every 14 to 20 storeys. Therefore the required breaks in the tower elevation became obvious locations for an outrigger and belt truss for lateral stabilisation, and a location for a mechanical equipment zone. These requirements give way to a louvred horizontal banding recognisable in the Shanghai Tower, but also in other tall structures around the city. Next, the variable floor plans enabled by the core design achieved some standardisation – this was important from a leasing standpoint – so that there would be some regularity to the commercial layouts on the tower floors. Finally, Gensler conceptualised the tower as a vertical city, with the idea that the diversity of urban life on the ground plane could be rotated vertically to bring richness to the programming of the tower itself. The idea was refined to a series of vertical *neighbourhoods* that were grouped in the 12- to 15-storey zones required by fire code. This led to the development of the vertical transportation system, in which a combination of express and local elevators are accessed from a common atrium floor for core efficiency. This transfer level also houses a sky garden, which is enclosed in the double facade.

The form of the building, which was vitally driven by the performance of the outside curtain wall, encloses an important amenity space of the tower and allows for a series of design opportunities within the building that were both expressive and efficient. The architects compare the vertical transportation sequence to how residents might experience their own urban neighbourhood as they embark on their day, stopping through a garden and commerce space before being delivered to their workplace via elevator.

10 Gensler, Shanghai Tower, Shanghai, China, 2008–14
Ground-floor lobbies differ based on the programme they serve, and were designed at a scale consistent with the tower itself. These multi-storey spaces expose the outrigger system that attached the building's curtain wall to its core. The lobbies are organised within the podium retail space at the tower's base.

11 Gensler, Shanghai Tower, Shanghai, China, 2008–14
The structural outrigger system continues up the tower and is exposed at many levels. These support the outer curtain wall and also create courtyards at each of the building's nine vertical zones.

12 Gensler, Shanghai Tower, Shanghai, China, 2008–14
The tower is divided sectionally into nine vertical zones or 'neighbourhoods' that vary between 12 and 15 storeys in height. This is in response to the local fire code, but also allows for distinctive programming over the height of the building as well as mechanical distribution of conditioned air. Cooling is delivered at the slab level to the offices within the building's circular core. That air is exhausted out of the offices at 25.5 degrees Celsius (78 degrees Fahrenheit) into the atrium, which in turn reduces heat load on the tower's interior facade. Air is ultimately exhausted out of the building through the floor above each atrium following a heat recovery process that adds further efficiency to the building's mechanical system.

12

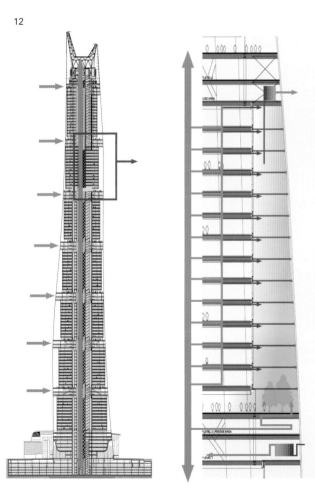

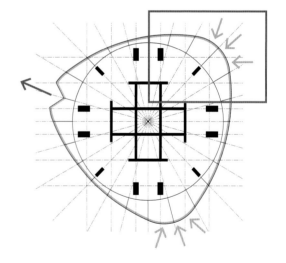

BUILDING ACTUALISATION

Gensler's contract stipulated that they would be responsible for concept design as well as schematic design and design development. Owing to the building's complexity, the Gensler design team worked closely with a local design institute (LDI) in Shanghai for the construction documentation and construction administration phases of the project. This included sharing the building information model, and a level of involvement far greater than the practice had experienced on other Chinese projects. There are construction administrators on the staff in Gensler's Shanghai office who also work closely with the contracting teams.

It was important for Gensler to explore efficient ways for actualising a building as complex as the tower with the general contractor, Shanghai Construction. There was already a great deal of empirical knowledge contained in the building information model the design team had developed, but how to share that knowledge with a contracting firm and subcontractors was an open question.

Several processes were put into place to ensure that construction tolerances and benchmarks were achieved. For instance, each of the water-jet cut parts of the curtain wall were laser scanned prior to being set in the field and checked against tolerances in the model. This ensures proper fitting of components on the project site. Once Gensler shared their model in a variety of software formats for information purposes, the general contractor quickly understood that they needed to utilise software for processes such as clash detection and the creation of scope for subcontractors. In fact there was minimal work done to the architectural model, which attests to the completeness of Gensler's BIM, which was intended to be a design model, *not* a fabrication model.

The Shanghai Tower will be completed in 2014. The building will stand approximately 632 metres (2,073'–0") high and will have 125 storeys, with a total floor area of 380,000 square metres (4,090,000 ft²). It will be the tallest building in Asia, the second tallest in the world, and promises also to be one of the most sustainable.

NOTES

1 Discussion with Benedict Tranel in San Francisco, 31 May 2013.
2 Ibid.
3 ibid.

IMAGES
pp 196–197, 198, 200–201, 202–203, 204–205, 206, 207, 208, 210, 211, 212 © Gensler.

13 Gensler, Shanghai Tower, Shanghai, China, 2008–14
At the time of its completion, the Shanghai Tower will be the tallest building in Asia. The building was topped out in July 2013 by Shanghai Construction.

8 | CONCLUSIONS: AUTHORSHIP AND LINES OF DEVELOPMENT

1

… The greatest industrial innovations have always, in the end, been communicational … Virtually all gains in efficiency are derived from being able to extract 'work' or value from social reservoirs. To say this [in] another way, we must acknowledge that 'communication' is a very profound and rich thing, and while it is the foundation of what we are, it is neither exhausted or explained by the one-dimensional activities and apparatuses within which we increasingly confine our lives.[1]

Sanford Kwinter, interviewed by Johan Bettum,
March 2007

There have been several prominent lines of development with respect to building information models and new modes of project delivery discussed within this text and elsewhere. At one end of the spectrum, the developers of software have created white papers that espouse BIM's ability to streamline the documentation process, advocating robust virtual environments that encourage collaboration and the sharing of data between parties.

At the other end of this spectrum is the current-day architect, as *author*, who uses such technologies in the creation of novelty, but has not necessarily adopted collaborative aspects of these new tools. To recall an example at the beginning of the book, the large Midwest contracting firm Mortenson Construction largely took on the responsibility of developing the Daniel Libeskind designed Denver Art Museum from a relatively crude solid model to achieve efficiency in trade coordination and steel fabrication. For Mario Carpo, '… the quest for the immediate visual recognizability of a designer product or a famous brand is probably a symptom of the crisis in the role of the author in the current techno-social context, and at the same time an effect of the crisis in the cultural logics of mass production which is being brought about by the new digital technologies.'[2]

1 Gehry Technologies, Museo Soumaya, Mexico City, 2011
Working closely with the architect and facade fabricator, the Gehry Technologies (GT) team went through a 'family optimization process' to achieve design intent while finding the largest number of similar parts – in this case metal hexagonal discs – as possible to make facade construction both efficient and economically viable. GT looked at different options to group and then assess the aesthetic impact on the facade of the building. The GT team rationalised the facade surface geometry of the building into a series of panel families as opposed to having thousands of unique panels. Area and gaps between panels were constrained through this process, which ultimately yielded 52 families that were suitable for cladding over 80 per cent of the facade.

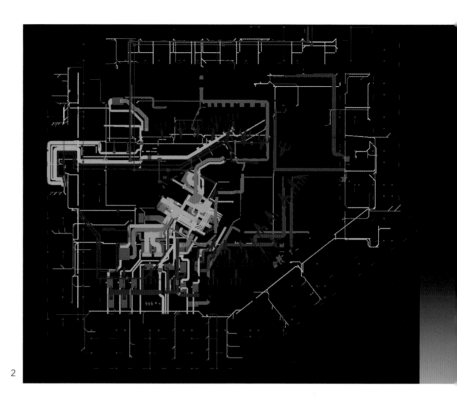

2

Neither of these positions, however, exactly satisfies the question of how the architect conceptually positions the use of new tools in the expanded design field; nor how the adoption of such technologies allows for the production of novelty within terms that are efficient, or manageable, for all parties involved in the design and construction of a building – at the very least the architect, owner and general contractor. In the description of digital design methodologies, developmental geometry and its relationship to an information model, as well as the analysis of architect, owner and general contractor responsibilities, we find a third, hopefully more nuanced approach to authorship that finds a mate in new technologies.

DIGITAL CRISIS?

The role BIM has played in design, and its effect on architectural practice, has evolved over the last decade. A white paper published in 2006 by Victor O Schinnerer & Company, a leading underwriter of professional liability insurance – the type of insurance US-based architectural practices generally carry – stated that BIM software can also 'inappropriately replace the need for professional judgment by forcing the model to redesign itself based on preset rules intrinsic in the design elements'.[3]

2 Gehry Technologies, Museo Soumaya, Mexico City, 2011
The GT team coordinated the mechanical system design and utilised conflict check studies to ensure that horizontal and vertical ducting were not in conflict with structural members or other building systems. While BIM systems offer a powerful environment to model and manage complex geometrical systems, such as the Museo Soumaya's facade cladding, they can also manage the integration of all building systems in large and complex buildings.

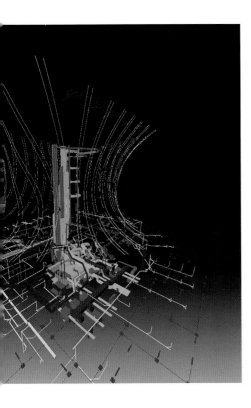

The opportunities for increased service, quality and collaboration that information modelling tools generally afford designers are illustrated; however, the paper also lists a series of unresolved issues with BIM.[4] Among them are a risk averse position on the creation of new business models, questions of control of both information and intellectual property, consensus allocation of risk as it relates to contract documents, and the very definition of design *elements*.

If the designer is working directly with new digital tools, and smoothly sharing the product with an expanded field of experts, a new idea about *control* develops. This new notion is not as top-down as it would have been with the master builders who emerged in the early Renaissance; however, it is not as complicated as the arrangements for designing and building based on 20th-century contract documents, where some vagary was believed to be good for everyone's sake. This is a sort of flexible control that allows for intuition while promoting a precision of concept through simulation and shared expertise. It is perhaps this sort of control, which allows for a self-organisation of teams based on expertise, that can foster novelty.

One of the premises of information modelling systems is that a user must have more general knowledge about design and construction activities, as the geometry, components and relations being developed have more specific consequences for the *actualisation* of a building. Such a premise is interesting for two reasons. First, it suggests that the division of labour commonly found in architectural offices, and theorised in the Renaissance by Alberti and others, might be collapsing – that there isn't a draftsperson taking direction from a project architect in the development of a design proposal. Instead, the new designer, as author, has the ability to drive the direction of a building solution based on actual criteria that can be tested within the virtual environment, while still relying on more conventional experience as well as intuition. In this model, the ability for others to collaborate on, and form, the final designed product refers less to a *design by committee* scenario than to one where the architect understands the need, perhaps for efficiency or perhaps because of a technical requirement, to give up a certain amount of control during the virtual development process to only gain it back in the actualised building. These very different aspects of creativity cannot be overlooked.

Mario Carpo, in cautioning about the impact of the digital 'turn' in architectural design, writes about an 'aggregatory' mode of development in which a combinatory pool of authors, or agents, can edit a digital design at will putting them at a state of 'permanent development … forever functioning only in part'.[5] There are obviously pragmatic limits to such posturing, as Carpo himself is quick to point out that 'architectural notations must be completed and finalized in order to be built; they cannot keep morphing and changing forever, like an animation sequence or a Wikipedia entry'.[6]

Perhaps it makes sense to reiterate with some irony the notion here that BIM is primarily made possible through advances in information (computing) technology, as opposed to advances in building technology. Sanford Kwinter emphasises the influence of the computer as a communication tool – via electronic mail, SMS text messages, micro-blogging sites such as Twitter, and cloud networks – which allows for the rapid dissemination of information at speeds we have never known. The communication technologies inherent in information modelling equip designers to translate information to *builders*, by which I mean literally both *those who construct our intentions*, and *computer hardware that can physically fabricate material concepts through digital data.*

It is interesting that users of these technologies have come to BIM through two related but different needs, as demonstrated by the projects included herein. The first is *pragmatic*: the desire for higher efficiency via a streamlined and coordinated documentation process makes information modelling attractive to firms with large and diverse teams of people working on large and complicated building projects. For them, increased communication and collaboration mean fewer errors in the field which in turn increases profits. To this end, Gehry Technologies was spun from Gehry Partners to allow others to engage in the experience the latter had gained in the construction of novel architectural solutions. It should be noted that some of the most adventurous and novel forms to emerge via such processes in the 1990s and 2000s were only made possible through digital fabrication technologies that allowed for cost-effective (pragmatic) production. Indeed, these curvilinear experiments in the actualisation of virtual technology spearheaded by Frank Gehry, Lars Spuybroek and others, have become symbolic – and in many ways iconic, of the use of such digital technologies in architectural design – an iconography that many in our profession are still not ready to engage or even acknowledge.

The second need is more *speculative*: by using software to communicate digital data to computer-controlled hardware, new types of fabrication or construction possibilities – in many instances borrowed from other industries – emerged. This work theorised and executed in small and innovative practices and schools of architecture has allowed for a new hybrid approach to construction to occur that is both novel and highly efficient by its nature. Playing out initially in installations and small-scale projects and exhibitions, computer numerically controlled (CNC) fabrication allows the designer to guide the formal organisation of a project or component from original concept or diagram through to its physical output. Perhaps then, the architect who fully embraces these technologies in design and construction arrives at a hybridised position that is at once authorial, as in one who authors a design direction or concept, but also agency based in that others, following the concept articulated by the architect, assist in the further development of the design, especially as it is actualised

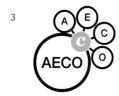

3

Technology Strategy

We leverage our broad exposure to help clients maximize their technology investments.

BIM Implementation

Our platform neutral training and support is focused on your project, not sales quotas.

Project Consulting

Our consultants bring deep insight from applying technology to real world projects.

Software Development

We bridge the gap between out-of-the-box software and your outside-the-box problems.

in construction. For Carpo, '*architectural authorship* might be succeeded by some form of mentoring or supervision, where one agency or person initiates the design process, then monitors, prods and curbs, and occasionally censors the interventions of others'.[7] In the BIM process, someone ultimately needs to decide who participates in the collaboration, and in that sense – assuming it is the architect making this selection – authorship is retained, but modified through enhanced collaboration.

THE EMERGENCE OF NEW PROFESSIONAL *MODELS*

Just as BIM has expanded the role of design in the construction process through productive iteration and created new staffing opportunities in professional practice in the form of the 'BIM manager', it has also allowed for the creation of a new type of consultant whose role it is to assist firms engaged in design and construction, in the more efficient delivery of a project through digital means, in effect filling a digital void where there is a lack of this expertise. One such firm is New York-based Case, a group that understands digital tools, is passionate about technology and is educated in architectural design. The firm has four main business units, through which it offers a variety of projects and that it uses to divide roles and responsibilities within the company.

The *Strategy Unit* generally works at the director or managing principal level in an architectural office and helps to adjust broader process change surrounding new and innovative technologies. This unit is primarily focused on helping firms to deal with technological change and workflow development. Through the *Implementation Unit*, the firm trains clients in BIM tools, focusing specifically on internal process improvement of its clients' firms. The *Consulting Unit* finds the firm working as consultants under the direct employ of an architectural or contracting firm.

Finally, the *Software Development Unit* will quickly become the largest offering Case has, primarily because integration between various and new platforms is becoming more and more necessary in the architecture, engineering and construction (AEC) industry, especially for large firms designing large and complex projects. This is the next stage beyond implementation, once a firm has a certain amount of maturity and is able to self-realise the issues that exist within its own workflows. Case does custom software development mainly involving geometric interoperability between various platforms. Much of this has do to with translating geometry natively from tools like Rhinoceros® or its popular Grasshopper™ plug-in, or Digital Project™ to Autodesk® Revit®, so that rebuilding geometry within Revit® is not necessary.

Case is also developing tools that extract data from closed and proprietary model-focused formats into more accessible, often web-based, interfaces that enable a much broader range of users to interact with this information. An example of this would be the translation of metadata associated with a Revit® model into web formats so a project manager, who does not necessarily have

3 Case, business units, 2013
Case offers a series of digital services to design and construction firms through four business units, the Strategy Unit, Implementation Unit, Consulting Unit and Software Development Unit.

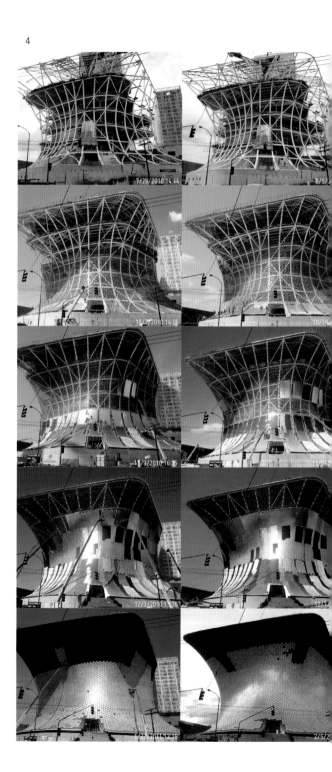

4

4 Gehry Technologies, Museo Soumaya, Mexico City, 2011
The GT team rationalised the construction sequence of the building facade into a series of layers that included the custom truss frames and hexagonal metal disks. The museum's mechanical, structural, and enclosure systems as well as the construction logistics surrounding them, were all taken into account throughout this process. The truss design was coordinated with Geometrica, a speciality fabricator that designs and builds domes and space frames for architectural, industrial and bulk storage applications.

experience with information modelling tools, can still leverage the robust information within the model for other purposes. As the information flows both ways, project managers can edit parameter fields with a tablet and feed that information back into the building information model itself. Web-based data visualisation tools will increasingly become an important way non-design members of a project team work with information models interactively. These opportunities have only recently become available because most information modelling applications now include application programming interfaces (APIs), which gain programmers access to functionality prebuilt into BIM systems that can be used to develop custom applications and plug-ins. Through such development, there exists the potential to access information in a model and integrate it across different platforms, something that has not yet been historically possible.

Steve Sanderson, a partner at Case, sees great potential in integrating these model-based, delivery-focused databases from traditional BIM and CAD systems with enterprise software and information solutions provided by companies such as Deltek; or with project information management software like Newforma®. For Sanderson, 'Seeing all of these diverse systems in an aggregated and integrated way presents an entirely new way of looking at project development and by extension provides insight into how projects are actualized.'[8] These operational concerns are held by all stakeholders across the design and construction process, and as such are larger than design-based information modelling operations.

Interestingly, Sanderson believes Case has the most freedom as designers on the software development side. This position brings new territory to the question of authorship, as the engagement of an information model goes well beyond the traditional design-bid-build process. This is significant for the AEC industry as it posits that the model, created by the designer or architect, is shared, edited and augmented in a way that ideally maintains the original design intent embedded in the model itself, much in the same way as Manuel DeLanda posits the changing role of the author in artificially intelligent systems.[9] The architect delivers creative content, and develops it through a system that is robust enough to interface with many trades or systems during the actualisation and operation of a building. Enter the master builder.

SAVE AS …

In closing, the adoption and creative use of BIM will ultimately have an impact on the state of future design practices. While not all will adopt the 'negotiated consensus' model offered by BIM, it should be recognised that it is not so different from collaborative models of the 20th century, just magnified by the power and speed of technology. For Stan Allen, 'architecture, you might argue, is a fundamentally slow discipline, involving many agents and large investments of capital. The work of architecture is weighty and durable; the building outlives its designer. There

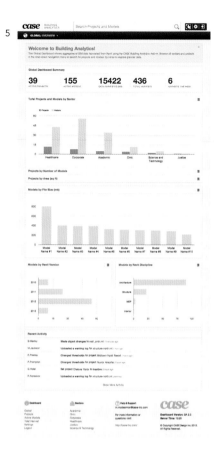

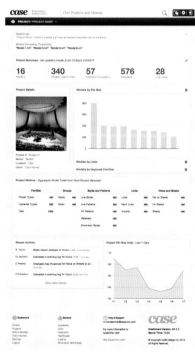

are those who believe the solution is a faster, more responsive architecture — an architecture that approaches the lightness of media, while others insist on architecture's traditional association with stability and survival over time.'[10] This must be considered with the authorial definition of architectural design since Alberti as a 'notational art',[11] one situated in drawing and *not* building. It seems that stability, whether a structural analogy for our buildings themselves, or that of our profession itself, is something worth engaging as we increasingly participate in the construction of our designs. Inherent to this is a level of *confidence*, as authors, as a more holistic embrace of design and construction technologies augments our collaborations with others, in some cases sharing responsibilities under our authorial supervision. The practice of architecture can no longer afford to resist market or other pressures applied to it as it unfolds to engage ever more complex sites and programmes, and less determinable typologies. As architects we need to embrace the increasing opportunities to engage these changes and to use technologies to confront them while continuing to assert a creative direction in our work.

NOTES

1 See: http://www.staedelschule.de/architecture/uploads/media/070303_interview_kwinter.pdf
2 Mario Carpo, 'The Bubble and the Blob', *Lotus International*, No 138 (2009), pp 19–27 (in Italian and English).
3 Victor O Schinnerer & Company, *Guidelines for Improving Practice*, Schinnerer and CNA, May/June 2006, p 2.
4 Ibid, p 3.
5 Mario Carpo, 'Digital Style', *Log* 23, Fall 2011, p 45.
6 Mario Carpo, 'Digital Darwinism: Mass Collaboration, Form-Finding, and the Dissolution of Authorship', *Log* 26, Spring 2013, p 98.
7 Carpo, 'Digital Style', p 50.
8 Discussion with Steve Sanderson in New York, 23 May 2013.
9 Manuel DeLanda, 'Philosophies of Design: The Case of Modeling Software', Alejandro Zaera-Polo and Jorge Wagensberg (eds), *Verb: Architecture Boogazine*, Actar (Barcelona), 2002, p 134.
10 Stan Allen, 'A Conversation between Stan Allen and Alejandro Zaera-Polo', *Rumor* 03.03, Princeton School of Architecture, Spring 2012, p 1.
11 Carpo, 'Digital Darwinism', p 98.

IMAGES

5 Case, Building Analytics, 2013
Case's Software Development Unit has developed Building Analytics' web-based 'Dash Board' applications that allow AEC industry companies to have a global overview of BIM information on a project basis, ultimately allowing BIM data to engage aspects of building maintenance and life-cycle assessment that go beyond completion of construction. Categories include grouping models by project type such as 'Healthcare' or 'Academic', as well as grouping models by Revit® version or discipline such as Architecture or MEP.

6 Case, projects overview, 2013
The Software Development Unit has also devised a web-based 'Dash Board' application to analyse and graphically organise projects and BIM data for AEC industry companies. Models can be queried by file size, links to other CAD or spreadsheet data, and numbers of BIM families. Project metrics, including numbers of families, groups and even line styles, are also graphically organised.

UNStudio

EDUCATION EXECUTIVE
AGENCY AND TAX OFFICES

While some of the practices included here have an overall strategy towards the *digital*, project development and integration is unique at UNStudio, or *United Network* Studio, as the practice is interested in the adoption of new digital tools and building information modelling as a way of producing novel possibilities and generating new types of architecture. The practice resists having an overall strategy to digital design techniques as its clients are increasingly diverse and bring different opportunities, however, the 'use of three-dimensional modeling in UNStudio's practice has been central to the active development of ideas and concepts, along with creating complex and challenging geometries and organizations'.[1]

UNStudio is a group of architects, engineers and technical consultants with offices in Amsterdam and Shanghai. Led by partners Ben van Berkel and Caroline Bos, UNStudio has executed a series of projects globally that have been notable in their formal organisation, novelty and technical accomplishment. The practice has long engaged digital technologies in the design, coordination and execution of its projects and a generation of these is now completing construction. In describing its design process and relationship to digital tools, the practice uses the term *attainability*, by which it suggests a mix of sustainability, affordability and responsibility. It is not simply a green facade or green roof – it is the whole system – the whole organisational quality of the work of architecture. Sustainability is integral to bringing a reduced cost solution to the client, something that has traditionally been at odds with an expressive piece of architecture. Attainability is achieved through what the practice refers to as 'Knowledge Platforms', which are combinations of intelligent computing techniques and solutions, and intuitive and innovative solutions by UNStudio *actors* – the design team.

2

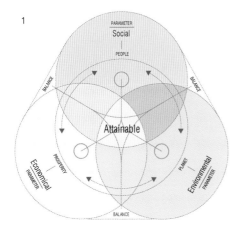

1

1 UNStudio, attainability diagram, 2011
By bringing together distinct Knowledge
Platforms established at UNStudio – the
Intelligent Operations Platform (Program),
the Architectural Sustainability Platform, the
Intelligent Material Platform and the Smart
Parameter Platform – the practice finds a
balance between design research and the
construction of its projects. In describing
these operations, the firm uses the term
attainability.

2 UNStudio, Education Executive Agency and
Tax Offices, Groningen, the Netherlands, 2011
In the design and delivery of a new, 92-metre
(300'–0") tall complex of undulating curves
in Groningen, UNStudio creates one of
Europe's most sustainable office buildings. An
aerial view of the completed project looking
south-west shows the heavily wooded public
garden to the west of the building. The natural
characteristics and wildlife present there,
including a bat colony, figured prominently in
the overall formal development and facade
detailing of the building.

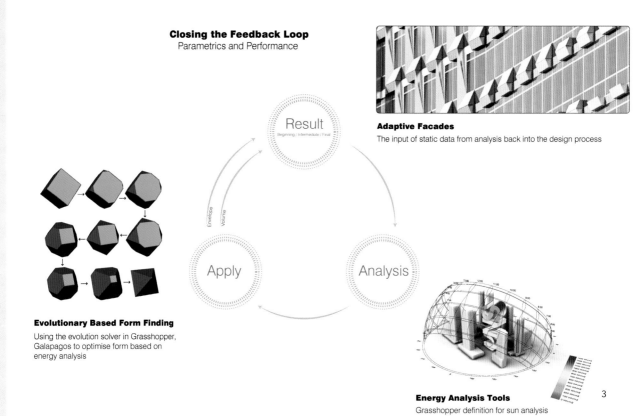

Closing the Feedback Loop
Parametrics and Performance

Result
Beginning / Intermediate / Final

Envelope
Volume

Apply

Analysis

Adaptive Facades
The input of static data from analysis back into the design process

Evolutionary Based Form Finding
Using the evolution solver in Grasshopper,
Galapagos to optimise form based on
energy analysis

Energy Analysis Tools
Grasshopper definition for sun analysis

3

THE ROLE OF *THE DIGITAL*

According to van Berkel, 'Similar to the role of a design model in the process from concept to building, the key function of the Knowledge Platforms is to act as a dynamic hinge between practice and research.'[2] The practice, which currently has 100 employees in Amsterdam and 40 employees in Shanghai, staffs project teams based on the scope of services required for each project, and team size is very much determined by a project's scale, complexity and planning. Van Berkel serves as the Principal Architect involved in all UNStudio projects. He is responsible for providing the design intent and remains involved in all major design decisions through construction phases. Caroline Bos serves as the practice's Principal Urban Planner and is a specialist in analytic programming. She contributes to projects her knowledge in planning, analysis and translation of the programme brief into an *organisational model* suitable for the site plan.

Within the practice exist various specialists who share their knowledge about specific software and digital processes, and employees have at least a basic knowledge of the specific software packages, increasingly Digital Project™ and Grasshopper™ for Rhinoceros®, used in project design and development. Interestingly, and consistently with other practices written about here, UNStudio relies heavily on physical models. According to

Marc Hoppermann, an Associate and architect at UNStudio, 'At UNStudio we believe that physical models help to provide an explanation of the ideas and concepts behind the design. For this reason sketching and also *sketch model making* during the design process is primarily about communication, they are used to study variants and set a dialogue about the various possibilities and solutions. You may start with a sketch or a model and then turn this into a computer drawing, or digital model.'[3]

In its use of digital tools, the practice looks to expand its architectural agenda making it more intelligent. Van Berkel describes the practice's process of finding the most optimal solution for a project as a 'way of distributing intelligence'.[4] For him, the grammar of architecture used to be quite simple, but now it has expanded greatly due to the possibilities of digital design techniques and building information modelling. This increase in the complexity of architectural grammar is not gratuitous; by using BIM to virtually understand the impact of sustainable goals or budgetary constraints on an architectural solution, the designers at UNStudio can calibrate the physical qualities of their buildings with the performance these buildings achieve. For van Berkel, this takes him back to the computational, which he thinks is important in allowing a designer to optimise far more than form. By optimising efficiency, UNStudio is also optimising the quality or direction of the design itself.

The way in which UNStudio works broadens the scope of BIM. Hoppermann leads the practice's Smart Parameter Platform, or SPP. Its role is pivotal in its interaction 'with the other platforms and with active projects. Through computation in its most specific and broadest senses (tools, software, thinking, design models), the SPP leads the initiative to bring together the various parameters that define a project'.[5] Computation at UNStudio, with parameters or constraints – both geometric and non-geometric – informs the design process as it moves from a virtual to actual state, but it also requires more *responsibility* of the design team so that computational initiatives do not simply replace inspiration or creativity. This is an important aspect of how authorship is retained at UNStudio. The design team, operating at a highly sophisticated level, must know when to work through problems computationally, while not making the design process automatic. This distinction allows the practice to exert a great deal of control in the design and development of its projects while fostering novelty.

HardBIM AND SoftBIM

The practice further defines its use of building information modelling as HardBIM and SoftBIM. HardBIM is commercially available BIM software – for UNStudio this includes Bentley® Architecture and Digital Project™ – used to compile data in an architecture project. SoftBIM is a looser concept and is not software specific. It is non-geometric information that exists in the design team's 3-D models that might be generated in Rhinoceros® or AutoCAD®, or non-three-dimensional software such as Microsoft

3 UNStudio, form follows energy diagram, 2011
In developing conceptual ideas about performance in the firm's design work, UNStudio studies the relationship of form-finding parametric tools, energy analysis tools and adaptive facades based on climate and energy data to generate formal strategies that increasingly perform at high levels in terms of energy production or conservation. In using what the firm refers to as a feedback loop it can increasingly tune project parameters for such performance – form follows energy.

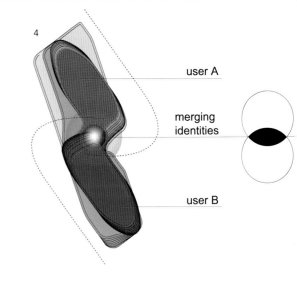

4

user A

merging
identities

user B

5

24th floor

1. central meeting area
2. open workspace
3. half open workspace
4. closed workspace
5. lounge workspace
6. quiet workspace
7. meeting room

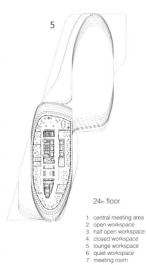

14th floor

1. central meeting area
2. open workspace
3. half open workspace
4. closed workspace
5. lounge workspace
6. quiet workspace
7. meeting room

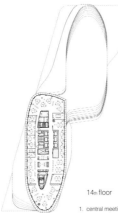

10th floor

1. central meeting area
2. open workspace
3. half open workspace
4. closed workspace
5. lounge workspace
6. quiet workspace
7. meeting room

8th floor

1. central meeting area
2. open workspace
3. half open workspace
4. closed workspace
5. lounge workspace
6. concentration workspace
7. meeting room
8. executive meeting room
9. director general

7th floor

1. central meeting area
2. open workspace
3. half open workspace
4. closed workspace
5. lounge workspace
6. quiet workspace
7. meeting room

2nd floor

1. call center
2. classroom
3. central meeting area
4. rest area

1st floor

1. central hall
2. central lift lobby
3. free flow
4. restaurant
5. grand cafe
6. meeting center
7. roof terrace

ground floor

1. entrance hall
2. reception
3. waiting area/help...
4. meeting center
5. helpdesk employ...
6. expedition
7. bike storage

N

0   5   10

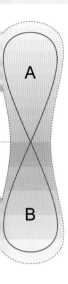

4 UNStudio, Education Executive Agency and Tax Offices, Groningen, the Netherlands, 2008
The 'knot' found at the centre of the building in plan allows for public and open spaces where the building's two 'identities' – programmes of the tax offices (*User A*) and education agency (*User B*) – merge. This diagram is carried through the project's design intent and development. Conventional wisdom is that this is where a building core would be located, but the two diverse programmes required separate cores to service different areas of the building. The tax office and education agency programmes overlap on the lower floors of the building allowing for a transition from one to the other by a main circulation path through the knot, where a central hall is programmed and which is opened as an atrium on floors seven to nine. Secondary circulation is provided to access discrete building cores and the plan of the building allows for visual connections between different parts of the building.

5 UNStudio, Education Executive Agency and Tax Offices, Groningen, the Netherlands, 2011
Building plans show a series of conference and meeting rooms, lounges and offices planned within the two 'bulbs' of the building. Upper floors are occupied exclusively by the education agency, which keeps the records of university students in the Netherlands. These floors have central and semi-private meeting areas, lounges and workspaces.

Excel®. This information is developed and input at a diagrammatic stage of project development and ultimately guides project design. These combine with geometric principles at the beginning of a design process. Van Berkel contrasts this method with the notion that many architects are simply fascinated with materialising geometry. In its use of digital tools, UNStudio calls for more adaptability of the internal and external regulations of its projects. These might include specific energy goals or bulk requirements that are used to *find* both a geometric solution, and more importantly locate the most effective total solution for the project – a notion that their architecture is expressive of much more than its geometric actualisation.

Use of BIM has allowed UNStudio to engage project budgets in a more integrated way – especially with the complexity of building in Europe. Design solutions must have very effective budget strategies for building construction, and BIM can take a certain amount of risk out of a project; for van Berkel, 'talking about risk is in vogue'.[6] The practice has adopted the export of bills of quantities as part of its new workflow as a way of optimising component costs and larger building variables, such as core-to-floor ratios.

The practice has always worked in close collaboration with consultants. Projects early on always had the idea of engaging all the other parties involved in the project and integrating this feedback as a way of driving the architectural design. With BIM the manner in which the practice collaborates has changed. Very quick interaction is possible, and often online, suggesting that collaboration is now in the form of digital knowledge and data exchange.

Collaboration occurs within the three-dimensional environment and, as two-dimensional drawing sets are still required in Europe and Asia, collaboration on the practice's projects can still occur in the two-dimensional environment. According to Hoppermann, 'Many people are still comfortable with 2-D drawing sets, but this now comes from clash detection and drawing generation in the 3-D environment.'[7] Consistent with other projects featured here, data exchange is especially important in the digital fabrication process, and the Dutch government is increasingly requiring a building information model to be tendered with the two-dimensional drawing set for public projects.

EDUCATION EXECUTIVE AGENCY AND TAX OFFICES

The Education Executive Agency and Tax Offices is a €130 million project in Groningen, the Netherlands that houses the national student loan administration and national tax offices. The commission from the Dutch National Buildings Service required the design team to consider the management and maintenance of building services and facilities for a period of 20 years. In addition, the building was required to contain 2,500 workstations and parking facilities for 675 cars and 1,500 bicycles in a below-grade garage. The site for the building is within a large public city garden with a pond and a multi-functional pavilion.

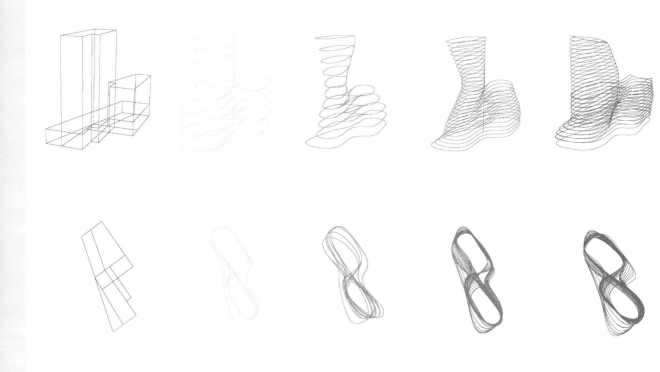

Envelop

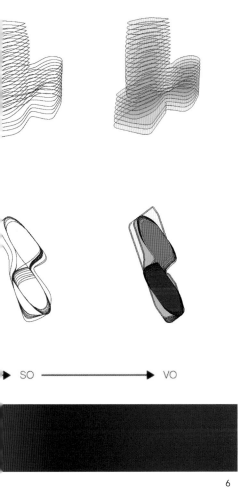

SO ———————→ VO

6

6 UNStudio, Education Executive Agency and
Tax Offices, Groningen, the Netherlands, 2008
The massing diagram shows the formal
resolution of the two main building
programmes. The building envelope was
originally massed as block forms that gave way
to curvature in the Concept Design (SO) and
Schematic Design (VO) phases as the building
development was informed by wind loading and
site criteria. The building's aerodynamic shape
lessens the impact of wind on the building's
facade and allows for interrelationships between
internal office programmes.

For the project, UNStudio worked in close collaboration with
the developer/builder consortium DUO² under a design/build
contract. It is not uncommon for government buildings, like this
tax office, to require life-cycle costing and facilities management as
part of the tendering process to the government client; however,
on the developer-side it can be very costly and difficult to develop
a life-cycle plan because material costs must be amortised over
a 15- or 20-year period. This presents opportunities for the
architect as the building will be held by the client for a stipulated
period of time following the completion of construction. Thus, the
amortisation requirement allows for the procurement of higher
quality materials and better performing facade and building
systems to be designed and implemented. The opportunity for
UNStudio to work with all parties from the commencement of
design – including the developer, general contractor, consultants
and maintenance company to maintain the building – allowed
them to better understand and allow life-cycle aspects to inform
the project's design. Arup provided structural and mechanical,
electrical and plumbing design for the building.

Building constraints were embedded in early Rhinoceros® models
as a way of verifying design. From a contextual point of view, the
building is next to an open and natural woodland that shelters
rare and protected species; so prevailing winds were considered
in the design of the building's overall form. Physical models were
used to confirm wind analysis studies using Grasshopper™ for
Rhinoceros®. The overall shape of the building became quite
aerodynamic and included a series of variable fins that provide
shading based on building orientation.

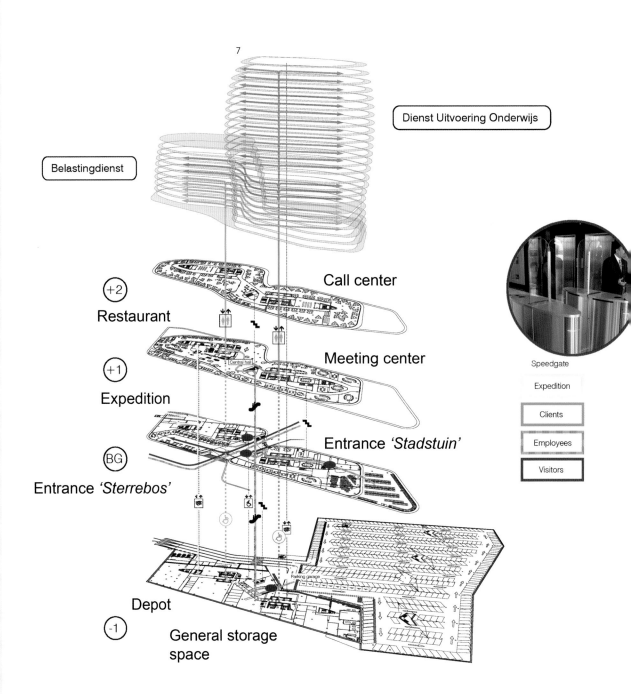

7

Dienst Uitvoering Onderwijs

Belastingdienst

Call center

+2

Restaurant

Meeting center

+1

Expedition

Entrance *'Stadstuin'*

BG

Entrance *'Sterrebos'*

Depot

-1

General storage
space

Central hall

Parking garage

Speedgate

Expedition

Clients

Employees

Visitors

BIM AND SUSTAINABLE DEVELOPMENT

For the project, UNStudio relied on Bentley® Architecture MicroStation® V8 XM to develop the building information model and set up a framework within that model to input and track various specifications made by the client and broader design team. These inputs were constantly compared to the design intent originally set forth by the UNStudio team, and were used to steer the project towards the available construction budget. For Hoppermann, at a detailed engineering level, 'the model could be utilized to come up with variables which helped in quickly deciding if solutions proved realizable, economic and coherent with our architectural conditions'.

The design process was quite short. For two months a 'consortium' of consultants, including the architects, contractor, engineers and technical advisors, and facilities and maintenance teams, worked in an office provided by the design/build contractor – everyone was physically working in the same space and lent expertise to a comprehensive discussion about the project's development.

The architectural response to this has been to strive for comprehensive understanding of the concept of sustainability, including energy and material consumption, as well as social and environmental factors. Sustainability manifests itself in reduced energy consumption (EPC 0.74), as well as significantly reduced material consumption. The design team dropped the floor-to-floor heights from 3.6 metres to 3.3 metres (11'–10" to 10'–10"), which resulted in a total reduction of 7.5 metres (24'–7") of height on the entire building. This drastically reduced the total building volume that needs to be conditioned and also lessens the impact of the building on the surrounding context, as the building is already considerably taller than existing buildings.

The UNStudio team developed a comprehensive virtual model that was used for cost estimating and the measuring of material quantities. The building information model also allowed the design team to precisely determine the perimeter condition, shape and dimensions of each floor slab, which vary given the building's overall form. Finally clash detections were generated to understand the integration of the building's concrete and steel structural system and forced air-conditioning system.

FACADE DEVELOPMENT

The building's aerofoil shape in plan allows it to shed wind while its supple geometry, referred to by UNStudio as a 'future-oriented form', provides a stark contrast to the mid-century corporate Modernism of many institutional buildings. This softness is further developed in the facade system's overall goals of achieving cost-effective and environmentally friendly solutions for the continued use and maintenance of the building over a 20-year period.

7 UNStudio, Education Executive Agency and Tax Offices, Groningen, the Netherlands, 2008
The exploded programme drawing notes horizontal and vertical circulation paths for specific user types. At the ground floor, the magenta diagonal line going through the building accesses the public garden to the west (*stadstuin* is 'garden side') – and the city (*sterrebos* is the 'city side'). The yellow line delineates a service path for the tax offices. The blue and orange lines delineate employee access to the tax offices (blue) and education agency (orange). A shared escalator allows employees to reach upper floors. The tax offices specifically occupy the first five floors and the education agency occupies the upper 16 floors.

8 UNStudio, Education Executive Agency and Tax Offices, Groningen, the Netherlands, 2008
The design team was required to satisfy requirements that winds, channelled from the building facade, would not drive away insects that provided sustenance for the bat colony and other wildlife existing in the wooded public garden. Wind tunnel testing was done to ensure that the overall shape channelled the wind down and off the facade around the building from an overall ergonomic perspective. Vertically, a horizontal fin system reduced wind speed and channelled winds above the trees of the garden. Wind tunnel testing was performed on scaled models and input into the building information model.

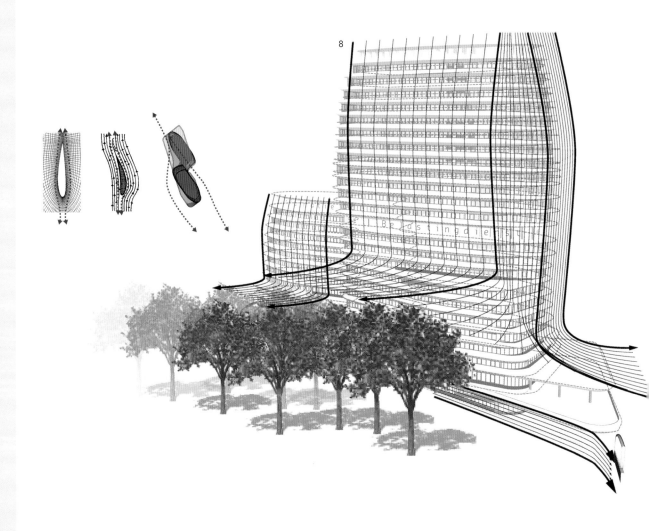

9 UNStudio, Education Executive Agency and Tax Offices, Groningen, the Netherlands, 2008
Operable windows allow for fresh air intake adjacent to the pressurised ventilation system. An interior shading system is also deployed on all glazed surfaces. The fin system disperses wind to lessen speed as fresh air enters the building for ventilation. Conditioned air is supplied through floor registers by an underfloor system above concrete floor slabs. The underside of these concrete slabs are exposed at the finished ceiling. Additional heating is supplied by a heat coil that exists on the perimeter of each floor at the interior base of the fin system.

10 UNStudio, Education Executive Agency and Tax Offices, Groningen, the Netherlands, 2013
UNStudio worked closely with BIM Specialist (http://www.debimspecialist.nl/), a firm located in the Dutch town of Nijverdal which supported the building information model development and coordinated other technical consultants. Strukton Engineering was the project's general contractor, whose work was supported by a structural engineering team from Arup in Amsterdam. Scheldebouw is the Dutch arm of the Italian facade manufacturer Permasteelisa.

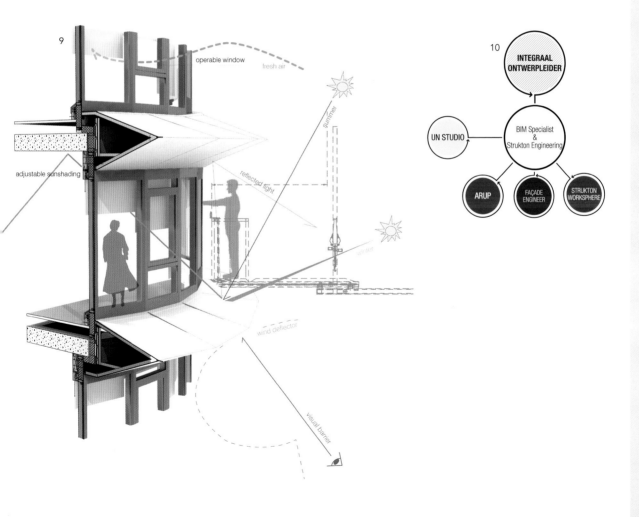

11 UNStudio, Education Executive Agency and Tax Offices, Groningen, the Netherlands, 2008
The design team used specific development criteria in the design of the fin system for different sides of the building. The fins generally reduce the vertical effect of the wind on the ground floor and neighbouring public garden. Conditioned air is supplied by a pressurised ventilation system, which additionally required the mitigation of strong winds on the facade. As a smooth glass facade – typical of an office building – would increase wind speed, the variable projections of the fins, based on orientation, provide an uneven surface for the winds to travel against. The southern fins are longer and narrow to shade the direct sunlight, while the east and west fins are taller in elevation with less projection. The northern fins were designed with the smallest profile and projection to take advantage of indirect sunlight. The fin system also reflects natural light into the building.

12

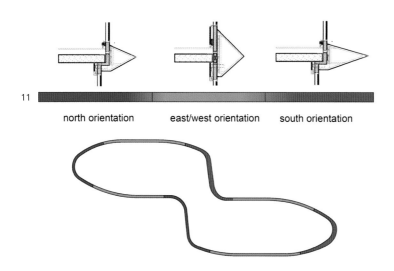

11

north orientation　　east/west orientation　　south orientation

12 UNStudio, Education Executive Agency and
Tax Offices, Groningen, the Netherlands, 2011
Each of the two main building programmes
has service desks to direct visitors in the
main lobby on the ground floor, adjacent to
a cafeteria. *Belastingdienst* is the tax office,
and *Dienst Uitvoering Onderwijs* is the
education agency.

13 UNStudio, Education Executive Agency and Tax Offices, Groningen, the Netherlands, 2011 An evening view from the northeast side of the building site showing the knot at the entry level, which connects to the public garden on the opposite side of the building.

14

Sustainability and energy reduction drove the development of the building facade and its continuous and variable-length fin system. The fin system is constructed of aluminium metal panels, which were chosen due to durability and their minimal environmental impact. The fin system integrates shading, wind control, daylight penetration and construction of the building facade. Parameters controlled in the building information model include the position, height, width and three-dimensional shaping of the facade fins.

The building's facade concept was rationalised through passive design strategies. The continuous fins – which project at different lengths based on their orientation and location on the building's facade – shade the building from summer sun decreasing heat gain, while allowing the lower and cooler winter sunlight into the building; they also serve to deflect wind from the building's facade. The fins ultimately keep a large amount of the heat outside the building, reducing the requirements for indoor cooling. Adjustable sun shading at all fixed and operable glazing augments the building's day-lighting strategies. By using operable windows, passive ventilation is also achieved.

The building was completed in late 2011 and has set a new standard for bringing ideas about life-cycle costs and building use into the design process. Ultimately, use of BIM technologies will allow architects to engage such questions and use BIM's simulation capacities to understand how often a building will need maintenance and how it will perform over time.

NOTES

1 Gustav Fagerström, Marc Hoppermann, Nuno Almeida, Martin Zangerl, Stefano Rocchetti, Ben van Berkel, 'SoftBIM: An Open Ended Building Information Model in Design Practice, ACADIA 12: Synthetic Digital Ecologies' in *Proceedings of the 32nd Annual Conference of the Association for Computer Aided Design in Architecture (ACADIA)*, San Francisco, 18–21 October 2012), pp 37–46, http://cumincad.scix.net/cgi-bin/works/Show?acadia12_37
2 Ben Van Berkel et al, 'Navigating the Computational Turn', *AD Architectural Design*, March/April 2013, p 83.
3 Discussion with Marc Hoppermann in Amsterdam, 10 July 2013.
4 Discussion with Ben van Berkel in Amsterdam, 10 July 2013.
5 Van Berkel et al, 'Navigating the Computational Turn', p 83.
6 Discussion with Ben van Berkel in Amsterdam, 10 July 2013.
7 Discussion with Marc Hoppermann in Amsterdam, 10 July 2013.

IMAGES

pp 224–225 © UNStudio, aerial photo Aerophoto Eelde; pp 224 (t), 225, 226, 228, 230–231, 232, 234–235, 236 © UNStudio; pp 237, 238–239 © UNStudio, photo Ronald Tilleman; p 240 © UNStudio, photo Christian Richters.

14 UNStudio, Education Executive Agency and Tax Offices, Groningen, the Netherlands, 2011
An interior atrium is located at the seventh floor, where furniture is organised for more informal meetings, and a circular stair allows for a quick connection to floors eight and nine. The round discs pictured are acoustic cushions for sound damping applied directly to the exposed underside of the concrete floor slabs.

SELECT BIBLIOGRAPHY

NAUTICAL DESIGN AND SHIPBUILDING (books)

- Monk, Edwin, *Modern Boat Building*, Charles Scribner's Sons (New York), 1973

NAUTICAL DESIGN AND SHIPBUILDING (essays)

- Andrews, DJ, 'Simulation and the Design Building Block Approach in the Design of Ships and Other Complex Systems', *Proceedings of the Royal Society: Mathematical, Physical and Engineering Sciences*, Vol 462, No 2075 (November 2006), p 3407–3433

  — 'A Comprehensive Methodology for the Design of Ships (and Other Complex Systems)', *Proceedings of the Royal Society: Mathematical, Physical and Engineering Sciences*, Vol 454, No 1968 (8 January 1998), pp 187–211

MASTER BUILDER (books)

- Benevolo, Leonardo, *The Architecture of the Renaissance*, Routledge (London), 2002

- Prager, Frank D and Scaglia, Gustina, *Brunelleschi Studies of his Technology and Inventions*, Dover Books on Architecture (New York), 1970

MASTER BUILDER (essays)

- Ackerman, James S, 'Architectural Practice in the Italian Renaissance', *Journal of the Society of Architectural Historians*, Vol 13, No 3 (October 1954), pp 33–11

- Adams, Nicholas, 'The Life and Times of Pietro dell'Abaco, a Renaissance Estimator from Siena', *Zeitschrift für Kunstgeschichte*, Vol 48, No 3 (1985), pp 384–95

- Briggs, Martin S, 'Architectural Models – I', *The Burlington Magazine for Connoisseurs*, Vol 54, No 313 (April 1929), pp 174–83

- Prager, Frank D, 'A Manuscript of Taccola, Quoting Brunelleschi, on Problems of Inventors and Builders', *Proceedings of the American Philosophical Society*, Vol 112, No 3 (21 June 1968), pp 131–49

  — 'Brunelleschi's Inventions and the "Renewal of Roman Masonry Work"', *Osiris*, Vol 9, March 1950, pp 457–554

- Toker, Franklin, in 'Gothic Architecture by Remote Control: An Illustrated Building Contract of 1340', *The Art Bulletin*, Vol 67, No 1 (March 1985), pp 67–95

DESIGN AND INFORMATION THEORY (books)

- Allen, Stan, *Practice: Architecture, Technique and Representation*, G+B Arts International (Amsterdam), 2000

- Broadbent, Geoffrey, *Design in Architecture: Architecture and the Human Sciences*, John Wiley & Sons (Chichester), 1973

- Deleuze, Gilles, *Bergsonism*, Zone Books (New York), 1991

- Hubka, Victor, *Principles of Engineering Design*, Butterworth-Heinemann (London), 1982

- Johnson, Steven, *Future Perfect: The Case For Progress In A Networked Age*, Penguin Group (New York), 2012

- Kwinter, Sanford, *Architectures of Time: Toward a Theory of the Event in Modernist Culture*, MIT Press (Cambridge, MA), 2002

- Spuybroek, Lars, 'The Aesthetics of Variation', *NOX: Machining Architecture*, Thames & Hudson (London), 2004

- Turkle, Sherry, *Simulation and its Discontents*, MIT Press (Cambridge, MA and London), 2009

DESIGN THEORY (essays)

- Allen, Stan, 'A Conversation between Stan Allen and Alejandro Zaera-Polo', *Rumor* 03.03, Princeton School of Architecture, Spring 2012, p 01

  — 'Diagrams Matter', in *ANY 23: Diagram Work: Data Mechanics for a Topological Age*, Anyone Corporation (New York), 1998, pp 16–19

- Carpo, Mario, 'The Bubble and the Blob', *Lotus International*, No 138 (2009), pp 19–27 (in Italian and English)

  — 'Digital Darwinism: Mass Collaboration, Form-Finding, and the Dissolution of Authorship', *Log* 26, Spring 2013

  — 'Digital Style', *Log* 23, Fall 2011

- DeLanda, Manuel, 'Philosophies of Design: The Case of Modeling Software', Alejandro Zaera-Polo and Jorge Wagensberg (eds), *Verb: Architecture Boogazine*, Actar (Barcelona), 2002

- Frampton, Kenneth, 'Intention, Craft, and Rationality', *Building (in) the Future: Recasting Labor in Architecture*, P Deamer and P Bernstein (eds), Princeton Architectural Press (New Haven), 2010, p 31

DRAWING THEORY (books)

- Evans, Robin, 'Drawn Stone', *The Projective Cast: Architecture and its Three Geometries*, MIT Press (Cambridge, MA and London), 2000

- Johnston, George B, 'Dialects of the Architect and the Draftsman in *Pencil Points*, 1920–1932', *Drafting Culture: A Social History of Architectural Graphic Standards*, MIT Press (Cambridge, MA), 2008

DRAWING THEORY (essays)

- Alberti, Leon Battista, On Painting, revised edition, Yale University Press (New Haven, CT), 1966

- Hewitt, Mark, 'Representational Forms and Modes of Conception: An Approach to the History of Architectural Drawing', *Journal of Architectural Education*, Vol 39, No 2 (Winter 1985), pp 2–9

20TH-CENTURY ARCHITECTURAL PRACTICE (books)

- American Institute of Architects, *The Architect's Handbook of Professional Practice*, 13th Edition, John Wiley & Sons, Inc (Hoboken, NJ), 2001

- Broderick, Mosette, *Triumvirate: McKim, Mead & White: Art, Architecture, Scandal, and Class in America's Gilded Age*, Alfred A Knopf, a division of Random House, Inc (New York), 2010

- Fenske, Gail, 'The Beaux-Arts Architect and the Skyscraper: Cass Gilbert, the Professional Engineer, and the Rationalization of Construction in Chicago and New York' in *The American Skyscraper: Cultural Histories*, Roberta Moudry (ed), Cambridge University Press (New York), 2005

20TH-CENTURY ARCHITECTURAL PRACTICE (essays)

- Bernstein, Philip G, 'Digital Representation and Process Change in the Building Industry', *Perspecta*, Vol 35, Building Codes, MIT Press (Cambridge, MA), 2004

- Heery, George T, 'A History of Construction Management, Program Management and Development Management', 2011, p 2, accessed via http://www.brookwoodgroup.com/index.php?sec=2&sub=7#histCMPM

INDEX

Figures in italics indicate captions.